Adolescence, Girlhood, and Media Migration

COMMUNICATING GENDER

Series Editors: Diana Bartelli Carlin, Saint Louis University
Nichola D. Gutgold, Pennsylvania State University
Theodore F. Sheckels, Randolph-Macon College

Communicating Gender features original research examining the role gender plays in communication. It encompasses a wide variety of approaches and methodologies to explore theoretically relevant topics pertaining to the interrelation of gender and communication both in the United States and worldwide. This series examines gender issues broadly, ranging from masculine hegemony and gender issues in political culture to media portrayals of women and men and the work/life balance.

Recent Titles in This Series:

Adolescence, Girlhood, and Media Migration: US Teens' Use of Social Media to Negotiate Offline Struggles, by Aimee Rickman

Consuming Agency and Desire in Romance: Stories of Love, Laughter, and Empowerment, by Jenni M. Simon

Michelle Obama: First Lady, American Rhetor, edited by Elizabeth Natalle and Jenni M. Simon

Women in the Academy: Learning From Our Diverse Career Pathways, edited by Nichola D. Gutgold and Angela R. Linse

Communication and the Work-Life Balancing Act: Intersections across Identities, Genders, and Cultures, edited by Elizabeth Fish Hatfield

The Global Status of Women and Girls: A Multidisciplinary Approach, edited by Lori Underwood and Dawn Hutchinson

Adolescence, Girlhood, and Media Migration

US Teens' Use of Social Media to Negotiate Offline Struggles

Aimee Rickman

LEXINGTON BOOKS
Lanham • Boulder • New York • London

Published by Lexington Books
An imprint of The Rowman & Littlefield Publishing Group, Inc.
4501 Forbes Boulevard, Suite 200, Lanham, Maryland 20706
www.rowman.com

Unit A, Whitacre Mews, 26-34 Stannary Street, London SE11 4AB

British Library Cataloguing in Publication Information Available

Library of Congress Cataloging-in-Publication Data
Library of Congress Cataloging-in-Publication Data Available

ISBN 978-1-4985-5392-6 (cloth : alk. paper)
ISBN 978-1-4985-5394-0 (pbk. : alk. paper)
ISBN 978-1-4985-5393-3 (electronic)

This book is dedicated to Jacqueline Rickman.
I love you very much, Mom.

Contents

Acknowledgments

My research resulted from a mighty amalgam of feedback, advice, encouragement, workshopping, distance running, and general kindness. It made this book possible. I am most fortunate for the valuable trust granted to me by the teens who allowed me to learn from them in this study. I am deeply indebted to my wise and generous academic mentors Christian Sandvig, Reed Larson, Soo Ah Kwon, and Robert Stake, and thankful for the interdisciplinary communities and research-focused funding I was given as a fellow with UIUC's Illinois Program for Research in the Humanities and the Center for Democracy in a Multiracial Society, as well as from the Myra Sadker Foundation.

I owe gratitude to many others for the help they gave me as part of writing groups, as members of my dissertation committee, and as meaningful presences in my life offering various types of inspiration along the way. Thanks to Mandy Tröger, Alexandra Calvallaro, and Rebecca Crist, award-winning members of the powerful TCB writing group; to Trixie DeMaria for inspiring this book; to Dvera Saxton, Caroline Cole, Anni Poppen, Ramona Oswald, Robin Jarrett, Mary L. Gray, Jorge Chapa, Jacqueline Rickman, Karrie Karahalios, Matt Crain, ShinJoung Yeo, Cheol Gi Bai, Meg Rickman, Beth DeMaria, Jolie Rickman, Mary P. Sheridan, Emily Fultz, Andy Kulczycki, Wendy Hundley, Sally Mundy, Laura and Peter Berk, David Wierzal, Clark Brooks, Mariel García-Montes, Meg Krausch, Shameem Rahka, Don Rickman, Darren Stevenson, Lisa Nakamura, Cope Cumpston, Mary Lee Sargent, Sandra Loeb, Sam Langford, Jill Langford, Loretta Gaffney, Ann Abbott, Marsela Raffaelli, Julie and Jenna Wirtz, Azure, Bianca, and Sasha Rubel, GirlZone, Jennifer Randles, Blake Zweig, Jan Slagter, Melissa Jordine, Loretta Kensigner, Jonathan Sterne, Michelle Denbeste, Carol Inskeep, Andrew Grznia, Chris Delis, Cap Vonderheide, Tracy and Christian Vonderheide, Geannine, Alan, Dirk, Leslie, and Trenten Kessler, Kaussaundra and Elijah

Slifer, Shawna and Brent Curry, UIUC's Graduate Employee's Organization and Department of Human and Community Development, the Esquire, Kathleen Hannah, Ian MacKaye, and to the undergraduate scholars in and out of my Youth and Social Media Research Lab who fuel my work with their curiosity, tenacity, and brilliance: Jasmine De La Torre, Sara Prieto, Kimberly Arroyo, Kendall Bailey, Rosielyn Rufo, Alecia Ram, Quanie Dildine, Melissa Winchester, Kristin Auzat, Iris Torres, Jamie Bomgardner, Kristin Migirian, Iris Perez-Reyes, Alexus Seiler, Veronica Romani, Sam Parchim, and Chelsey Crossin.

Much appreciation to my wonderful editor, Nicolette Amstutz, at Lexington Books for her belief in this project and decision to place it in the Communicating Gender series, to Jessica Thwaite, and to the anonymous reviewers whose incisive, invigorating feedback bettered my writing in many ways. Thank you to Patience Milrod and Paul Pierce of the Dorothy Parker writing group for regularly rewarding kept deadlines with sharply insightful commentaries and generous, joyful, and always highly topical spirits, and to Meghan, Jacob, Silviano, Jacob, Ron, Juan, Nam, Henry, Jason, Patrick, Jeremy, and the other good souls at Spokeeasy for sharing my excitement throughout the writing of this book. I am immensely grateful, finally, for Spencer Vonderheide, who helps to remind me every day how much support matters. Thanks for making it all worth it, love.

Chapter One

"I Guess I Can Be Myself There, Instead"

I am sitting across the table from 14-year-old LaToya in her family's kitchen. Out the window behind her, the road bends by her front yard to loop through her housing development, veering away from the low, blonde cornfield spreading as far as the eye can see.

LaToya tells me about her week. She did well on a test again. School was boring, but fine. She was allowed to volunteer Tuesday at the Youth Center, but they did not need help so she "just sat there again." A boy she likes from afar got in a fight at the park in the neighborhood and the police came, so everyone is talking about it in school. LaToya was not in the park that day. "I really don't go outside," she explains. Despite not directly seeing the altercation, LaToya tells me she knew all the details before going to school the next day from Twitter. She opens her laptop computer and shows me a long list of tweets discussing the boy before continuing to recap. "I am always babysitting," she states. She says she feels all she does is go to school and watch her two younger sisters. As she explains this, her scrolling Twitter feed catches her eye and she responds, tapping on the keyboard with a wry smile. "I have to share everything with them: my room, the television, everything." I ask her to explain what is happening on the computer. "My friends. They crazy," she says, turning the screen to show a tweet telling her she is "cryyyyng" without her "boo." Noise spills from the hallway and sisters run through the kitchen, stopping behind a chair to peer at us. "Can we use the computer?" one asks. LaToya raises her eyebrows and quietly replies: "Go back upstairs."

LaToya and I have had four meetings in her home since we first met last month. Each time, she has been the oldest family member present. "It's hard," she explains. "My mom likes to keep me in the house because she

1

says, 'I don't want you to get in trouble.'" This is not the first time LaToya has discussed her limited social permissions. Curfews, rules, boredom, and adults' fears have come up regularly in each of our talks so far. When school is out, LaToya tells me she has little time away from her pesky siblings, and few friends nearby. Her mother believes she is too young to date, so she does not discuss her boyfriends at home. She can rarely attend the events people later talk about. This causes her to feel constrained and cut off from the world. It is unfair, she says. LaToya explains that she works hard to try to show the adults in her life that she deserves to be trusted and respected by doing well in school, helping out at home, and not being "a whore, like some other girls," with little success. After listing off a number of recent efforts, LaToya shakes her head. "I'm a kid. That's just how it goes."

As a female "kid," LaToya feels powerless and limited by others. She regularly shows herself to be responsible, able, and trustworthy, but this has never convinced her mother to extend her curfew or to let her hang out with friends in the park after school. She has little control over her life and little hope that her conditions will improve. Her mother will not budge. She knows of no teens in her neighborhood with jobs, and she doubts that she could find a way to earn money to move out on her own where she could make choices for herself. This is frustrating to her, but these frustrations are lightened by her ability to interact with friends on social media while confined at home. "My friends are online. They get me," she says. LaToya is not pleased about having her interests judged and involvements monitored by adults in her life, but, to her, this seems inevitable. She shrugs and nods toward her scrolling Twitter account. "I guess I can be myself there, instead."

This book details an ethnographic study of ethnically, economically, and racially diverse female, rural adolescents aged 14 through 19 from the Midwest region of the United States. It investigates how these young women call upon social media in everyday attempts to address and mediate the marginality they face in their offline lives in adolescence. While a variety of recent research focuses on social media and some of this work considers US adolescents, our current understandings of girls are both myopic and quixotic. This book raises important new points. First, it finds that focusing on the context of rural life, focusing on young women, focusing on some in economic hardship, and focusing on the meaning and context of actions taken on Facebook and Twitter that are judged by adults and institutions as risky provides an important new perspective from which we can better understand childhood, identity, involvement, safety, and justice.

Second, it argues that looking past the dominant discourses of peril, protection, victimhood, and recklessness is necessary to fully see and understand teens' involvements with social media as related to their own interests—as a group—in meaning, identities, well-being, and survival, as well as to young women's desire to fight trivializing cultural subordination by claiming social spaces, demanding new social understandings, and finding new ways to exist in the present. Lastly, this book calls on readers to ask the question: What are young women, acting from the containment and subordination of gendered US adolescence, willing to do and to sacrifice online in an effort to gain increased social power, respect, and relevance? This book finds young women's social, ideological, and geographic marginality fueling their interests in social media, and heightening their trust and engagement in online environments in ways that affirm their subordination and further their marginality. As teens use social media to attempt to mediate their offline experiences, this book explores how involvement in online social spaces also actively mediates young people's interests in social reordering.

ADOLESCENT GIRLHOOD AND MEDIA MIGRATION

Adolescence is a problem in US culture. Labeled by developmental theorists as a distinct and biologically informed developmental stage between childhood and adulthood,[1] adolescence is also, importantly, a socially produced holding period in which industrial society deprives youth of economic, political, and civic rights for the sake of exposing them to a "long period of indoctrination into acquiescence and acceptance of existing power structures as normal, natural, good, and benign."[2] There are few things "natural" about adolescence. Trivialized and denied rights, adolescent girls represent a socially marginalized group in the United States routinely dismissed from society.

In adolescence, young people are defined by others, most typically in unflattering manners. They are commonly perceived to occupy a stage of becoming rather than a state of being, and institutionalized developmental perspectives have encouraged society to view both them and their realities as ephemeral rather than real.[3] When their present status is considered, young Americans are not well regarded, and they are commonly scapegoated for larger and far less tangible societal problems.[4] Mainstream social perceptions in the United States connect young people with thoughts of laziness, consumerism, decadence, and entitlement. As individuals and as a group, youth are widely perceived as problematic, incomplete beings who will eventually be incorporated into adult structures, not as actual people who occupy valid existences in the present.[5] Young people in the US are generally not listened to. When they are, they are not taken seriously. In addition to not being heard, youth are regularly denied the ability to be known for their positive traits and realities. They are not seen as competent, able, sexual, and deserving of full rights.

While negative representations are easy to find for youth in general, females, queer youth, poor youth, and youth of color are even more commonly constructed as deviant and outsider within hierarchal American society.[6] However, the lived experiences of these adolescents are rarely heard. Mary Celeste Kearney explains that patriarchal ideologies in academia contributed to coding the term "adolescent" as "male," leaving girls out of foundational research purporting to understand adolescents and their realities.[7] And research on adolescents and on girls has historically also lacked attention to intersectionality, presenting the "normal" adolescent not only as male, but as white, heterosexual, cis, able-bodied, and middle class.[8]

Girls are marginalized in adolescence; adolescence is a problem for girls. Despite the hardship that this time period causes young women, researchers note that the period of adolescence is lengthening deep into the third decade of life due to economically driven social changes.[9] As such, young people in the United States today face increasingly complex and less certain access to social locations that grant full status and rights,[10] and an indefinite extension of social marginalization within the social perceptions and containment of adolescence.

In contrast to the material world, the online world offers young people the promise of vast amounts of information and guidance, connections to people well outside of the immediate environment, purportedly limitless choice, opportunities for "branding" and other kinds of self-retooling within social space, and promises of potential incorporeal involvement and equality.[11] Females value such opportunities, but, as in offline worlds, they face challenges in online forums. Girls and young women fare poorly in popular media and in popular opinion in the US. Like social understanding offline, the collective image of the girl Internet user is not, by any assessment, complimentary, with their acts and intentions comfortably explained away in the binary framing of girls being either "at-risk" or "risky." Many believe young women require protection and are in constant danger of being taken advantage of by ill-intentioned strangers in their online involvements. Others see them as risky in their own acts, putting themselves in harm's way and needing to be controlled for their own good. And similar to how the presence of hoodies and other "humble objects"[12] effectively cast social dispersion on the characters and motivations of young people, girls using Internet-accessing mobile devices are commonly rendered narcissistic, entitled, and otherwise less worthy of empathy, care, and support. And yet it is in this forum that we can learn how young, rural females in early twenty-first century America understand, respond to, and act within cultural assumptions and ideologies that girder the social infrastructures of US girlhood.

Using a metaphor of "migration," this book focuses on teenage girls who, facing frustrations in restrictive, monitored, censoring, and contained life in their homes and communities, attempt to flee to "spaces"[13] in social media where they are able to gain social involvement and perform their identities without fear of reprisal. Within the rhetoric of adolescence, this idea of fleeing, seeking, movement, or relocation can be understood to be part of juvenile exploration, disinterest in stability, and "trying on" ways of being.[14] It can be seen as volitional, with teens moving from space to space by choice, because they want to, perhaps as a fleeting fancy. However, as scholars of culture understand, choices made when performing an identity and seeking to advance standing are complex social acts. Accordingly, the choices girls make to migrate to and between social media spaces are based on much more than individual desire. They are relocating in search of lesser containment and greater opportunity, just as people depart and return to their home countries. And this phenomenon, what I call *media migration,* offers a way to help readers understand both the choices and the calculations that young women make as part of a larger social context that constructs a particular decision as an opportunity in the first place.

THE STUDY

This study was based on ethnographic interview, in-person participant observation, and social media–based participant observation. In contrast to most research on teens and social media drawing data from one interaction, this ethnographic research was based upon more than 12 months and 300 in-person hours in on- and offline interactions in "the field" with the rural teens in my study (my "interlocutors"). Rural communities can offer many wonderful opportunities for girls. They also present unique geographic and social challenges that might make social media particularly appealing to minors. However, rural populations are largely overlooked in research considering youth and social media.[15] Catherine Driscoll notes this problematic gap in the literature in her essay, "Girl Cultural Capital."[16] She writes that her own research on rural girls has led her to attend more to teens' own valuing and evaluation of both girlhood and culture within a wider context where they see girl culture as a system of exchange. With this in mind, this study set out to better understand the local meaning, experiences, and lived realities of these particular rural girls.

Adolescence and girlhood, as concepts, exist within very specific frames of understanding.[17] Many understandings of girls and adolescents are based on psychologist Erik Erikson's 1968 coining of identity as "a subjective sense of continuous existence and a coherent memory"[18] resulting in personal "sameness" and "continuity."[19] Erikson's definition ignores the privilege involved in not having to code-shift to survive. It ignores that girls are commonly not granted this privilege in US society. As a result, the design of this study is guided by critical scholars who consider girls' identities as necessarily discursive, performed, multifarious, socially functional, and socially negotiated rather than as a solitary internal truth or essence. In line with interdisciplinary scholars of girlhood studies such as Mary Celeste Kearney, Angela McRobbie, Clare Bradford, Mavis Reimer, Sinikka Aapola, Marnina Gonick, and Anita Harris, this book focuses on girlhood not as a process of becoming but as an important state of being.[20] It also understands that there is no universal girlhood or adolescence. In the inaugural editorial of the journal *Girlhood Studies,* Claudia Mitchell, Jacqueline Reid-Walsh, and Jackie Kirk explain: "Girlhood is not monolithic, but rather diverse and multiple."[21] Girlhood, like adolescence, cannot be essentialized; this book seeks to understand the lives of specific rural, American, and primarily lower-class girls. To do so, it follows the lead of critical race theorist Kimberle Crenshaw, of feminist scholars, and of media scholars Sharon Mazzarella and Lisa Nakamura in taking on a lens of intersectionality, considering how gender, age, race, class, sexuality, and other power-based social locations mediate teenage girls' ability to "be" themselves on- and offline.[22]

This book is informed by critical youth scholars who argue that attributes given to adolescents and to girls are not inherent to youth, themselves, but rather that they are "intrinsic to the person living under a particular set of societal constraints and dictates."[23] In viewing youth marginality to be a result of social relationships, social perception, social action, and self-discipline, this approach is in line with the theory of structuration that regards everyday actions as the mechanisms behind structures of power, and framings of power as manifested and affirmed in perceptions and interactions between people.[24] Taken together, these perspectives suggest that social media technologies offer opportunities for youth agency within significant cultural, structural, and historical constraints.

The work of Nancy Lesko was especially influential to this study. In her book *Act Your Age*: *A Cultural Construction of Adolescence*, Lesko draws attention to how social policy, practice, and discourse on youth have relegated young Americans to marginalized social positions in which they have very little power or credibility. And though an adolescent has little social clout, adolescence, itself, is mighty. Adolescence, Lesko writes, has become "a handy and promiscuous social space, that is, a place that people could endlessly worry about, a space that adults everywhere could watch carefully and that could be imagined to have many visible and invisible instabilities."[25] Indeed, adolescence serves as an important cultural project in US society. Challenging the idea of adolescence as a linear phase borne of nature moving youth toward more "developed" adulthood, Lesko and other critical youth researchers charge that adolescence is not a natural necessity but a racially minded social stricture set upon young people rooted in the belief that adolescence and adolescent immaturity are biological facts, a belief that helps to justify youth surveillance, control, and subordination. This approach argues that young people in the US have many real and rational reasons to want to both engage in and try to get around society. This study was informed by these important cultural understandings of girls.

Design and Method

Participants

Fifteen female adolescent-aged rural teenagers participated in this study as interlocutors. Each chose their own pseudonym. I selected teens with varying interests, involvements, identities, resources, and backgrounds, and I learned from them carefully over time. These interlocutors do not represent all teens. They do not represent all young women, or even all rural girls. However, the insights shared by them raise important—and often overlooked—issues that are essential considerations and contributions to wider efforts working to understand youth, girlhood, and social media.

Amelia is a 15-year-old sophomore from the town of Brown, population 262, where she lives with her mother, father, and older brother. She describes herself as "Caucasian" and as "athletic, outgoing, creative. I show cattle during the summer and sometimes in the winter. And I play volleyball and I'm a middle hitter. My favorite things in the world are food, glitter, sleep, close people like friends and family, and animals." Amelia spent most of her time on Facebook when we first met, and she moved over to Twitter, which she joined about a month into our meetings because of friends telling her she was posting too much to Facebook.

Amy is a 14-year-old freshman from Townsville, population 12,600, where she lives with her mother, father, younger sister, and younger brother. She describes herself as "African American and black" and as "nice, funny, and outgoing. I am a nice person, a girl who cares about your feelings. I'm cool to hang with. I'm a Facebook user and I use Twitter. I'm not really a Twitter fan. I'm a Facebook fan. I like to go for walks, but if it's real, real far, I won't be going. . . . And I don't like putting people down, and I don't like to see people putting people down because it's not cool. And I'm just a person who can just be there for you." She uses Twitter, but mostly Facebook.

Annie is a 17-year-old sophomore from Townsville, population 12,600, where she lives with her mother, stepdad, little sister, and big brother. She describes herself as "African American" and as "shy, aggressive, polite, unique." She uses Facebook.

Cassidy is a 17-year-old senior from Willow, population 975, where she lives with her mother, father, and sister. She describes herself as "Caucasian" and as a "very nice, shy person. Always wanting to do my best and help others. Friendly." She uses Facebook and Twitter.

Carollynn is a 17-year-old senior from Flatville, population 750, where she lives with her mother, father, and brother. She describes herself as "Caucasian" as well as "energetic, happy, easy going." She uses Facebook and Twitter.

LaToya is a 14-year-old eighth-grader from Townsville, population 12,600, where she lives with her mother, stepfather, and two younger sisters. She describes herself as "African American" and as "a fun outgoing person who likes to try new things and take risks." She uses Facebook and Twitter.

Marcin is a 19-year-old junior from Concord, population 102, where she lives with her mother, father, and older sister. She describes herself as "white" as well as "funny, loves to talk." She uses Facebook.

Molly is a 16-year-old junior from "in the country between Prairie and Flatville," where she lives with her mother and father. She describes herself as "a very country girl. I live on a farm and raise cattle. My family and friends are all really close, and I love to hang out with them!" and also as "Caucasian." She uses Facebook and Twitter.

Naomi is a 14-year-old freshman from Brown, population 262, where she lives with her mother and father. She describes herself as "Caucasian" and as "funny, outgoing, blonde, reckless." She uses Facebook and Twitter.

Noel is a 17-year-old senior from Flatville, population 750, where she lives with her mother, stepfather, and sister. She describes herself as "Caucasian and white" and as "short, skinny, nice." She uses Facebook and Twitter.

Rosie is a 14-year-old eighth-grader from Townsville, population 12,600, where she lives with her grandmother, grandfather, aunt, sister, and cousin. She describes herself as "African American" and also as "funny, smart, active." She uses Facebook and Twitter.

Sarah is a 15-year-old sophomore from Flatville, population 750, where she lives mostly with her mother and stepfather. She describes herself as "Caucasian" and "very active in sports, a hard worker in school." She uses Facebook and Twitter.

Shelly is a 14-year-old freshman from Prairie, population 193, where she lives with her mother, stepfather, and two sisters. She describes herself as "Caucasian" and says about herself: "I like to have fun and I like to laugh." She uses Facebook and Twitter.

Stevie is a 14-year-old eighth-grader from Townsville, population 12,600, where she lives with her mother, father, and her two little brothers and two little sisters. She describes herself as "talented. I'm a prodigy at cooking and cleaning and stuff. I want to get a job so I can get my own clothes. I like singing, and reading books, coloring, playing with my brothers and sisters, a lot of stuff. I like hanging out with my friends, going to the mall. And I'm quiet and shy when I meet new people." She does not use Facebook or Twitter. She used to be part of Club Penguin, an online virtual community game by Disney, but she no longer visits the site. Her mother does not let her join Facebook because she won't let her lie about her age to get an account. While Facebook's minimum age limit is 13,[26] when I asked Stevie what age you need to be to get a Facebook account, she replied: "18."

Violet is a 16½-year-old junior from the edge of Brown, in unincorporated Carroll, where she lives with her mother, father, grandmother, older and younger brother, and her brother's girlfriend. She describes herself as "Hispanic and Caucasian" and as "fun, caring, thoughtful, generous." She uses Facebook and Twitter.

Setting

All interlocutors lived in the same rural region of the US Midwest, and used at least one of two specific social media platforms.

Offline, all interlocutors in this study lived in and around Townsville, the pseudonym for a rural Midwestern town located more than 100 miles outside of a metropolitan city. In Townsville, I worked with some teens from the Eagle Bluff neighborhood. Eagle Bluff, referred to as "The Bluff" by teens, is a Section 8 housing unit on the north side of Townsville made up of low-slung two- and three-bedroom duplexes lining three main curvy roads crossing into a rough figure 8. In 2013, families of four could earn no more than $19,600 to be eligible to rent a home in this neighborhood. In the 2010 census, Townsville reported a population of nearly 13,000. Some 76.7% of Townsville residents identified as White, 16.9% identified as Black or African American, 2.7% identified as Latino or Hispanic, and 1.8% identified as Asian. Townsville and its surrounding areas suffer from a depressed economy. A military base closed in the early 1990s, leaving unemployed workers and a number of toxic dump sites in the town. According to 2015 census data, 31% of families with related children under the age of 18 had annual incomes below the poverty line in comparison to the US average of 18%. Townsville is the only hometown in the study large enough to appear on the US Census Bureau's reports; others had much smaller populations and lower incomes. The other towns my interlocutors lived in—Brown, Carroll, Concord, Flatville, Prairie, and Willow—range in population from 975 (Willow) to 102 (Concord).

Online, this inquiry involved two online social media sites: Facebook and Twitter.

Facebook is currently the most popular social media platform in the United States. Facebook ended its first year of operation in 2004 with fewer than 1 million active users. In 2013, Facebook grew beyond one billion accounts. As of June 30, 2017, they reported 2.07 billion users worldwide.[27] In 2015, the Pew Center on Internet and Society found that 71% of US teens aged 13 to 17 used Facebook; despite the broadening of social media options and involvements, Facebook remained teens' most frequently used platform.[28]

Teens were found to be involved in Facebook at similar rates across gender (72% male versus 70% female) and geographic location (77% urban; 75% rural), but older teens were more likely to be Facebook users than those who were younger (80% 15–17; 57% 13–14). Non-Hispanic Black teens were also slightly more likely to be Facebook users (75% versus 71% White non-Hispanic, 70% Hispanic). Facebook has specific requirements for users to hold only one account. It is quite relevant to note that this rule was explained by Facebook CEO Mark Zuckerberg in chiding terms that echo Erik Erikson. "You have one identity," Zuckerberg stated. "Having two identities for yourself is an example of a lack of integrity."[29]

In earlier years, Facebook defined its mission as: "To give people the power to share and make the world more open and connected."[30] In June 2017, this mission changed to focus on communities.[31] Facebook is most likely not going to be a space young people spend time in forever. But it does boast the greatest teen involvement of all social media sites in the US at the current time,[32] and, unlike its predecessors, its popularity has steadily increased over the past decade. Also, as this research began, studies noted Facebook as a surprising departure from earlier tech-based environments in that females, as a group, reported feeling high levels of confidence in their use of this technology.[33] It is due to this comfort as well as to Facebook's widespread popularity as a youth "hang out" that this study chose to examine Facebook usage.

Twitter is a social media site that launched specifically for use on mobile technologies in March of 2006. With a mission to "give everyone the power to create and share ideas and information instantly without barriers,"[34] Twitter offers space where users craft, disseminate, and aggregate brief social communications to and from others using "tweets" limited in size to 140 characters. Twitter describes itself as "dedicated to building a platform where all voices can be heard,"[35] and is understood to be both "about broadcasting daily short burst messages to the world, with the hope that your messages are useful and interesting to someone" and "about discovering interesting people online and following their burst messages for as long as they are interesting."[36]

Unlike Facebook, Twitter allows users to hold multiple accounts, and it hosts accounts and users' handles, or account names, that do not need to include the users' offline name. Also unlike Facebook, the vast majority of Twitter accounts are public, allowing anyone—not just followers—to read users' tweets. Twitter also allows users to post photos, direct message ("DM") other accounts, and demarcate appreciation of others' tweets with a star icon and note to the original user through "favoriting," and to "retweet" or repost others' tweets. Retweeting is most commonly a sign of appreciation, though it can also be used to spread pictures or other tweeted information for less supportive and beneficent reasons.

In June 30, 2016, Twitter hosted 313 million "active" accounts.[37] Though growth rates are higher in other nations, 21% of all Twitter accounts are based in the US, making the US the nation with the most users worldwide currently. The number of teens on Twitter doubled between 2009 and 2011 to surpass adults.[38] The Pew Internet and American Life Project found that 33% of online 13- to 17-year-old teens in the US used Twitter in 2015.[39] Of these teenaged Internet users, Twitter users represented a higher proportion of females and non-Hispanic Black teens. While young adults aged 18–29 are most likely to use Twitter, older teens were more likely than younger teens to use Twitter. Girls aged 15–17 represent the main teen tweeters, with 49% using Twitter.[40]

The Data

This book is based on interviews and observations with teen interlocutors.

Interviews

I conducted formal, semi-structured interviews with each of my interlocutors multiple times throughout this study. Most teens met with me at least five times as part of this research. Rural communities in the US often lack spaces for youth to gather with others outside of school.[41] The sites in this study proved no exception to this; finding locations to hold interviews proved a challenge. Many of the farming communities outside of Townsville offered boarded-up downtowns and no indoor public spaces, restaurants (fast food or otherwise), or tables inside their few, lonely gas stations. There were many Christian churches in the area, but none that had meeting space we could use. I interviewed some teens in their homes, but most told me they had little space in their houses, so we found other places to meet: storage rooms, the youth center, rooms made available by their high school, a roadside diner, the park. Many times, my car served as a mobile research unit. Lacking other spaces, I often picked up teens and drove through the country to discuss the week on the road. Other times, interviews were held in my car as it was parked outside of one of their houses. Winter is long and harsh in the Midwest. Finding a space was especially a challenge in the cold weather, when spending time outside was not an option. When warm weather returned, I interviewed some interlocutors as we walked around their neighborhoods and met with others on their front lawns or back yards.

Finding a space that allowed us to talk without being overheard in these areas was an even greater challenge. Flatville was the only town outside of Townsville with a library, and it was an echoing, one-room operation with a table in the front, a small computer room in back, and a volunteer staffer at a desk who kept a watchful eye (and a visibly listening ear) on both spaces.

First interviews began with a set of questions asked to gain broad information, and to help us establish some general rapport. From then on, the questions I asked of teens in interviews were primarily emic, or emerging to follow the most pressing issues and topics at hand. I was interested in learning from my teens, and aware that my perceptions of what was important to know on any given day about their social media involvement might not align with what they encountered as meaningful. Because of this, our meetings were designed to be led by teens' interests, insights, and experiences. While I always entered meetings with questions, I often abandoned most of them to follow lines of thought raised in discussion.

Meetings were recorded using a small digital audio recorder. As part of our first meetings, I told the teens about the recorder, and I showed them how to operate it, telling them that they could begin the recording each time we met when they were ready to start. All interviews began with a teen pressing "start" on the recorder, followed by me saying the date and my interlocutor introducing herself. Recording would start and I would say: "Ok! Today is Tuesday, November 12 and I'm here with . . . " to which the teen would respond with her pseudonym. After our first meetings, I would start by asking my interlocutors what was new on Facebook or Twitter. I would ask questions to get further clarity, details, or examples, but I generally let the teens talk. Throughout our discussions, when it felt appropriate, I would ask follow-up questions noted from review of their previous interviews, and I would query them about information observed on their social media pages outside of our meeting. I took notes on recorded interviews, which were later transcribed.

Observations

Beyond interviews, I also observed teens both in person and online as part of this study.

I arranged to spend extensive in-person time with my interlocutors, but I found myself faced with difficulties attempting to interact with them as part of their naturally occurring life "in the world," as might be imagined in a typical ethnography. These teens went to school all day. Some had sports after school. They went home after the school day and practices were over. Many had responsibilities to meet younger siblings at the bus and to supervise them until parents arrived home from work. All had curfews and limited ability to go out of their house once they were home. With few spaces to gather and permission needed to leave the house, these teens had no regular "hang outs" outside of the home where I could drop in to observe them in an organic environment that was part of their world. Because of this, we scheduled meetings and searched for meeting spaces. This, they told me, was something they also did. While their highly scheduled and monitored lifestyles presented limitations to participatory observation, by creatively working with them to find spaces to host private conversations, I was able to interact with them within a subsection of their natural environment.

Some meetings would involve my interlocutors using social media while I observed them. Often in these sessions, I would ask them to talk through what they were doing. In these times, I wanted to see what they were doing and know what they were thinking, and why they were taking certain actions. Other times, I would tell teens to log on and to do what they would normally do, no descriptions needed.

The number of observations varied from teen to teen. For those who could not meet with me at their homes and who did not have wireless access on their phones, it was very difficult finding meeting places with Internet access, especially in areas outside of Townsville. There were no restaurants within 30 miles of Brown, Carroll, Concord, Flatville, Prairie, or Willow with public wireless service. The Flatville Public Library had odd hours that were unexpectedly shortened due to difficulties finding volunteer staffers. The new times were posted on a handwritten sign in the library window, but not on the website. This library also had two public computers with Internet access. However, on two occasions, an interlocutor and I logged on to find their wireless service down. The volunteer staffing the library said she was unfamiliar with computers, and unable to remedy the situation. "I think they might be having problems," she told Noel and I the second time they did not work. And Brown High School blocked wireless signals, shutting down cell phone service within its walls and in a section of its parking lot. It also did not allow students to access social media on their library computers. This prevented us from going online when meeting in this space. Despite these obstacles, I was able to observe all of my interlocutors in their daily lives, and most of them using social media.

I also observed these teens' lives on social media. I friended them on Facebook. Teens who were on Twitter gave me their Twitter handles—all of which gave no hint about their "real" name. All of the teens' pages on Twitter were public, so I did not need to follow them to observe them in this space. However, I gave them my Twitter handle, and told them that, if they wanted, they were welcome to follow me, and that I would follow them back until we ended our time together. I regularly observed and downloaded interlocutors' Facebook and Twitter profiles, regarding these platforms as sites for observation of my interlocutors as they lived in social media. I took screen shots of different parts of homepages, and saved these images to files that were also coded.

I reviewed my interlocutors' profiles a number of times before every interview, and I referred to them often when meeting with teens to ask about interactions and to clarify involvements that both aligned and differed from what teens said they did online.

Self-Presentation in Research

As a researcher, I bring certain experiences and approaches to my work. Growing up outside of Chicago, I had some firsthand experience with constraints that might be presented by rurality, adolescence, and gender. Through age 13, I lived with my family in the country some 50 country-road miles west of my mother's large Southside Chicago family. In the country, my house filled a corner acre. One side of our yard was bordered by a gravelly side street that led to the stream where we looked for frogs in the spring, and that passed the house of the older twin boys who pushed me down at the bus stop every winter. The street ended suddenly at a barbed wire fence branding a "No Trespassing" sign that we, on occasion, heeded. Beyond the thorny blackberry bushes, another edge of our home was flanked by the long, hilly, main rural road that looped around our unincorporated area, spilling out from either end onto the highway. Turning right from the side street, this road took us by a handful of homes, a field of cows, and a wetlands preserve before T-ing into the two-lane highway. Turning right again, it cut for miles through fields, then under a four-way flashing red light, then past the high school, the junior high, and a small neighborhood full of houses before eventually slowing down to enter the downtown.

Living in the country, I knew space. In being situated away from most others, our house in the country often felt safe and secluded. In many ways, as a child, I cherished the openness around us. We were allowed to roam within the area, and, with three sisters, I never felt lonely in my explorations. We climbed trees and chased our Old English Sheepdog around the yard in the daytime, and played ghost in the graveyard late into the night. We wandered through houses under construction after work crews left feeling confident no one would see us, and rode sleds tied to the back of the car over ice and snow with our parents knowing they would not have to worry about encountering other cars. The space encouraged some forms of active involvement. But as I got older and had little sisters to watch, friend visits and Halloween trick-or-treating requiring rides, and no money, transportation, or permission to spend time at the pool, the library, the mall, my friend's house, or in the speed-skating contests at the roller rink on the other edge of town, I also recall beginning to feel some of the constraints of open space in the country. Although there were still trees to climb and frogs to catch, I felt far away from other things I was beginning to believe mattered, things outside of my immediate environment that made me feel important, and made my life feel interesting and meaningful.

In eighth grade, I reluctantly moved with my family to the south suburbs of Chicago, bribed by a new 10-speed Schwinn. This was before the days of the Internet, and long before I had a license and a car, so I knew leaving town meant leaving friends I loved. With a laid-off father, money was tight. We were permitted very few long-distance phone calls, and trips back to our former town were infrequent. Still, I kept up to date with close friends through letters. "There's not much to do around here," I recall a friend telling me on a rare, but cherished, visit back. I bring this background to my research.

I also come to this research after studying and working with girls for many years. My path through graduate school was less than direct, and I ultimately benefited from this. I completed a degree in Educational Psychology before taking a position with a local engineering college where I coordinated engineering camps for female teens and considered factors impacting the recruitment and retention of female engineering students. During this time, I also co-founded and directed GirlZone, a feminist, grassroots program that hosted female-led workshops, festivals, shows, and mentoring for girls and young women.[42] In GirlZone, I was able to expand and apply my understanding of critical pedagogy by studying feminism, culture, and power, and by working with girls to consider the multiple cultural contexts that mediate and inform identities, interests, understandings, and involvements. This work inspired and shaped me in many ways. It also led me into my doctoral program in Adolescent Development. I was in the final years of this program when I began fieldwork for this book.

Throughout my fieldwork, I worked to create an approachable and safe-feeling environment for my interlocutors' involvement. I volunteered at a youth center to help connect with some teen volunteers who eventually joined this study. Both there and in individual meetings with teens in the study, I dressed casually but presentably. I wore my hair down rather than up as I typically did when teaching at the university, and asked teens to call me by my first name. I let them know that I wanted to hear what they really felt and thought. I reminded them that their comments would never be linked to them, specifically, and that what they shared with me would not be able to be traced back to them by anyone. I said I was not there to judge them on what they knew or on how they acted, but to understand more about the experiences of teens like them. I tried hard to create a comfortable and open environment in which my interlocutors would feel safe sharing their experiences and ideas. The repeated meetings established a trust between me and my interlocutors that helped us move beyond stock responses the teens were well prepared to give about Internet safety and their own involvements. However, despite this, it is important to acknowledge that I am still an adult, a white woman, a researcher from the university. As such, the way I was able to participate in the field created particular relationships with my interlocutors that shaped their disclosure and involvements with me.

As a 30-something-year-old university-affiliated adult, I arrived to the field with a certain level of authority that these teens, as people deemed "minors" in society, probably recognized as important to heed. For example, one girl's parent alerted her to my arrival by announcing through the screen door into the house: "The teacher is here!" As a white woman interacting with teens who, as racial and ethnic minorities, had experienced racism, I very easily could have been viewed as someone who would not understand, like, or want to accept their experiences. While I let my interlocutors know that there were no "right" answers, and that they were free to skip any questions I asked or end our meetings whenever they felt like it, my social position doubtlessly influenced their participation. The teens talked to me about many subjects that might be considered taboo. However, in speaking with me, all of these teens must have deliberated to some extent on which of their realities to make visible to me, and which to make invisible. Should they say what they really think, or say things they thought I would want to hear and avoid those things they thought I would not like? I worked hard to build trust to help with disclosure. Still, because of who I am, and because of the way race, age, ethnicity, and class contribute to hierarchies in US society, I brought to the field a very specific power that surely complicated teens' ability to disclose, especially initially.

I let those in my study know that I, like them, grew up in the country. I let them know that I also used social media (primarily Facebook). I made clear to my interlocutors that I was meeting with them to learn from them about their experiences, but I told all of the teens that they were welcome to ask me questions as well. The relationships I was forming with these teens opened up opportunities for them to take me up on this offer. Some asked me how my week had been. Others asked for specific assistance. For example, Annie discussed her difficulties trying to find information about admission requirements for universities during her Internet searches. Being the first to consider college in her family, she detailed receiving little help on this from adults in her life at home or at school, or from Facebook friends, and she spoke at length about getting lost online while trying to locate this information. At the end of this discussion, she asked me if I knew how to find admission criteria for Harvard. I told her I could help, and worked with her to find the page she was seeking. Another time, while discussing privacy settings, Violet was surprised to see that her phone number was listed on her Facebook account. She was not able to figure out how to remove it using her phone, and said she had no access to a computer to make this change. She asked if I could help her delete it from her page. I said I would look into it and get back to her, which I did. As an ethnographer, I saw this type of dialectical reciprocity as essential in building the trust and openness needed to learn from—and to respect—interlocutors in this setting.

Beyond this, it must be said that it is difficult for young women to be honest about many of the experiences they have within a dominant US society that views them as appropriately asexual, necessarily interested in boys, easily corrupted, and ideally pure, good, and smart. The teens in this study knew they were "not supposed to" smoke, drink, swear, use drugs, sneak out, act upon their sexual interests, or sneak around on or offline. They knew there were ways adults wanted to see them, and things they and other teens did that adults typically would not approve of. Although I repeated through-out our time together that no one they knew would ever be told about them saying any specific comments, and that what they told me would not be able to be traced back to them, my interlocutors surely grappled with the notion that they might get in trouble by giving voice to some of their on- and offline realities. Also, to varying extents, I could tell they wanted me to see them as worthy of attention. Ethnography proved invaluable in ensuring repeated visits with interlocutors that allowed us to move past superficial responses to more complex and multiple realities. However, getting teens to talk beyond the rhetoric of appropriate childhood and girlhood is a challenge to all studies that seek to learn from and about adolescent-aged females, as is getting girls to talk honestly about social media use and other parts of their lives that are laden with unrealistic advice telling them how to be "safe" or "good."

Analysis of the Data

In his influential text, *The Interpretation of Cultures*, Clifford Geertz writes that "what we call our data are really our own constructions of other people's constructions of what they and their compatriots are up to."[43] In data analy-sis, I interpreted and organized these constructions throughout this study to find relational meanings, considering interviews along with in-person and social media participant observation notes. Interview transcripts and observa-tional data received line-by-line open coding to note concepts and actions discussed by teens across ages that they used to explain and conceptualize their experiences. This presented me with codes that I compared to one another to identify larger domains, or shared meanings around actions, be-tween them. I checked in with teens as domains were being formed to ask if these concepts held meaning to them, and both memoed and reflected upon their feedback in further consideration of categories.

The domains were further sorted and compiled, worked and reworked through componential analysis to gather them together and break them down into 72 broad categories that I reviewed within and across to find shared meanings. No distinctions were found between younger and older interlocu-tors. I compared data with one another, and with my notes from interviews, reflections, and observations, and I identified overlapping and contradicting sentiments, experiences, and statements among them. From this, I broke these broad categories into more specific themes and sub-themes reflecting overlapping and more detailed patterns observed in the data. As interviews continued, these categories grew large with data. Categories and themes were further refined by comparing them to one another in reflection upon notes and memos to consider the data as "constitutive of" specific conditions within which they exist. Categories were collapsed and expanded into one another to embody these conditions in these data. This re-organized the data in a way that created themes capturing shared processes and experiences of the girls within each larger category.

Vignettes

Each chapter begins with a vignette portraying interlocutors' lives and social media use in wider context. Girls are avid social media users, but they do not commonly speak candidly to adults about this use. Similar to their wider social involvements, US adults tend to regard female teens' social media involvements with suspicion, fearing for them and expecting them to be up to no good in these spaces. Teens hear about this regularly from parents, teachers, law officials, and in school assemblies. Also, parents commonly recognize social media as a distraction from other obligations such as homework, as well as from face-to-face interactions. Girls realize that their social media use worries the cherished adults in their lives and threatens trusts they worked to gain from them. For example, LaToya explained: "My mom doesn't really know what I do mostly on [social media]. I don't know what the deal is, but she's always telling me to get off and do something else." As a result, LaToya lived actively on various social media platforms, but she felt nervous and guilty about these involvements. She knew that certain pictures and flirtatious exchanges with boys in these platforms would certainly upset her mother, but she did not know if other acts would cause alarm. Rather than risk getting in trouble for raising a controversial involvement, she did not talk to her mother about her life on social media. Others felt similarly. Social media is a taboo subject for US girls. Teens who hope to impress the adult in front of them know not to broach the subject of their social media use. They know doing so is risky and reckless when considering their larger interests. They know they will not be understood.

These teen's online lives were found to have deep roots in their offline realities. With the repeated and long-term engagement allowed by ethnography, my interlocutors were able to talk and explain and contradict and construct themselves to me as they discussed their experiences and perspectives. In an effort to trace the threads of social media interest, involvement, and identities woven in and across on- and offline platforms, and to capture the essential larger context of media migration that is necessary to accomplish what sociologist Dawn Currie terms "listening 'beyond and around' girls' words,"[44] this book is guided by thick description[45] of experiences of—and interactions with—interlocutors encapsulated in vignettes.

CHAPTER OVERVIEW

Focusing on lives on- and offline, the remaining chapters examine how these teens used social media to mediate US adolescence and girlhood. To do so, I have organized chapters around regular challenges, frustrations, and issues they faced in their daily lives that motivated their media migrations. Setting the stage of each chapter is a vignette.

Chapter 2, "It Just Felt Like There Was a Lot More Space Around Here Before": Crowded Isolation introduces the themes of isolation and crowdedness that run throughout my interlocutors' lives offline in their homes and communities due to the social positions they occupy as female adolescents in post-recession US society. It unpacks the specific economic, social, and cultural contexts faced by these girls, and discusses how feelings of isolation and crowdedness inspire them into media migration where they are able to feel less constrained and more respected in their social involvements.

Drawing off these teens' experiences, chapter 3, "This Is About as Good as It Gets": Negotiating Involvement, looks more closely at what adolescents are doing offline and in online social spheres, specifically on Facebook and Twitter. In addition to examining the technical and social factors that influenced their willingness to stay and become more invested or to move on from these sites, this chapter considers the challenges rural life brings them offline that they attempt to tackle online.

Zooming in to more a granular examination of these practices, chapter 4, "I Don't Want Them Knowing My Business. And They Don't Have To": Negotiating Performances of (In)Visibility, explores the ways teens perform their identities both to maintain important relationships while curating controversial identities within and across commercial social media platforms, and to claim these identities for their own use as the spaces they are in simultaneously aggregate these same identities for their own immediate and vaguely defined future use.

Chapter 5, "I Think It's Pretty Private": Negotiating Safety, Risk, and Recklessness consider various framings of young females' safety in light of these teens' experiences in social media. Examining teen confidence in safely using social media, this chapter explores areas of safety and risk raised by teens' experiences with media migration and asks whether existing conceptualizations of youth and social media safety and risk are sufficient to keep daughters informed in ways that ensure their safety online and offline.

Chapter 6, Adolescent Marginality and Media Migration synthesizes issues addressed throughout the book to examine how marginality can be understood to be a context that informs and directs young people's actions on- and offline in US society.

Looking beyond stock binary cultural framings of girls as "at-risk" and "reckless," this research seeks to tell a detailed story about teenaged young women who, as part of everyday life, strategically and intentionally use social media as part of their larger efforts to be taken seriously, to have meaningful involvement in the world, and to make something of their lives in today's America.

NOTES

1. Laurence Steinberg, *Adolescence* (Chicago: McGraw Hill, 1993).
2. James Côté and Anton Allahar, *Generation on Hold: Coming of Age in the Late Twentieth Century* (New York: NYU Press, 1994), 26.
3. Mary Celeste Kearney, "Coalescing: The Development of Girls' Studies," *NWSA Journal* 21, no. 1 (2009); Johanna Wyn and Rob White, *Rethinking Youth* (London: Sage, 1997).
4. Nancy Lesko, *Act Your Age: A Cultural Construction of Adolescence*, 2nd ed. (New York: Routledge, 2012); Jason Sternberg, "Young, Dumb, and Full of Lies: The News Media's Construction of Youth Culture," *Screen Education* 37 (2004).
5. Sunaina Maira and Elizabeth Soep, *Youthscapes* (Philadelphia: University of Pennsylvania Press, 2005).
6. See Richard Delgado and Jean Stefancic, *Critical Race Theory: An Introduction* (New York, NY: NYU Press); Nicole Fleetwood, "Busing It in the City: Black Youth, Performance, and Public Transit," *TDR: The Drama Review* 48, no. 2 (2004); Henry Giroux, *Disturbing Pleasures: Learning Popular Culture* (New York: Routledge, 1994); bell hooks, *Black Looks: Race and Representation* (New York: Random House, 1981); Angela McRobbie, *Feminism and Youth Culture: From Jackie to Just Seventeen* (New York: Routledge, 1991); Katherine Bond Stockton, *The Queer Child, or Growing Sideways in the Twentieth Century* (Durham: Duke University Press, 2009).
7. Mary Celeste Kearney, "Coalescing: The Development of Girls' Studies," *NWSA Journal* 21, no. 1 (2009).
8. See Dawn H. Curry, "From Girlhood, Girls, to Girl Studies," in Clare Bradford and Mavis Reimer, eds., *Girls, Texts, Cultures* (Waterloo, Ontario, Canada: WLU Press, 2015); Lesko, *Act Your Age*; Claudia Mitchell and Jacqueline Reid-Walsh, "How to Study Girl Culture," *Girl Culture: An Encyclopedia*. Vol. 1, ed. Claudia Mitchell and Jacqueline Reid-Walsh (Westport, CT: Greenwood, 2008).
9. Reed Larson, "The Future of Adolescence: Lengthening Ladders to Adulthood," *The Futurist* (2002, November/December); Reed Larson, Suzanne Wilson, and Aimee Rickman, "Adolescence across Place and Time: Globalization and the Changing Pathways to Adulthood," in *Handbook of Adolescent Psychology* (2nd Ed.), ed. Reed Lerner and Lawrence Steinberg (New York: Wiley, 2009).
10. Larson, "The Future"; Jeylan T. Mortimer et al., "Tracing the Timing of 'Career' Acquisition in a Contemporary Youth Cohort," *Work and Occupations* 35, no. 1 (2008).
11. See danah boyd, "Why Youth (Heart) Social Network Sites: The Role of Networked Publics in Teenage Social Life," in D. Buckingham (Ed.), *MacArthur Foundation Series on Digital Learning—Youth, Identity, and Digital Media* (Cambridge: MIT Press, 2007), 119–142; danah boyd, *It's Complicated: The Social Lives of Networked Teens* (New Haven: Yale, 2014); Mizuko Ito, Sonja Baumer, Matteo Bittanti, danah boyd, Rachel Cody, Becky Herr-Stephenson, . . . and Lisa Tripp (Eds.), *Hanging Out, Messing Around, and Geeking Out: Kids Living and Learning with New Media* (Cambridge: MIT Press, 2010); Howard Rheingold, *The Virtual Community: Homesteading the Electronic Frontier* (Cambridge: MIT Press, 2000); José Van Dijck, *The Culture of Connectivity: A Critical History of Social Media* (Oxford: Oxford University Press, 2013).
12. See Dick Hebdige, *Subculture: The Meaning of Style* (London: Routledge, 1991), 18.
13. Although online environments are not literally places, "space" and movement are metaphors I will use throughout this project in referring to the social settings teens engage in online.
14. Amy L. Best, *Representing Youth: Methodological Issues in Critical Youth Studies* (New York: NYU Press, 2007); Jens Qvortrup, *Childhood Matters: Social Theory, Practice,*

and Politics (Aldershot, UK: Avebury, 1994). Also see Esther Dyson, George Gilder, George Keyworth, and Alvin Toffler, "Cyberspace and the American Dream: A Magna Carta for the Knowledge Age," *Release* 1, no. 2 (1994).

15. For example, two recent research reports on youth social media involvement put out by the Pew Center on Internet & American Life (Madden, Lenhart, Cortesi, Gasser, Duggan, Smith, and Beaten 2013; Madden, Lenhart, Duggan, Cortesi, and Gasser, 2013) were based on data gathered through focus groups held across the greater Boston area, in Greensboro, North Carolina, and in Los Angeles and Santa Barbara, California, which built upon findings from a undefined yet "nationally representative" phone survey. Details given by one (Madden, Lenhart, Duggan, Cortesi and Gasser, 2013) specify that rural youth were identified as only 12% of the 789 teens surveyed. There were 50% fewer rural teens than urban teens in the study, and rural teens represented less than a fourth of the number of suburban teens involved. The Pew's work on youth and Internet is taken quite seriously by those studying teens and Internet involvement, but this study's low representation of rural teens in a "nationwide" sample highlights a common overlooking of the experiences of rural teens in research providing insights on "teens" and "youth."

16. Sharon R. Mazzarella, "Reflecting on Girls' Studies and the Media: Current Trends and Future Directions," *Journal of Children and Media* 2, no. 1.

17. See John Clarke, Stuart Hall, Tony Jefferson, and Brian Roberts, "Subcultures, Cultures and Class," in Stuart Hall and Tony Jefferson (Eds.), *Resistance through Rituals: Youth Subculture in Post-War Britain* (New York: Routledge, 1975), 9–74; Phil Cohen, *Rethinking the Youth Question* (London: Macmillan, 1997); James Côté and Anton Allahar, *Generation on Hold,* 1993.

18. Erik H. Erikson, *Identity: Youth and Crisis* (New York: W. W. Norton and Co., 1968), 61.

19. Ibid., 50.

20. Sinikka Aapola, Marnina Gonick, and Anita Harris, *Young Femininity: Girlhood, Power and Social Change* (New York: Palgrave Macmillan, 2005); Clare Bradford and Mavis Reimer, eds., *Girls, Texts, Cultures* (Waterloo, Ontario, Canada: WLU Press, 2015); Kearney, "Coalescing"; Angela McRobbie, *Feminism and Youth Culture: From Jackie to Just Seventeen* (London: MacMillan, 1991); Angela McRobbie and Jenny Garber, "Girls and Subcultures," in *Resistance through Rituals: Youth Subcultures in Post-War Britain,* eds. Stuart Hall and Tony Jefferson (London: Harper Collins Academic, 1976).

21. Claudia Mitchell, Jacqueline Reid-Walsh, and Jackie Kirk, "Editorial," *Girlhood Studies* 1, no. 1 (Summer 2008).

22. Kimberle Crenshaw, "Mapping the Margins: Intersectionality, Identity Politics, and Violence against Women of Color," *Stanford Law Review* 43, no. 6 (July 1991); Sharon R. Mazzarella, "Reflecting on Girls' Studies and the Media: Current Trends and Future Directions," *Journal of Children and Media* 2, no. 1 (2008); Lisa Nakamura, *Cybertypes: Race, Ethnicity, and Identity on the Internet* (New York: Routledge, 2002); Lisa Nakamura, *Digitizing Race: Visual Cultures of the Internet* (Minneapolis, MN: University of Minnesota Press, 2008).

23. Aapola, Gonick, and Harris, *Young Femininity*; Bradford and Reimer, *Girls, Texts, Cultures*; Kearney, "Coalescing"; David W. Proefrock, "Adolescence: Social Fact and Psychological Concept," *Adolescence* 26 (1981): 858.

24. Anthony Giddens, *The Constitution of Society: Outline of the Theory of Structuration* (Berkeley: University of California Press, 1984).

25. Lesko, *Act Your Age,* 5.

26. Facebook, "Statements of Rights and Responsibilities," accessed October 31, 2017 https://www.facebook.com/legal/terms

27. Facebook, "Stats," accessed October 31, 2017 https://newsroom.fb.com/company-info/

28. Amanda Lenhart, "Teens, Social Media & Technology Overview 2015," Pew Research Center, April 2015. Accessed January 3, 2017. http://www.pewinternet.org/files/2015/04/PI_TeensandTech_Update2015_0409151.pdf.

29. David Kirkpatrick, *The Facebook Effect: The Story of the Company That Is Connecting the World* (New York: Simon and Schuster, 2010), 199.

30. Facebook, "Our Mission," accessed March 5, 2013, https://newsroom.fb.com/company-info/; Gillian Reagan, "The Evolution of Facebook's Mission Statement," *The Observer* (July 13, 2009), accessed October 31, 2017, http://observer.com/2009/07/the-evolution-of-facebooks-mission-statement/.

31. Facebook, "Our Mission," accessed October 31, 2017, https://newsroom.fb.com/company-info/; Mark Zuckerberg, "Bringing The World Closer Together," *Facebook,* last modified June 22, 2017, https://www.facebook.com/notes/mark-zuckerberg/bringing-the-world-closer-together/10154944663901634/.

32. Lenhart, "Teens, Social Media."

33. danah boyd and Eszter Hargittai, "Facebook Privacy Settings: Who Cares?" *First Monday* 15, no. 8 (2010). Accessed May 2, 2017, http://firstmonday.org/article/view/3086/2589.

34. Twitter, "Mission," accessed October 31, 2017, https://twitter.com/about.

35. Twitter, "Our Company," accessed October 31, 2017, https://twitter.com/about.

36. Paul Gil, "What Exactly Is 'Twitter'? What Is 'Tweeting'?" (2012). Accessed October 4, 2016, http://netforbeginners.about.com/od/internet101/f/What-Exactly-Is-Twitter.htm.

37. Ibid.

38. D. Bailey, "Shifting Twitter Demographics: Twitter Less about Teen Drama, More about World Politics," *The Content Standard* (January 14, 2013). Accessed March 23, 2017, https://www.skyword.com/contentstandard/marketing/shifting-twitter-demographics-twitter-less-about-teen-drama-more-about-world-politics/.

39. Lenhart, "Teens, Social Media."

40. Lenhart, "Teens, Social Media." Some 37% of females are Twitter users compared to boys' 30%. Some 45% of Twitter are users non-Hispanic Black teens compared to 34% Hispanic and 31% non-Hispanic White teens. Some 42% of older 15-17-year-old teens use Twitter compared to 21% of 13–14 year olds.

41. See A. Yousefian, E. Ziller, J. Swartz, and D. Hartley (2009). "Active Living for Rural Youth: Addressing Physical Inactivity in Rural Communities," *Journal of Public Health Management and Practice* 15, no. (3), 223–31. doi:10.1097/PHH.0b013e3181a11822

42. An excellent book was written on GirlZone. See: Mary Sheridan-Rabideau, *Girls, Feminism, and Grassroots Literacies* (New York: NYU Press, 2008).

43. Clifford Geertz, *The Interpretation of Cultures* (New York: Basic Books, 1973), 22.

44. Dawn H. Currie, "Talking with Girls: Methodological Challenges and the Need to Sharpen Our Methods of Inquiry," *Journal of Children and Media* 2, no. 1 (2008).

45. Geertz, *The Interpretation of Cultures.* See also Robert E. Stake, *The Art of Case Study Research* (Thousand Oaks, CA: Sage, 1995).

Chapter Two

"It Just Felt Like There Was a Lot More Space Around Here Before"

Crowded Isolation

The school bell rings, announcing the end of the day. From my car, I scan faces as students pour out of the doors of Brown High School in pairs and ambling groups, climbing steps to board one of the four waiting buses or heading for a truck or car in the parking lot (the makeup of the lot has the odds leaning toward a truck). I am looking for Marcin, but she is nowhere to be found. The vehicles in the lot fill quickly and motor away from the brick building, passing a handful of students walking down the gravel drive and leaving an empty school yard.

I drive away from the school's cell phone signal jammer to where the bars on my phone begin to build, and pull over to send Marcin a message on Facebook. *I am at your school, but must have misunderstood where we planned to meet today,* I write, followed by mention that I will be swinging by her home in Concord to see if she is there. I drive out of Brown, population 262, and, after twelve minutes, take a left to enter the city of Flatville, population 750. Over the next five miles, I pass two cars and a sprawling silver grain elevator before stopping at the sole stop sign in Marcin's hometown. The road T-s into a row of low, white houses making up Concord, population 102. I turn left toward the post office and park in front of Marcin's family's single-wide mobile home behind a high, white fence. I begin to text again when Marcin appears outside of my window, waving, freckles and gray-green eyes standing out against her pale skin. It's a blustery winter afternoon with whipping winds spitting snow, and Marcin, a 19-year old high school junior, braves the cold in a sweatshirt and jeans. She raises her eyebrows, smiling and hugging her arms while rocking back and forth in the cold. I motion to her to come around and jump in. She opens the passenger side door and climbs into the seat, shrugging as she buckles her belt. "I totally forgot we were meeting."

We know our plan. There are no publicly accessible buildings in or near her home. The closest restaurant is six miles away, but it is only open at night for dinner. The nearest fast food place will take at least 25 minutes to reach if we take the interstate highway. The only library within 20 miles is closed on Wednesdays and, with only one room, it is sometimes lacking in privacy when open. We knew of nowhere to meet, so we have—again—decided to just talk as we drive, an activity Marcin tells me is a common way for her to spend time with friends when they want to have time together. "We hang out at each others' houses mostly," she says. "But you always have to deal with people around, brothers and parents and stuff. A lot of times when we want to have some space just to kind of do our thing, we just drive around. We don't really go anywhere. We just drive." Today, we do just that, driving through the low brown fields sitting fallow for the winter with small farmhouses and barns in the distance.

We pass huge, white wind turbines standing in the fields in various stages of assembly along our aimless route. In driving through the area over the past year, I have watched the number of these spinning giants grow. One year ago, there was one small stretch of them in a field far from the highway, spinning tiny on the horizon. Now, they are scattered throughout the region, passing outside of both of our windows as we leave Concord. A driver's quick glance off the road around Marcin's home is now just as likely to meet open fields as they are to hit upon blocks of white turbine trunks reaching upward beyond view. I can't think of one drive I have taken to Concord in the past six months when I did not meet a convoy of trucks carrying immense windmill arms to a local construction site, or a late drive out of the area when a constellation could be found through the blinking lights. A break in our conversation about the past week gives me an opportunity to ask Marcin what she thinks about the turbines. She replies:

I guess it's been a big change having the windmills here. Big but not really big. Things look really different. . . . I just kind of feel it's overcrowding. Like, it kind of feels like they're kind of taking up more space than they are. . . . It just felt like there was a lot more space around here before. It looks kinds of weird, but it looks cool too. Like, the blades just look weird at nighttime, all you see is red dots. But it looks kind of cool because it makes a shape, kind of. And it makes the sky all red. You can't really see the sky or the stars as much, but it's still kind of cool. But it's kind of crowded. They're everywhere and they're so close. That's all you see when you look out: windmills. I don't think about it much. Just sometimes, there's a glare. And the crowding. I guess it just feels different now.

CROWDED ISOLATION

Marcin's comments echo what teens in my study told me life was like for them as young women in their rural towns. Throughout my fieldwork, the teens I met with repeatedly described a constant awareness of space, with their lives marked by feelings of both isolation and crowdedness. In their descriptions, these feelings were not presented as binary, "either-or" categories. Rather, with few places to be on their own and ample opportunity to feel alone, isolation and crowdedness were presented by youth as complicated categories that were discussed as ever-present, intermingled, and frustrating. Rural girls in early twenty-first-century America are not novel in this; feeling contained and constrained is a common experience for American teens. Indeed, adolescence, itself, is predicated upon deeply seated, century-old views claiming that youth should be simultaneously isolated and crowded.

In his 1904 "discovery" of adolescence, for example, psychologist G. Stanley Hall—borrowing recapitulation from biology—called for the increased containment and heightened supervision of those he described as occupying a hormonally driven, "savage, pigmoid" lower state so they could develop beyond what he deemed the pathology of pubertal youth into mature, self-governing adults. However, as much as removing youth from the mainstream encouraged adolescents' isolation, the demands for their extended cultivation and guidance in the home, at school, and within other age-graded institutions of cultural learning encouraged these adolescents to be crowded with adult monitors and peers. Hall's views on recapitulation were refuted and ultimately dismissed by biologists and critical scholars,[1] but attitudes about sequestering and monitoring youth justified by biological explanations remain dominant. The project of surveilling youth and removing them from meaningful societal involvement in the US continues to charge ahead, with females facing additional restrictions due to gender bias. The frustration this causes is exacerbated by teens having no clear pathways to move toward fuller standing in their futures as the period of adolescent non-adulthood extends later into life for Americans.[2]

As these teens felt isolated, watched, and cut off from the world, they turned to social media, taking part in crowded online social spaces that broadcast their contributions with those of many others, and that put them on show to family members, friends, and other disparate communities rarely merged offline. Yet whereas adults might view social media as expanding the boundaries of their social lives, adolescents often need to find ways to carve out spaces that will allow them opportunities to negotiate the social marginality they regularly encounter in being crowded by people, rules, and oversight in geographic and social isolation on and offline. Crowded isolation is a feature of teens' daily lives. It is also a context that motivates teens to move their attentions.

Isolation

"There's nothing around" was a phrase used by all the teens when talking about where they live, and each discussed feeling disconnected and alone in a number of ways. To start, they felt isolated due to their geography. Teens who lived in towns had parks where they could meet up with others to be social in warm weather, but both those in town and outside of them in "the country" said they had very few things to do during the colder months that spanned nearly half the year. For example, 15-year-old Amelia's comments illustrate how little some US communities offer teens in the way of available—let alone entertaining or exciting—social space:

> I live in town, but, I mean, we're not a very, we don't have places to go. We don't have like a Casey's [General Store] or anything, so the only thing to do is just walk around. Usually in the winter, we just drive places. So like the movies or whatever. I guess you hang out in the park, you could but you'd be very cold. No one does that. And, well, sometimes we just drive around.

When I asked Amelia how long it would take for her to get to the movies, she said the closest theatre to her home was 45 minutes away.

Other teens also discussed how their physical environment increased their isolation by offering few options for meaningful involvement. Living geographically far away from school, from town, from theatres, malls, skating rinks, swimming pools, and other physical spaces where teens might regularly spend out-of-school time, they felt cut off from things they imagined were important. "There's not much to do," 17-year-old Noel explained. "There's nothing—no stores or anything. You can't shop. Everything is so far away." Other teens in other small towns agreed. "There's nothing to do here," said 17-year-old Annie, with a sigh.

Further complicating matters is that spaces that often accommodate teens require money. Not only are there costs for admission and involvement, but for transportation and gas, limiting access for US teens facing both rising child poverty and the highest unemployment rates for workers their age since data first began being collected by the Bureau of Labor Statistics in 1947;[3] these economic disparities were even more pronounced in rural communities that already had very high and persistent poverty levels. Some of the teens whose families were better off believed that all teens had cars. Molly, for instance, observed that "most people do have a vehicle to get places. I mean most people over 16 that go to [my school]." But this was not the case, and not having access to a car made it very difficult for teens to avoid isolation once they were home from school—especially for teens like Annie, who had no computer or phone in her Eagle Bluff home, and no cell phone. Amelia explained:

There's two people in my class right now that have their license, but they don't live in this town. . . . It's not like I can just ask them [for a ride] 'cause I feel bad 'cause they, like they don't have a job yet. They just got their license, so then it's like a waste of gas money and then I don't have a job and I don't even have my license.

My meetings with Marcin—which often happened in car rides to nowhere—echoed these sentiments. At the end of one of our drives, Marcin and I sat in the car outside of her house and finished talking as fat snowflakes covered the car windows. I asked what there was to do in her town. Marcin tilted her head, paused, looked down the street, then back to me, and replied:

Well, there's church. Post office. They're thinking about making that into a grocery market, which would actually be really awesome, because then we could just walk down to the grocery store. That would be awesome. Now, we just walk around. There's nowhere to go. There's a cemetery down there. We just walk around. Go to the cemetery.

In a sprawling town with no public transportation options and no car, most teens had to rely on walking, but even that was not always viable. One early winter day, for example, I sat in 16½-year-old Violet's kitchen and asked her how long it would take to walk to the nearest neighbor's house. "To walk there?" she responded, incredulous. I expanded my question to include driving. She replied with a laugh, looking out the window at the immense low brown field past the driveway spanning to the horizon. "To drive there it'd be only like a few minutes, but it'd be quite a long walk." No kids her age lived in the area, she said, and the one friend who she mentioned earlier on in our meetings as stopping by most days on his way home from work to do homework crashed his car, and no longer could come by. "I don't really see anybody except my family once I come home." I asked how far away her closest friends are. She replied:

From Brown, like it's like fifteen, twenty minute drive. But everyone pretty much lives in Brown or Flatville, and maybe me being far out in the country is kind of, I don't know, I think it's inconvenient. . . . I live in the middle of, like, three cornfields. I have one neighbor that's kinda far away. Mom and Dad are the only ones who have cars and they both have jobs so I don't get to use a car. So we don't see anyone, and no one wants to drive that far and just come to my house.

Teens' geographic isolation impacted their daily lives. But for many, the social marginality they experienced as a byproduct of their physical isolation also felt like the result of inescapable forces the teen believed would impact them for years: "I'm gonna graduate from high school," Violet explained. "Not gonna have a job yet or a car, so I won't be able to get a job, so I'll just be stuck at home. And I won't see anyone ever." Suggesting isolation was related to failed identity, Violet continued: "I want to be someone someday. I don't want to end up like my brother's friends, just sitting at home until they're thirty, doing nothing." Violet's concerns articulated a sentiment common among her peers.

In addition to having little access to physical spaces in which they could socialize with other adolescents, all of the teens in this study said they had few peers living in their area. "No one lives by me," Annie said with a shake of the head and slow grin. "And no one will let me walk anywhere because they don't want me to fall in the street." Most of the teens had only a small number of friends (if any) who lived near enough to easily see after school, causing them to feel even more disconnected and on their own in the world. "You'd have more friends if you were in a bigger city," Noel stated. And as Violet explained: "People and teens in cities, they live closer to civilizations. They probably get more recognition than people that live in the country."

Naomi had one person near her age living close by her family's home in Brown, her "best friend since kindergarten." She added that her other friends lived at least a 10 minute drive away and were often busy after school with sports, as she had been before suffering a recent injury:

> Well, my other best friend, she has volleyball in morning before school and then she had a game after school and then sometimes she'd have to come home and just go do her homework and stuff and then sometimes she would go to school and have back-to-back volleyball and cheer practices and then get off at seven thirty, which makes it even hard to just talk to her about anything. I'll be like, "Can I call you really fast and tell you about what happened or something?" and she'll just be like, "Wait, I gotta do my homework."

Different schedules impacted the challenge to connect, but so did distance. At 14, Naomi was too young for a driver's license and, like some of the others, said she had few prospects for getting a car when she became 16, making it harder to stay in touch with friends who did not live in the area.

Physical distance remained a challenge, but it was not the only reason teens felt isolated. Many described feeling socially isolated, too. As adolescents in general and adolescent girls in particular, the teens in this study often spoke of being regularly blocked and monitored. Parents and the community worried that the teens were too young and too naïve to navigate a world of unknowns; therefore, teen's actions and interactions beyond home and school were constrained by formal and informal rules on where they could go and with whom. Laws, for example, scripted the number of teens allowed in one car and where teens were allowed at particular times of the day; community parks closed at dusk; certain shops permitted entry to no more than two teens at a time; teens needed to vacate school property if they were not participating in school-sponsored activities; and while all teens under the age of 17 had to be off the streets by 11pm on weekdays and by midnight on weekends, state nighttime driving restrictions forbid them from driving past 10pm during the week and 11pm on Fridays and Saturdays.

Enhancing these restrictions were those created by the teen's family. Some teens were prohibited from dating (although they still did). Most were not to attend parties in the woods (although they did this also). Amelia said her father set her curfew at 7:30 pm, and explained this by telling her: "You're not gonna be out with a guy after dark because I know how they think." She said her mother approved of this curfew because she did not want her to get pregnant. Such actions—meant to protect—merely reinforced the sense of isolation from conventional social networks: friends, classmates, and other immediate peers.

Further adding to the isolation teens felt was their lack of connection to communities outside of their immediate environment. Social media helped teens join and feel part of conversations and efforts they considered important. Locally, however, this was more difficult. For example, LaToya lived more than 1,000 miles from the Florida town where Trayvon Martin, an unarmed Black teenager, was fatally shot by George Zimmerman. Although LaToya did not live near Trayvon Martin, and though she did not personally know him, as a Black youth, she nevertheless affiliated with him and recognized him as a member of her community. As such, LaToya was outraged by the killing and by the shooter's ability to walk away from police following the incident. But despite her anger, she was not able to connect with others who felt the same way to discuss and process the events she considered both highly personal and reflective of wider systems of inequity and injustice. Most in her local communities and in her immediate social circles, for example, were Caucasian, which led some of them to see the Trayvon Martin story as a just another report about crime fighting dominating the media. Therefore, even though LaToya expressed her anger about events to a few close friends, she said most of her classmates did not feel the same, making her perspective controversial and largely unpopular with her peers. "We had a discussion of it in study hall," LaToya explained, "and the teacher was good but everyone else was like 'Well, what if [Trayvon Martin] punched Zimmerman in the face?' and 'Well, what did that boy do to make it happen?' and stuff."

LaToya said that she knew of no protest efforts in her school, neighborhood, or town to add her outrage to, and that her mother and after-school babysitting responsibilities at home would probably prevent her from joining any group that did exist. As such, she felt alone and unsupported in her beliefs. The lack of opportunities to share her views and contribute to conversations and actions that could improve her life and those in her community— no matter where her community was located—reinforced LaToya's feelings of isolation:

My teacher said they're going to have a trial on April 10, and I think that's when they're going to decide if Zimmerman is going to jail. And I hope he does! And if I could be at that trial when they have it, I would be there. But I can't. I mean, I don't think my mom is going to let me. But I would go and I would sit there in the back and I would probably have some comments. . . . Because if it was a Black person who shot a Caucasian, we would go to jail, 25 years to life, no bond, no bail. But it's different. . . . I just think that everyone should have the same equal rights, like equal justice laws, there should really be a law. And if I was old enough to go up and say, "this needs to be a law, this should be a law" and propose it, I would! But I'm not old enough, so I can't.

Teens felt cut off from the world they wanted to contribute to and be a part of. Annie explained:

Kids have very little opportunities. Say you know someone who's in trouble and you want to help. . . . (I)n real life, you can't help anyone because of your age and the minimum freedom that you have. Say you're a teenager, you're 14, 15, 16, and you see someone who's in need. You don't have any power, so you can't do anything. Like if they need something and you're in school, you can't just get out of school. You have to have a parent's note.

As much as teens craved opportunities to connect with others, they were still particular about those they wanted in their network. In other words, it wasn't just a matter of having people around; the teens wanted connection with those who they felt shared their interests and concerns. Teens missed siblings who moved away and parents who worked nights. LaToya, who lived in the Section 8 Eagle Bluff neighborhood of Townsville, explained that just being surrounded by other teens did not lessen isolation:

A lot of my friends moved, so I really don't go outside that much because I really only have a couple friends here, and that's all right, but most of the kids out here, it's a lot of little kids or its a lot of high schoolers that I don't really talk to. I know high schoolers, but I'm like "Ok, I don't really talk to you."

In this case, LaToya had people around, but the fact that they were older or younger, rather than immediate peers, meant they had little in common at a critical time when teens are encouraged to look to one another for guidance and understanding. Indeed, in her seminal text, *Act Your Age: A Cultural Construction of Adolescence*, Nancy Lesko[4] stresses that peer systems of support for teens have been intentionally nurtured:

Peers were understood as able to demand an inner discipline and comradeship from each member, something neither school nor parents could do. This emphases on peers as the primary source of values and discipline would become a foundational element of modern adolescence in the United States.

Having few options of people from whom to learn about different interests and with whom to share, test out, and refine their ideas meant these teens had few immediate allies and, thus, minimal support for the things that mattered to them.

As discussion indicates, the teens in this study often felt isolated in ways that were magnified by their geographic isolation. Yet their desires to connect were more complicated than simply having people around them. After all, the very elements that created the teens' feelings of isolation on one hand also made them feel overcrowded on the other. The following section examines this tension.

Crowdedness

Teens felt isolated, but the spaces they were able to occupy were filled with people, just not the interested, supportive people the teens wanted. Rather, these spaces were filled with people who did not trust them and who watched and judged them constantly. They were people who established strict curfews and set rules that diminished options and constrained their lives. As 15-year-old Sarah explained: "My parents are always checking on me, and if I say something bad, I get in trouble." As such, the spaces teens occupied felt crowded by oversight as adults policed their involvements and identities. And teens found such surveillance intrusive. "[P]arents are always asking you questions and they never leave you alone," said Sarah.

Teens believed they needed to be socially involved to prepare themselves and advance in life but, they said, their parents forbid them from doing so. For example, Amelia felt the many years she spent working on her family farm had caused her to miss out on important social interactions with peers—such as sleepovers and parties—that would have aided her in developing social graces. But even after her family sold its business, she said her involvements in social activities were still limited. Amelia recognized that her shyness did not help. In fact, she was quite cognizant of the fact she needed to "get over" her shyness if she wanted to do well in her future:

> You can't just, you have to, like, confront the person when you want to apply for a job. You have to confront them, you have to tell them about it, hand them your resume and everything, and you get called in for an interview and, I mean, if someone's too afraid to talk to someone in person, that's not going to go over very well.

Reflecting on understandings gleaned from reality television shows, Amelia also recognized the consequences if she could not develop the interpersonal abilities she needed to work toward her career goals as a fashion designer. "When you go into design," she said, "you have to show your design to, like, CEOs and stuff and go and try to sell what you have, and you have to be up in front of the company, so you have to be able to be an attention-getter and be able to do that stuff." But if she were to develop the social skills she needed—something she and other teens felt they could control—to hopefully earn respect from others and, eventually, better her life, Amelia believed she would need to be more socially involved. However, the people in her life, most notably an overprotective father, disagreed and were unsupportive in these efforts:

> Yes, social is everything nowadays, I guess. I mean, I don't know what it was like back in the day, but my dad was like, "Social life isn't everything, it doesn't matter!" And I'm like, "Dad, that's everything!" Especially in design. . . . You have to be, like, really straightforward and go to a lot of socials and stuff.

Furthermore, as female minors, teens were subject to curfews, laws, and adult fears that limited their ability to do as they pleased. Teens felt crowded by adult expectations for female youth, and by protocols that governed their relationships, involvements, identities, and lives. They felt further constrained by their inability to explain their need to gain adult support in freeing themselves of these restrictions. As a result, teens said they learned to seek out new routes to self-advocate. "When there's too many rules," Marcin explained, "we just want to go out with friends and stuff and hang out."

In addition to rules and regulations restricting their lives, teens were often physically constrained. One May afternoon, I was meeting with Annie in the kitchen of her home. Not long into our discussion, we heard the front door open and a small girl who appeared to be no more than four ambled into the room. The child grabbed Annie's hand and leaned in, gazing up as Annie continued talking. After a little while, the child pulled at Annie's arm. "I'm hungry." Annie stood up as she continued talking to me, removing a plastic container of cut fruit from the refrigerator, and opening it up. "You know where forks are," she said as she set it down on the counter next to a bowl and returned to her chair. "Yeah," the child replied. She prepared her bowl, and came back over to Annie, staring at her as she ate. The door opened again and two girls a bit older than the first came into the kitchen, asking Annie what she was doing. "I'm busy," Annie replied, looking straight at them, then back at the front door they left open. "Go!" They ignored her directive, and both grabbed onto her in extended hugs. Annie shook them off with a good natured but serious "stop it!" and they moved to stand by the other girl, laughing. Both joined in on watching Annie talk for a few moments before one nudged the other, and the two turned and ran out the way they came in, slamming the door behind them. A couple of minutes later, the door opened and two adults were heard talking as they continued on into the living room. Next came Annie's brother, who said a quick hello as he passed through the kitchen. "That's sort of my cousin," Annie explained, nodding toward the child eating the fruit. "She's always around. Well, her and all of the others."

Despite living in a rural town, Annie joined other participants in explaining that her offline life was crowded, with little "me time" or uninterrupted space at home to do what she wanted, or to focus in on things that interested her. She took on formal and informal babysitting duties for extended family members and neighbors, and her house was always filled with people—especially in cold-weather months. But even on beautiful spring days, the empty house filled quickly both with adults, who had special rights to living room couches and to the one television, and with bothersome kids looking for something to do. Annie found this later group particularly annoying:

> I get no space. I'll be watching a movie, and out of nowhere one comes in and sits in my lap. I push them off and they'll put their butt on one leg and put their legs on my other leg. I push them off. Then they do all that and put their arm around my neck. I push them off me and say, "Please get off me, I'm trying to watch TV," and then they'll be like "Ooh, is this a scary movie? What they gonna do? What's this movie called? What are they gonna do?" Whenever I'm trying to watch TV, they always come up to me. I don't even know why. I try to watch a scary movie because most of them are scared of scary movies. But ain't much scary movies on these days.

Annie's situation was one of the more obvious cases among teens trying to find a place for themselves, alone, in the physical space they occupy, but others spoke of similar challenges. Teens' homes often also held siblings and extended family members, offering few places in which the teens could be by themselves. Many of the teens had to share a computer with siblings or other family members, and some shared a bedroom with their sisters. Most were charged with childcare responsibilities on weekends and after school.

A couple had no home or personal phone, and relied on their mother's cellphone.

Life at home was certainly crowded for most, but these claustrophobic feelings were evident elsewhere. Teens had packed afterschool schedules and communities where "everyone knows everyone's stuff." Teens found little space as they had to compete with others for the attention of their teachers, coaches, and guidance counselors. They discussed consolidated high school classrooms filled with far more students than in earlier years of schooling led by teachers with little time to know them. Amelia struggled to find friends at her school that were not "bad influences." Marcin was overlooked in assemblies and announcements that recognized farmers, football players, and cheerleaders. "I'm a little bit listened to in school," she said:

> But the popular kids do things, and teachers just kinda like forget you. It's easy
> to not feel popular. People act like they're better than everyone else. It makes
> me want to get out of here. Like, I don't mind living in a small place, but I just
> feel overcrowded.

All of these things contributed to their life feeling crowded. Even spaces
where teens gravitated—if and when they were able to get there—could feel
crowded. For example, many teens attended home football games, but the
space also attracted teachers, neighbors, and parents. As a result, adolescents
engaged in these spaces knowing chances were high that they were being
watched by an adult who typically supervised them. The public library closest to most of the teens offered a place to gather and access to computers with
Internet connection, but sound traveled in the small, two-room space, and
one of the librarians watched teen visitors intensely. Eagle Ridge had a large
public park that could have hosted teen games and gatherings, but it was
known to be highly monitored by police, and those teens who might spend
time there knew they were not likely to use this space without getting has-
sled. Because of this, they stayed away. And the Youth Center in Eagle
Ridge welcomed teen volunteers, but large numbers of young participants
and little volunteer oversight made teens feel both uncertain of how to contribute and, ultimately, unneeded.

Each space reveals how different configurations, populations, and uses of
space can constrict its participants, but a critical component of these environments for the teens in this study is the way these spaces become forums in
which the teens' constraints are the result of those outside of themselves. In
other words, where, when, why, and how the teens are allowed to move
through these spaces are often dictated or controlled by others—their rules,
their scrutiny, their expectations, their setup, their wants and needs, and so
on. The teens could complain, but they knew it would do little. LaToya
explained:

> Like, you just can't walk up and say, "Ok, this is what you need to do, this is
> why I think" and put your point across, because sometimes they're gonna be
> like, "Well, you're just a kid, so what do you really know?" Nobody would
> listen to what we had to say.

As a result, the teens found little in their immediate worlds that would let
them focus on themselves, learn about and experiment with other interests,
share and be validated for their views, and, perhaps most importantly, do so
with privacy and control.

Teens' feeling of both isolation and crowdedness made social media and
its promises of like-minded communities, forums, and opportunities for engagement especially appealing to these adolescent girls—so much so that
crowded isolation became a primary "push" factor in teens' media migra-

tions. Social media beckoned teens to move to and through spaces that seemed more beneficial and exciting than those they could find offline as female teens. And the teens responded enthusiastically, welcoming these technologies into their lives with the hopes of gaining access to a wider, more connected world. Yet for all that media migration offers, there are also concerns. The following chapter examines both of these areas through consideration of teens' involvement in social media.

NOTES

1. For biologists, see William Coleman, "Limits of the Recapitulation Theory: Carl Friedrich Kielmeyer's Critique of the Presumed Parallelism of Earth History, Ontogeny, and the Present Order of Organisms," *Journal of the History of Science in Society* 64, no. 3 (1973): 327–350; Walter Garstang, "The Theory of Recapitulation: A Critical Re-Statement of the Biogenetic Law," *Journal of the Linnean Society of London, Zoology* 35, no. 232 (1921): 81–101; Thomas Hunt Morgan, *The Scientific Basis of Evolution* (New York: Norton, 1932); N. Rasmussen. "The Decline of Recapitulation in Early Twentieth-Century Biology: Disciplinary Conflict and Consensus on the Battleground of Theory," *Journal of History of Biology* 24, no. 1 (1991): 51–89; Waldo Shumway, "The Recapitulation Theory," *The Quarterly Review of Biology* 7, no. 1 (1932): 93–99. Also, critical scholars point out a history of social forces aligning to prevent young people from active involvement with the world outside of family through adolescence. For example, Nancy Lesko (2012) argues that the surveillance, control, and subordination that youth experience comes in large part because of the socially held belief that adolescence and adolescent immaturity are biological facts. See also James Côté and Anton Allahar, *Generation on Hold: Coming of Age in the Late Twentieth Century* (New York: NYU Press, 1994); Sunaina Maira and Elizabeth Soep, *Youthscapes* (Philadelphia: University of Pennsylvania Press, 2005); Morrow, 1995; Waksler, 1986.

2. See Reed Larson, "The Future of Adolescence: Lengthening Ladders to Adulthood," *The Futurist* (2002, November/December). Also, in 2000, Jeffrey Arnett proposed a new developmental period of "emerging adulthood" to explain the experiences young people in their late teens and twenties face not feeling they have direction, not knowing where their lives are headed, not finding meaningful careers, not being able to support themselves financially or knowing how to procure health insurance. Arnett's theory asserts that certain societal shifts— such as later marriage and longer schooling—have led to a delay in typical markers of adulthood for many in the US. The framing of emerging adulthood, however, does not question the economic forces or the political policies driving young people to seek more stability, experience, or training in a failing economy that hit them hardest. Instead of questioning structural factors shaping social identities, the period of emerging adulthood normalizes delayed adulthood as an universal and immutable given. In this, it scientifically formalizes a lack of meaningful social involvement, directionlessness, and partial rights as a part of life for a new, even older group recognized as "non-adults."

3. Some 43% of children under 18 in the US are low income or poor. Yang Jiang, Maribel R. Granja, and Heather Koball, "Basic Facts about Low-Income Children," National Center for Children in Poverty (January 2017), accessed from http://www.nccp.org/publications/pub_1170.html. Also, in April 2010, the job market offered young workers aged 16 to 24 years old the highest unemployment rates since data first began being collected by the Bureau of Labor Statistics in 1947: US Congress Joint Economic Committee Staff, "Understanding the Economy: Unemployment among Young Workers" (May 2010). Accessed from http://www.jec.senate.gov/public/_cache/files/adaef80b-d1f3-479c-97e7-727f4c0d9ce6/understanding-the-economy---unemployment-among-young-workers.pdf. In 2011, the job market boasted the lowest number of 18-to-24-year-olds in the labor market on record: Paul Taylor, Kim Parker, Rakesh Kochhar, Richard Fry, Carey Funk, Eileen Patten, and Seth Motel, "Young, Underemployed, and Optimistic: Coming of Age, Slowly, in a Tough Economy," *Pew Re-*

search Center (February 9, 2012). Accessed from http://www.pewsocialtrends.org/files/2012/02/young-underemployed-and-optimistic.pdf.

4. Nancy Lesko, *Act Your Age: A Cultural Construction of Adolescence*, (New York: Routeledge, 2012), 43.

Chapter Three

"This Is About as Good as It Gets"

Negotiating Involvement

It is an unseasonably hot early Friday spring afternoon when I drive to meet Annie for our fourth formal interview. On the way, I race alongside tractors moving over rich brown fields, leaving streaks of dark, overturned earth in their wake. The area has just come out of one of its warmest winters on record and, as the mild weather spills over into April, the land blooms with colors and activity.

Approaching Townsville, fields are replaced by low buildings—many of which sit empty. The highway passes by a road on the edge of town that, after a mile or so, leads to the public library, then by the public swimming pool across the street from a graying motel whose gravel driveway is shared with the prison ministry next door. I drive on, passing through a light at a busy intersection. Leaving the highway, I drive alongside sprawling, and mostly retired, military base buildings behind a fence on one side, and a worn field on the other. Past the field in the distance sits a school. Sidewalks begin running along the road here, but, after a couple blocks, the sidewalks end as abruptly as they start. A few school-aged youth wearing backpacks kick up dust as they walk through the field toward the road.

A few minutes later, I turn off into Eagle Bluff, a Section 8 housing neighborhood, driving past tightly spaced ranch townhomes alternating from blue-gray to beige, with an occasional brick, robins' egg blue, or white house depending on the block. An open grassy park sprawls out behind some of these houses, but this park sits surprisingly empty. Some of the driveways in "The Bluff" host folding chairs filled with adults looking out into the street as they chat; others hold young people standing together in long, closed oval-

37

shaped groupings. A few of the yards host sitting teens. My car passes young kids walking and biking in the street, most no older than eight years old.

Typically, when I would pull up to Annie's house for a meeting, I would either find her inside or see her in my rearview window headed home across lawns from family members' houses. Sometimes, I would walk over to a family member's house or to the youth center to look for her. She was always in the neighborhood and had never missed a meeting. Today, again, no one is at her house, so I head down the street to her grandmother's, where she typically spends time after school. As I near, I see adults sitting around a table at the top of the driveway talking and playing cards. Discussion quiets as I walk up the drive. I call out a hello and hear, in reply, a "Oh—it's the teacher. Hello!" I say "hi" directly to Annie's mother's boyfriend, and say I am looking for Annie. He smiles and walks to the door, calling her name into the house. 17-year-old Annie soon comes out. She had fallen asleep, she says with a sleepy grin, but was just on her way over.

Annie suggests we go to her house to talk. We walk back across lawns and I ask her about the neighborhood's empty park as we pass by. She tells me no one her age goes there. "It's not safe," she says. If a teen were involved in a fight or some other altercation in the park, Annie explains, they would receive harsher repercussions than if this happened elsewhere in the neighborhood. Annie was astute in her observation. Although parks appear to be an ideal space for youth gatherings, state law allows for a doubling of fines and sentence time for drug possession or dealing within 1,500 feet of areas deemed a public park, and other legislation enables police to arrest those considered "gang members" for associating in public.[1] Annie wasn't in a gang. She didn't know of any gangs in the neighborhood. She also didn't deal or dabble in drugs. But she knew fights happened and that drugs were used by some in her neighborhood, and she knew she could be blamed for this. She also knew that adult assessments of teen involvements could be unfair, imposing understandings upon teens that doubted and misrepresented their realities; she could easily be guilty by association by being "in the wrong place at the wrong time" during a crackdown in the park. So while the park suggested a space for gathering and interacting with peers, Annie understood it to be a risky space of surveillance and broadly cast penalties, promoting her to spend little time in the park that allowed her ample space involvement, but also little control. "You can get in more trouble there than anywhere," Annie says. "That's why we don't hang out there."

Annie unlocks her front door and turns on the hallway light, waving me toward the round table in the kitchen. We sit down and begin talking about her CityVille involvements. Everything in the city is going well, she says.

Annie uses Facebook mainly to play CityVille, a very popular game "app," or third-party application, owned by Zynga. Accessible only through Facebook, where it was available in five languages, CityVille boasted the most active monthly user base ever of all Facebook apps when it was released in 2010.[2] CityVille allowed players to plan out and maintain a virtual city "of their dreams," and to perform limited helpful tasks in other player's cities to earn reputation points and other game currency.[3] Annie tells me that she feels important, knowledgeable, and powerful in her involvements with this social media game. When playing CityVille, Annie states, "I am in charge." Asked whether this was appealing to her, she replies: "Yes it is. Because it goes how you want it to go. If you want to do something, you can do it how you want to do it." She goes on to explain that the way she feels while involved in CityVille is very different than how she feels at other times. "I play it because what I'm doing, I won't do in real life, basically. This is about as good as it gets as far as opportunities go."

Annie's attraction to this Facebook game spoke to her interests in certain involvements she wanted within the wider world—interests that were seldom met in her daily life. In offline living, Annie stated that kids her age "don't have any power, so you can't do anything." "Kids don't have control," Annie explained. "Well, they do have control when it comes to people younger than you, like if you got to babysit, or if you have a pet. But otherwise, no. They don't have control." In Facebook's CityVille, however, Annie found that she had both the power and the ability to do many things and that, she said, is why she went online every day to spend hours tending to virtual crops, workers, community, and city planning. Like many teenage girls, Annie has found that social media avails to her life opportunities that are difficult, if not impossible, to have offline. In her social media involvements, Annie knew she could feel powerful. She could learn rules that lead toward gratifying ends. She was able to invest in a world that not only welcomes her, but values and benefits from her contributions. Offline, these things were not possible. In social media, Annie felt she found a safe space to bypass limitations upon her sense of direction, her social relevance, and the control she felt over her life. As an adolescent-aged girl, Annie felt she had few offline options for meeting these needs.

There are three dominant, yet widely unsubstantiated, narratives in the US used to explain teenagers'—and teenage girls'—enthusiastic social media involvement. Using terms such as "digital natives," "tech kids," and "Net generation," the first narrative suggests that teens are somehow naturally predisposed to Internet involvement; this work forwards the notion that, having grown up surrounded by technology, young people should all be expected to have technological proclivity.[4] Another narrative tries to explain teens' high rate of social media involvement as a product of uncontrollable, innate, and even biological social obsessiveness somehow inherent only in youth.[5] The final narrative specific to females frames teens' involvements in social media as girls "gone wild," an irresponsible rebellion against civility as they voluntarily put themselves in harm's way by being naïve, out of control, and reckless.[6] It is true that US youth are increasingly growing up with Internet technologies deeply woven into their home, school, and social lives. This could justify their framing as "tech kids" and part of a "Net generation." But the attraction to social media held by the girls in this study was not found to be rooted in any type of natural technical adeptness, nor did it stem from peer or Internet compulsion, or even from indiscriminate "teen-age" acting-out.[7] Instead, their social media involvements occurred in response to the offline experiences they faced as young females growing up in twenty-first-century rural America. In other words, teens used social media as a tool to try to address and get around obstacles they encountered in their daily lives as adolescent girls.

Mainstream media and dominant discourses in the US depict young peoples' lives as overflowing with freedom, choice, and rewarding options, but this is not the case. Adolescence is a time of normalized partial rights.[8] In this context, young people in adolescence are a socially marginalized group routinely dismissed from consideration and from meaningful societal involvement, ironically at the very moment they are being told they must prepare themselves for life in society. Consistent with research on adolescent identity development,[9] the teens I worked with experienced low levels of guidance and high levels of uncertainty as they tried to figure out how to move toward a "future" with social relevance and full rights. Further complicating matters were these young women's frustrations with their social condition and belief that they were unable to effectively negotiate the marginality, crowdedness, containment, powerlessness, and constraints they faced in their life offline with adults. Combined, these factors led them to enter into "media migration."

MEDIA MIGRATION

Teens like Annie reported that social media provided more promising life options than what was available to them as adolescent-aged girls offline. As a result, they regularly made calculated decisions to move to social media; they directed their attention and efforts to and through online social spaces in the hopes of fleeing harsh social conditions and locating more supportive environments and opportunities. They engaged in what I term *media migration.*

Globally, migration involves pull and push forces.[10] Some seeking a better life are pulled into migration, leaving their home countries and towns in search of greater opportunities. Others leave due to unbearable local factors that make it difficult to survive and that push them to make a change. Often, according to the push-pull model of migration, these forces are combined. Those who are forced—or "pushed"—to migrate make a decision to leave.

They then identify places that they believe will give them the chance for a better life, or that otherwise "pull" them. In line with these migrants who leave because of hardship but who focus on the positives ahead, these teens reported also attempting to leave hostile conditions as they relocated themselves optimistically within new online settings.

Offline, teens explained that the material and ideological conditions of crowded isolation and the lack of options for improved status motivated their interests and involvement in social media. For example, as a group, the girls involved in this study identified the problem of voice as a major issue of concern in their life, and as an impetus to their media migration. They said they commonly are not listened to. They do not feel they are taken seriously. In addition to not being heard, they report also not being seen or validated for many of their realities, and, instead, being maligned and discredited by widely held social understandings. These factors served to "push" teens to try to find better options in social media. At the same time, social media "pulled" them further online with offers of opportunities for information about the world, opportunities for social relevance, and opportunities for various forms of control that they desired but were regularly denied access to as rural, female teenagers. And these opportunities provided channels for teens' eager willingness to hustle to make something of themselves.

Of course, households aren't sovereign nations and parents aren't governments. An earlier era of Internet research made this mistake, framing all of offline or "real" life as the opposite of online life or "cyberspace," which was seen as necessarily a kind of new country or an "electronic frontier."[11] Let me be clear that I am not proposing a return to the utopian talk of "netizens"[12] and "e-citizens"[13] who commence "homesteading"[14] the Internet. Facebook is not a country, yet there are useful parallels that make migration a powerful explanatory framework for the social milieu discussed in this book. Writers such as Howard Rheingold[15] and John Perry Barlow[16] mistakenly saw every Internet user as someone fleeing the outmoded apparatus of government and the unwelcome strictures of real life to find a new land.[17] However, for the group of people in adolescence, this characterization is not a mistake but a truism. Adolescent girls *do* experience their environments as though they are the subjects of an outmoded apparatus of government, and real life consists of a long series of unwelcome restrictions they long to escape.

Using the framework of media migration, social media isn't uncharted territory; instead it is an option—a choice where you might invest effort because the potential results from your labor might be more advantageously realized there. It is also not an empty frontier where anything is possible; instead it is a highly structured corporate environment that has already been designed, yet each particular corporate platform may offer options that are more desirable than other choices in some circumstances. As a conceptual experiment, consider these adolescents within social media as people relocating in search of lesser containment and greater opportunity, just as people depart and return to their home countries. Although an immigrant leaving home for another country is not the same as a teenager choosing to spend time on Facebook, the evidence from this ethnography suggests that territorial migration should be seriously considered as an incisive metaphor for the way that rural female adolescents understand and manage their lives. The metaphor of media migration provides access to adolescent understandings of their own situation while also highlighting the overarching issues in play.

Thinking of social media use as a migration emphasizes that it is a structural and societal phenomenon as well as a circumstance that can apply to a particular individual and involves personal choices. Migration is complex, but it is also, importantly, based on identifiable and controllable systemic factors. It is not incomprehensible. As a metaphor for social media use, this framing helps present the situation in terms that adolescents would understand, revealing their motivations and thinking to outsiders, while at the same time it presents the situation as multilayered, subject to specific macro-level social, political, and economic events, and more than any single person's decisions.

Media migration thus became an intentional and strategic act taken with an interest in both advancement and self-preservation within marginality. Rather than continue frustrating restrictions and futile negotiations offline, teens reported that they decided to migrate controllable parts of themselves online to Facebook; some of them later made this choice again, shifting from Facebook to Twitter. In doing so, teens found ways around barriers and carefully curated their involvements across various social media platforms in an attempt to self-advocate and improve their lives while maintaining important relationships with adults they valued and, in many ways, needed. The extent to which girls could make this shift, however, was shaped by technical factors.

TECHNICAL AFFORDANCES OF SOCIAL MEDIA INVOLVEMENT

Teens' involvements in social media were shaped by two critical elements of technology: access and affordances. The following discussion offers an overview of each.

Access to Technology

The ownership and access to technology varied widely among the teens in this study, affecting the extent to which teens could participate in online forums. All of the girls in this study reported having access to hardware needed to use social media available to them during the school year. Those without their own phones used computers shared with family members or others to get online. This, however, did not always enable social media use. 17-year-old Carollyn, for instance, often used school computers as a member of the Yearbook Club. But like the rest of my interlocutors, she was not allowed to pull up social media on these or other computers available to students. Although the girls had to work their access to Facebook or Twitter around these types of constraints set by school, activities, and parents, they were able to find ways to log onto social media throughout the week.

All of the teens had access to a computer, iPod, and/or cell phone, but there was significant diversity in their access to these items. For instance, all but one had access to social media through a computer while at home, but 15-year-old Amelia had to share the computer she bought with her older brother. 16-year-old Molly had her own computer. 16½-year-old Violet logged on using the family computer in her living room, 14-year-old Amy checked updates on a family member's computer, and 14-year-old Shelly's mother took away her laptop until her homework was completed. Annie used the Internet on a computer owned by a family friend a few doors down who allowed Annie access when the friend was not fighting with Annie's mother.

Though computers were available, teens said they preferred to access social media through mobile telecommunication devices. Access to cell phones helped bridge the gap for almost all of the girls, but here, too, there were access challenges. Amy borrowed her cousins' cell phone to take and post pictures to her Facebook account. Annie borrowed her mother's. And four teens had phones with "pay-as-you-go" phone plans that were left off for at least one month that we worked together. One of these teens, 19-year-old Marcin, regularly used her friends' phone to check Facebook when her phone was turned off for the month. "I don't have time on my phone," she told me. "People can't really get in touch with me if they want to. They can through Facebook, though."

As these cases show, access to hardware shaped not only when or if the teens could participate in social media. But the technology also shaped how the teens could be involved in social media.

Affordances of Technology

Providing the teens had access to technological hardware, either via computer, iPod, or cell phone, Internet service affected teen involvement in social media. Many spaces within the rural communities surrounding these teens had spotty, unreliable, or no Internet access. Teens reported that Facebook took longer to load onto their phones than did Twitter, but some teens' computers also struggled to load the image- and digital media–intensive pages common among Facebook users; when pages did load, teens reported

Facebook's bandwidth requirements often resulted in slow or partial updates, annoying the teenage users. These issues of technological affordance informed their social media involvements.

Twitter needed less bandwidth to work, and the teens with smartphones said this was one reason they began spending more time on Twitter; Twitter feeds appeared quicker and more efficiently onto their phones than did Facebook.[18] As Violet explained. she spent most of her time on Twitter "'cause everybody has a Twitter now and Twitter loads faster. And it's just kinda simpler. And there's less to it." Shelly agreed, noting in one meeting that "the only thing that loads on my phone is Twitter, so I was on that a lot." When I asked her to elaborate, she replied:

> [Twitter] just takes up a lot less space. So I do have 3G on my phone, but I kind of live in, my house, um, like it's 3G only in certain spots, so, Twitter just loads a lot easier without 3G than Facebook does 'cause it has so many pictures and profile pictures and everything.

Finding that Twitter worked most efficiently within her less-than-reliable Internet environment, Shelly began using Twitter more than Facebook, demonstrating the way possibilities outlined by technologies—or "technological affordances"—can shape teens' involvement with social media.[19]

Within the unreliable Internet infrastructure of their rural communities, the technological affordances of specific hardware further shaped how usage happened. Specifically, these teens reported that their cellphones made it quite difficult for them to change their Facebook profiles, to de-friend Facebook friends, to block people on Facebook, to stop following Twitter accounts, or to change privacy and account settings on both platforms; they said they concerned themselves less with these matters on their mobile phone than they did when they accessed social media accounts on computers. Molly explained it this way: "On my phone I can't change the people I block or unblock. But I'm always on my phone, and it's just difficult and seems like I never press the right buttons and I get really frustrated. So I end up saying: 'forget it.'" Shelly, who also primarily used her phone to access social media, said that, if she wanted to block or unfriend someone on Facebook, she "would have to wait until I get to a computer most of the time." She confessed that this extra step decreased her likelihood to follow through with her plan. "I'd have to wait for [the computer] to start up, then go through all of the steps. And then," she said, "I don't know. I might forget, or decide not to spend the time to do it."

At the same time, teens' mobile devices offered new possibilities for shortcuts to social involvement through social media. Cassidy used Facebook more after receiving her own cell phone. "Getting on the computer will take more effort and time than getting on social media through my phone," she explained. "I get on Facebook more now that I have my phone for sure. I'd rather just be lazy and be like 'oh, let's just click this button and get on it since it's in my hand.'" Teens said social media use was simple on cell phones, and mobile technologies heightened the interoperability of social media into their daily lives by eliminating many steps they, as rural female minors, traditionally needed to take to try to be involved with a wider world outside of family. On mobile devices, social media use was a convenient option for teens' involvement at various times and despite supervision, rules, and curfews. But even those with fewer constraints found themselves drawn to mobile social media. Molly regularly chose to be on her phone during her free time despite having her own car and permission to come and go as she pleased. Like the other teens, she described being social through social media as compellingly expedient and satisfying.

> I have this thing on my iPhone where I, like, pull the top down and I can just tweet. It says "send tweet," or whatever, and I just do it right there. And it makes it easy to always be on. Like, if I'm just sitting at home and I don't have anybody to talk to, I just talk to Twitter. It's easy. A bunch of people hear. And I always have my phone in my hands.

Confusing and cumbersome processes on mobile devices thus discouraged the teens from adjusting their Twitter and Facebook settings in ways they might have if they were on computers, while other device features added conveniences that encouraged their involvement in social media. These are significant findings given that teens are increasingly turning to cell phones to access social media, and that youth who use mobile technologies are found to be more avid Internet users than their peers.[20] The Pew Center on Internet and American Life reported in April 2015 that 91% of US teens access the Internet via mobile devices. They write: "94% of these mobile teens go online daily or more often compared with 68% of teens who do not use mobile devices to go online."[21] Considering that most "nationwide" studies on teens or youth underrepresent rural teens,[22] and considering that rural teens tend to access the Internet *mostly* on cell phone, we must examine how involvements availed, encouraged, and complicated by these technologies guide these young people's own interests and involvements.

MOTIVATIONS BEHIND SOCIAL MEDIA INVOLVEMENT

In many ways, teens I spoke to participated in social media because their friends participated in social media. Originally, most of the teens in this study started Facebook accounts to get around obstacles that prevented them from staying connected with friends outside of school. As discussed in the last chapter, living in rural communities with large distances separating most of them from their friends, teens had to make significant effort to see or talk to friends after school and in summer. Public transportation or private cars were seldom available to some, and phone calls across town from landlines often incurred long distance charges—an issue for the three participating teens who did not own a cell phone at the time of this study. In this climate, teens reported that social media made their life easier by helping them feel less isolated from their friends, as Naomi explained when discussing how hard it was to see her best friend in person: "I can just tweet to her and stuff and tell her what I need to say and like or message her on Twitter," Naomi explained. "It's kind of like we're together."

But being with friends was just the start of why these teens lived in social media. The remainder of this chapter will examine some of the other reasons.

Involvement to Gain Information

The interlocutors in this study said they were involved in social media to gain information about their lives. Although they rarely used the word "information," they often said that knowing things was extremely important: "Having information kind of helps you get more attention," "It's all about impressing other people," "Nobody wants to be known as clueless," "You need to know what to do to, like, do things in life," "Like, if I didn't know anything about that, I know I'd feel real uncomfortable," "We want to know the whole entire story because there's nothing else better to do." In brief, these teens believed that having the right information could help them become an interesting person, an important person, an admired person. Quite often, however, they also seemed to understand that the "right" information was not what *they* knew, but what *others* knew.

Teens had many questions about life. Beyond the varying levels of importance they placed on book learning in school, all recognized certain types of non-academic information as highly useful to their efforts to navigate and succeed in their worlds, to meet goals, and to form and maintain relationships. As such, teens strategically gathered a range of information through social media to try to hone their understandings of—and engagement with— the offline world. For example, wanting to become more active participants in the larger world, my interlocutors wanted to know how to act to be taken seriously in and outside of their communities so they could direct their attention to matters people considered important. They were highly concerned about growing up well; getting "on the right path" to their futures, in Naomi's words; and, ultimately, getting to the point where they could "be somebody someday," as Violet said. But outside of doing well in school and not getting in trouble, they were confused about what these paths were, or how to get on them. Social media gave them the tools to look to others for advice and direction on how to be "right" in the world.

Consider, for instance, information as simple as what to wear or how to behave in unfamiliar settings. Naomi said she learned about "popular" homecoming dress options from pictures posted by Facebook friends at other schools, and said she used these pictures to choose her own dress. Molly, whose enlisted fiancé was stationed away from home, said she learned about other Air Force wives' plans for weddings using military colors on Facebook. And Cassidy summed up the information she gathered from social media as shaping how she chooses to present herself to the world: "Facebook, I guess it gives me ideas of how to be. Or how not to be."

In addition to offering advice on how to present themselves in the world, social media offered ideas and direction for how to move through the world. Annie, for example, said that she was considered the high achiever of her family: "All these dropouts," she said, speaking of her extended family. "They're such bad influences, but I try . . . to stay positive. Not many of them have even graduated from high school. I'm trying to be a positive influence on myself and on the kids younger than me." But while Annie, a sophomore, aspired to go to college, she had few people in the offline world to help her navigate how to get there. Her high school guidance counselor would not see students who were not seniors, providing no help to younger students like Annie thinking about college several years before they would be applying. An aunt—the only person in Annie's family who went to college—volunteered to take Annie to a historically black college, but this aunt lived out of state, and Annie said, "I don't know if I really want to go to one of those schools." And she had a local youth program leader who, helping her apply for part-time jobs, piqued Annie's interest in a post-secondary institution:

> She told me that Harvard is wanting to get more diversity in the school, which is making my chances more likely, I just need to get my grades up. I think I can get in there with a full-paid music scholarship. That'll work, that'll be so helpful.

Annie loved playing the flute, and she said, "I feel good when I play it, [because of] the fact I'm so good." Yet while she expressed an intent to earn a music scholarship to put herself through college, she also acknowledged, "I just need to know how to do that."

Further complicating matters is that her rental instrument had become too expensive for her family to maintain, so she decided to "take a break" from playing: it had been over a year since she had played the flute.

Not playing an instrument did not trouble her life plans, but she was worried about her grades. They were low freshman year, she admitted, but they were better this year. "All my grades are up," she stated. "I just have two Cs that are really bringing me down." She added that she was close to gaining approval to take honors English next year, but believed she probably still needed to improve her grades a bit to get into Harvard.

Trying to make sense of all she would need to do to prepare for college, Annie said she looked to Facebook in planning for her academic direction. Early on in our meetings, Annie posted questions on Facebook asking friends things like "Where should I go to college?" and "How do you go to college?" By the end of our time together, however, Annie said she had given up this tactic, crediting a lack of response: "Nobody really ever put comments on those posts" about college. She added that she did not plan to look to Facebook for information on how to apply for a music scholarship for similar reasons, saying, "Nobody has much of an opinion on that kind of stuff, I guess."

When I asked her how she did learn more about admissions requirements and scholarships for colleges that interest her, Annie explained that her frustration with the lack of response on Facebook prompted her to take her question to the larger Internet. "Everything you need to know is there somewhere on some page," she told me, though she also recognized that seeking specific information on colleges online was not easy:

> I looked online. I don't even think I know how to look at colleges online. I don't know how to at all. It's confusing. I don't know. I don't know what to do. I was trying to look and see where was the closest one and stuff. I just ran into some stuff. I was looking at Harvard and then I ran into the "Top Ten Colleges and Universities" [page]. I just started clicking away and that's where I ended up.

Further discussion revealed that the "Top Ten Colleges and Universities" page was an online article produced by a commercial entity not affiliated with Harvard.

Annie described moving from official university websites to outside pages frequently in her online college searches, seldom noticing when or how her clicking redirected her from conventional university sites. "I don't know how, but I always end up being on the University of Phoenix [website]," she said, laughing. "I'm looking for Harvard, but I end up there. I don't know what happens." Annie hadn't heard of University of Phoenix before she began online college searches, but the fact that she was often bounced to its website while researching her college of interest led her to believe that University of Phoenix was on par with Harvard. "Nothing's as good as Harvard," she said. "But this is probably pretty much like it." Unfortunately, the other teens in this study faced similar challenges in using social media for their post-secondary information gathering and planning. However, lacking few other resources, teens continued to look to social media to try to gain information about the world. There, they found posts and links to articles and videos that gave these teens insights into the local, national, and globally recognized people, events, and ideas that these teens said others knew and spoke about.

LaToya, for example, learned of the killing of Florida teen Trayvon Martin from Facebook, and she was able to hear perspectives defending his actions that she said were not common in her school. Violet, meanwhile, used social media to learn about the upcoming presidential election, citing information she learned from Facebook about some of Republican presidential candidate Mitt Romney's social positions. "They were talking about how he's against having an abortion if you're raped but there's, I don't know, a lot of stuff. I don't agree with anything he had to say about that." When I asked if she would have known this without Facebook, she replied: "No, because no one here really talks about it. They're just anti-Obama. And they never said anything about Mitt Romney. It's like, always like, 'he should win and Obama should not.'" Social media thus helped teens get alternate views, (re)consider what they believed, and, at times, validate some of the feelings they had on topics they could not affirm locally.

Related to world events, teens explained that social media also exposed them to ideas and viewpoints about popular culture they seldom encountered offline, helping them broaden their interests and perspectives. For example, Amelia aspired to be a fashion designer, but she found it difficult to own her sense of style in her small town where she said everyone wore only boots, jeans, and hoodies. "I really love pumps," she said, referring to the high-heeled shoes. "Like a lot. Even though I don't wear them around like school or whatever. People would be like, 'Are you trying too hard? Are you trying to be in *Pretty Little Liars* here?' . . . It's just not how we dress around here." But on Facebook and Twitter, Amelia said she was able to hear and share thoughts about fashion with friends outside of the area who shared her appreciation for design, and who did not attempt to reframe her interests as inappropriate and attention seeking. "Twitter kind of like gets me out," she stated. Similarly, Sarah explained that Facebook presented points of view that she did not often hear often in her day-to-day life:

> But the more knowledge you have, maybe it's good. . . . Say, evolution. People hear brief mention of it, and they're like "Oh well, that's not true because of god." But the more you learn about it, you can understand it, so you can kind of, like, appreciate a new approach, but you don't have to believe in it.

Although she might not agree with these new perspectives—as was the case with her beliefs about evolution—Sarah explained that social media did provide more complex framings and elaborate details on subjects than she experienced offline, thereby enabling her to build and affirm her own understandings of topics. "Kind of like with sex," she continued, drawing parallels between discussions that pit religious beliefs against scientific ones, as well as topics involving personal and social issues. "With more information, you can understand it more, but that doesn't mean you have to do it."

Social media also helped these teens learn about and leverage highly valuable interpersonal information about their peers. Teens sought some of this information because it was, in their words, "entertaining." For teens, social media provided a platform for continued involvement with their peers, often in a titillating and spectacle-filled manner that gave plenty of personal information to discuss later when gathered again in person. "It's very entertaining," Violet said of the interpersonal exchanges she is able to observe on Twitter and Facebook through posted comments. She continued:

> I just love to read people's comments on pictures and stuff. Some of them are negative and some of them are positive. And there's a lot of Facebook fights. I like the comments of any type but those are the most interesting: the discussions. The arguments.

Molly also commented on the entertainment value of such information, describing a fight that occurred on social media between students from her school and students from a rival team. "[There] was, like, a big football game this weekend, so those kids . . . They were just arguing about it [on Twitter]. . . . I was always updating my page to see what they said next [laugh]." Making this information particularly engaging is that, as Noel stated, these types of interactions on social media do not stay online; they continue on in school the next day. "Facebook's usually like little fights and stuff," she said. "I hear a little bit on Facebook and then like I usually hear in person the next day all the details and stuff." Such online conflicts thus provide information about peers that can prove useful for offline social sharing. Amelia, for example, discussed "subtweeting"—a tactic used on Twitter to indirectly but publicly talk about peers—as a source of enthusiastic offline group discussions of classmates:

> People do tweet things that are interesting . . . like I said, people breaking up and then I also, I follow those two people who fight a lot on Twitter too. So it's kind of interesting to see, like, how it all unfolds and . . . if they talk about each other, 'cause when you subtweet, it's when you tweet but you don't mention the person, you just kind just put it out there and kinda hope that the person knows it's about them. So you can tell who it's about, and it's just a lot more drama on Twitter.

The teens considered such information valuable because it allowed them to stay connected with and be entertained by their peers beyond face-to-face exchanges. It also enabled them to acquire scintillating insights they believed others would care about.

The other category of leveraged information teens gained from social media involved details that helped them better know people. Social media has been noted as making it easier for individuals—especially those who may be shy—to find someone's online account and ask to start up a relationship in a low-pressure environment, potentially leading a new social connection on- and offline. Such was the case for the teens in this study. For example, Naomi said that Facebook made it easy to contact people who didn't have each other's number, and it also helped people meet when there were opportunities to do so. "Like, you can connect with more people," she said of Facebook. "Like, people that you wouldn't be able to see in these small towns like [pause], I bet you know this, like there's no big towns around here like, they're just really little."

To demonstrate, Naomi shared a quick exchange she and her friend had with a couple players from the rival team at the boys' basketball game the previous weekend. Naomi said she and her friend looked up the players on Facebook when they got home and sent them friend requests, which the boys accepted. "We wouldn't have never saw 'em again if we wouldn't have asked their name and added 'em on Facebook!" she said. Facebook thus became a tool to connect to new potential friends, but it also provided an easy way to "check out" and vet these potential friends. Naomi explained:

> Like, if they seem like they're okay in person but they're like all creepy and like, trying to talk to everybody and creep on all these girls online, then I wouldn't want to talk to them. Like I know a kid that, he's cool to talk to in person and then online, he just won't stop talking to you and won't stop talking to you. And then like, you're like, "Oh wow, is this just me?" and then you're like "Wait. He's doing this to like [pause] 700 other girls." Not really 700, but a lot!

In offering a forum in which to gather details about people of interest that Naomi could use to make purposeful choices about who, beyond her social circle, she should befriend, social media once again proved itself to be an invaluable source of information. Others had similar stories of making friends through social media. Amelia explained:

> Yeah, that's how I've met a couple of my friends. I went to a couple homecomings and went to one this year and I met a couple people there and they friended me on Facebook and [pause] we're pretty good friends now. I mean, not like, I tell them everything about my life, but we still talk and hang out and stuff.

Involvement to Gain Social Relevance

In addition to gathering information about their world, teens were also involved in social media to advance their interests in social relevance. Teens' efforts to bolster social relevance often used information gained in media migration.

All of the teens in this study were active participants in their communities. Four of the teens were involved in at least one afterschool sports team, with most taking part in two or more. Three had jobs. Almost all of them talked about in-school activities they were involved with, such as student government, FFA, yearbook, or the step team. But when asked about their involvements once they got home, all of my interlocutors reiterated the words, "there's nothing to do here" throughout this study. For instance, Naomi loved sports, but, suffering from an injury that prevented her from joining teams her freshman year, she found little to do afterschool for those who didn't play sports—especially during the winter. She said she had one classmate her age in her town, and, together, they frequently visited the town's public soda machine: "[A neighbor] put up a pop machine and you can get a pop for fifty cents. So we'll walk up to the pop machine and walk around the block and then go straight home, which takes like ten minutes."

Some teens reported that the involvements in the neighborhood that were both financially and physically accessible to them held little interest. Amy, for example, used to volunteer for the new youth center in The Bluff. As a teenager, she was years older than most youth who attended the center for tutoring help, games, crafts, open play time, and, late into our meetings, computer access. By our third meeting, however, Amy said she was no longer going there. "I just don't want to go back," she explained. "It's just boring." Outside of moving from grade to grade, she and others could identify very few ways they were promoting themselves in life. Teens cited adult supervisors' low expectations and the absence of opportunities for challenge, advancement, recognition, validation, and responsibility in available options as other reasons they didn't feel needed or engaged in socially meaningful ways, making social media all that more important to create meaningful opportunities in their offline world.

But social media made teens feel important. Teens' social media involvements helped them stand out as relevant to others and gain their interest. For instance, Marcin explained: "Facebook kind of helps me get attention. Say you're going to Florida or something. Then people kind of know, and respond. That's real nice to have happen." Others concurred; teens were pleased to see likes and comments on posts. They enjoyed finding out that others regarded them in positive ways. As Sarah explained, they liked getting noticed.

> Like, people just want to be known. I live in a small town, but I want this person from far away to know that "this is Sarah." You kind of want to make a name for yourself because no one knows you, basically. So you just want to be known, even if it's a good or bad thing.

Sitting at computer terminals in the empty school library under signs that read "Computers for school work only. No Facebook!!" Cassidy discussed how having her profile on display made her think about what others would respond to:

> Sometimes, people will brag about things they did on Facebook to get attention, because Facebook is a place where you are supposed to get attention. If you don't, like if your posts don't get any "likes" or comments, you kind of look like a loser. You kind of feel like one too sometimes.

She and others passed on videos, news, and other details they believed others would want to know, and they gained attention as a result. They looked forward to logging on and finding new likes, retweets, and messages and comments to be read. "You never know who is gonna 'like' your stuff," 14-year-old Rosie explained. "It's like Christmas every time!"

Unlike offline, teens also found that their presence and efforts made a difference in their social media communities as they tended to—and improved—virtual game spaces, real relationships, and individual images. Social media gave teens an outlet to display themselves with things they prized—their friends, their song lyrics, their cell phones, their family—and to both identify and present themselves in desired ways to communities they wanted to be relevant to and part of. Some of these displays were a continuation of teens' daily lives, but others went beyond typical offline involvements. For instance, even after budget cuts ended the art program at La-Toya's school, she was able to regularly post her digitally altered photographs on Facebook and gain notice for her artistic talents.

Similarly, in their media migrations, teens took on serious involvements that made them feel important that were difficult for them to achieve or unavailable to them offline. They interacted with admired peers, brands, and celebrities and displayed these interactions for others to see. They took on central roles within family by sharing passwords with grandmothers to help them earn more Bingo points, teaching parents how to use hardware and platforms, presenting themselves as "good" in ways that reflected well on parents, and serving as a liaison passing on information to distant family members. And they maintained important social connections with peers. For example, teens posted compliments and other positive comments on friends' pictures and posts to overtly give them support and to affirm connections. "Writing nice stuff and 'you're pretty' on someone's picture makes them feel good," explained Shelly. "That's why I do it. They like it and it shows you're a friend. You can't do that all the time in school when you're in different classes and stuff, or when you're at different schools."

And teens also used social media to be more present in romantic relationships they cared about. Sarah explained how she used social media to coordinate secret in-person meet-ups with her boyfriend, who lived far away from her. Since phone conversations could be overheard and texts could be read in parents' random phone checks, Sarah said she found Facebook messaging to be "safer" to strategize an in-person rendezvous with her boyfriend after curfew, while her parents were asleep. "They check my statuses and page," she said of her parents' monitoring of her Facebook page, "but they don't know how to check my messages." Direct messaging through Facebook ("IM"ing), therefore, provided a work-around:

> IMing with him on Facebook, I can kind of break around the rules [draws a curve on the table with her finger]. By saying: "I want to do something to-night." "Ok. I'll meet you at the community building." "Ok, that's fine." And we'll sit there and actually talk and have the time I don't get during the day to see, like, "how was your day? How did you do?" Facebook helps by, like, [being] just another connection of talking with him and figuring out, "Well, what can we do?"

By living in social media, Sarah was able to negotiate wider social involvement in her life offline that helped her feel more valued, meaningful, and connected.

This was significant, as all of the teens in this study expressed feeling powerless and frustrated by their inability to gain meaningful involvement offline that might better their status in life. As minors, most conceded that they deserved fewer rights than adults. In Amelia's words: "I think you should have to be a certain age to do certain things, like voting. You have to be eighteen, I think that should stay in a way because, like, our minds aren't fully developed." As females and, for some, non-white youth, the teens had also learned to begrudgingly accept that being treated unfairly was just a part of life. While they knew of no way to secure social mobility beyond these corporeal constraints that bounded them as second-class citizens, they recognized they had a chance to gain *social status* mobility by knowing things about others, and, importantly, by knowing things that others wanted to know. Status was a rare form of power teens had access to; teens used social media to attempt to improve their own relevance and popularity, and many of these efforts drew upon the information they collected in their media migrations.

The teens consulted social media for information they could use to parlay into different social settings. By gathering information that might be interesting to peers they saw in their day-to-day lives, as well as those they encountered less frequently online, the teens in this study saw ways to add to their clout and power. This information could be shared socially with all of these people for personal gain. "People I know are really into the clique of knowing things," 15-year-old Sarah stated. "It's like a competition of who knows what." Knowing something that was going on with a peer or a celebrity,

Sarah continued, encouraged people to seek them out to learn more, thereby enabling and, at times, increasing social interactions with and status among their peers. But even if their peers did not see them as a source of information, simply knowing about topics allowed them to participate in conversations and appear to be "in the know" about a range of issues. Teens explained that social media helped with this, as information garnered online for personal knowledge could be parlayed into offline social settings. Sarah discussed this type of information gathered from social media as important in appearing adequately knowledgeable in social situations. She explained that this knowledge helped enable social interactions with peers:

> I, personally, I want to be in the social media and know who is doing what, and knowing, just because it's just curiosity of knowing how everybody's doing, and knowing stuff. And when they have conversations about what happened on Twitter, it's nice to know, like "oh, I can participate in this conversation." Like, I know what they're talking about.

With and through social media, the teens in this study were often able to learn about what people thought was important or popular, and to step into the esteemed role of an information broker in social settings, passing what they learned from social media on to peers to increase their own social relevance in hopes of improving their social standing. On Facebook, for example, the teens talked about seeking out socially esteemed material by following links to funny stories and videos liked by friends, reading memes shared by friends and by businesses their account "liked," checking out pictures on third-party applications ("apps") like Pinterest and posting them to friends' pages, and listening to YouTube music videos that showed up on their newsfeed. On Twitter, they learned about songs, videos, gossip, products, and new Twitter accounts from friends, celebrities, and other accounts they followed, sharing their interests even as they validated their own values. To demonstrate, Molly explained "favoriting" tweets with certain song lyrics to stand out to certain people. "When they see that I favorite it," she said of tweets with lyrics, "they're probably like, 'oh, she likes country music like me.' Like, you have to understand what [the song is] talking about. . . . You have to understand to show you understand them."

The type of information gleaned from social media that was often most entertaining also provided them with powerful social currency recognized by their peers: information that others wanted and, therefore, fodder for attention and interest. Scandalous, new, or personal details that would be considered "breaking news" to people who knew the participants was of great interest. Molly discussed learning about changes in peers' haircuts and relational statuses through Facebook, giving her "juicy details" that helped her start conversations with others in school. All of the teens also followed celebrities on their social media pages, and they used this information to learn about and share the relationship status, interests, and recommendations of celebrities in ways that made them appear knowledgeable and relevant to their peers. For example, three of the teens each told me that they learned of Selena Gomez and Justin Bieber's breakup "before everyone else" through Twitter, and passed this on to their friends. Similarly, the other teens passed on Facebook posts and tweets from celebrities that they felt their friends would want to know about. Having this type of information before others— or at all—made them owners of a valuable social commodity: dirt. They were brokers of coveted information others wanted to know and talk about. And this information, Carollynn explained, gave those who had it power:

> I keep saying this over and over but, at school, they'll talk about a tweet someone made last night or a post someone made or [pause] if something happens or if somebody posts a like, risqué picture, they'll be gossiping about how inappropriate it was or how wrong it was. And it's just, it's how things are.

Interestingly enough, however, is that although social media brought them entertaining information about peers that they enthusiastically shared, unless the poster was a close friend, the teens in this study said they were reticent to follow up offline directly with people who posted personal information, scandalous or not. "I'd feel like it was weird," Violet said when I asked if she would talk to others at school about their tweet. "I don't know," she continued. "I kind of feel like I'm bringing up something I shouldn't know about." Teens found relevance passing on dirt they learned in social media, but they were often nervous to check in with the source of the "leaked" information. Still, having the information was enough to share, to attract their attention back to social media, and to validate their involvement with widened offline social permissions.

Teens used social media to advance other forms of relevance, as well. Amelia used social media to achieve greater offline involvement with her peers. As she explained:

> I like knowing what people are doing, I mean, I kind of think that's the point of Facebook is knowing what everyone's doing. It's not like I'm stalking anyone, but if I just go through the newsfeed and see it's like "Oh. They're going to the mall. That sounds like fun," so [I'll] just message a couple of my friends and go to the mall.

Giving teens details of where people are hanging out—be it an upcoming party, a high school game, the park, or some outing—social media allowed teens to follow up and participate in various ways, making them feel in-the-know, less left out, and, as such, important. Sometimes they called to get involved. Sometimes they texted. Other times they sent tweets or private messages. Usually, however, the method they chose was influenced by their technical affordances of their rurality and their objectives.

Facebook and Twitter, for example, were both common go-to platforms for teens with limited cell phone service. Amelia demonstrated this during our conversation about how kids in her area find out about social events outside of school:

> If one of my friends is having a party or bonfire or something and, like I said, I don't get good service in my house, so we just message through Facebook, and that's how we make plans.

With no neighbors nearby and lots of last-minute planning, Amelia said that it would be very difficult to know about these social gathering opportunities without Facebook or Twitter. "I mean it's not like you just text people and be like 'Hey. I'm going to the mall,'" she said. "I mean, you just see it on Facebook and you text them. It's like, 'You want to hang out at the mall? I'll meet ya there!'"

While social media provided one forum to learn and share information, the teens often then brokered this information in offline and online forums to try to enhance their status. For instance, on Facebook, Amy learned about the very popular "Cinnamon Challenge" in which groups of teens recorded and posted video of one another's failed attempts at eating a spoonful of cinnamon. Demonstrating how social media could encourage specific, mainstreamed ideas for creative teen action and involvement offline, Amy used this information to enlist cousins and friends into her own funny expletive- and gagging-filled Cinnamon Challenge video—a project she and her collaborators then posted on their Facebook pages and shared with pride both offline and online.

Amelia told of frequently using Twitter to address transportation obstacles she faced as a teen without a driver's license. "Yeah," she sighed. "There's issues getting places out here. You have basically no way to get anywhere," but she said Twitter helped overcome these issues. Specifically, when she would hear about last-minute parties and gatherings of interest, she would use Twitter to send direct messages out to local friends with licenses to let them know about the party. In doing so, she regularly got offered rides for passing on the information, and a group to hang out with at the party. "So Twitter kinda helps you know about things going on," she explained. "But then passing on that information helps you actually get there." By using social media to learn about information she knew would be of interest to her peers and by brokering that information through social media outlets to access face-to-face involvement with peers, Amelia was able to mediate her offline marginality as a minor and a female in a rural community, gaining opportunities for social interaction and heightened relevance.

Teens turned to social media seeking increased relevance. Once there, they found opportunities to perform acts and pass on socially salient messages that made them feel connected, valued, meaningful, affirmed, and esteemed, and that made them excited to log back on for further involvement.

Involvement to Gain Control over Their Lives

Social media offered a rare private space in which teens could focus on topics and people they found interesting and use that information to promote their value among peers. But it also gave them a way to feel more in control of their lives. Take, for instance, the obstacles of transportation and economics. Although my interlocutors often said there wasn't anything to do, when there was, they often said they had trouble attending because of transportation and financial obstacles, magnifying the fact that they had little control over when, how, or even if they could participate in the world. For example, Amy's family had no car, and Townsville had no public transportation. Only a few sidewalks lined the busy road from Eagle Bluff into either town or the library. Yet while Amy is allowed to walk wherever she likes, she doesn't usually go far because of the two friends she has in her neighborhood in Eagle Bluff. "They don't like to walk anywhere," Amy explained. "They like to sit on the couch."

Annie's mother also did not have car, affecting what Annie could do beyond class time. Annie was a member of the school dance team at the start of the year, but she had to drop off the team by late fall because she had no way to get home after practice. "I couldn't make it because my mom doesn't have a car anymore." She went on to say, "That's always been my biggest issue, which is why I never tried out for anything. I want to try out for the basketball team, but I don't have a ride."

When asked if there are other ways for students her age to get around town without a ride, she answered:

> There's no public buses that I know of. There used to be a bus . . . for people who were at school still either from practices or whatever. It's not running anymore, which is why most people haven't been staying at school anymore, because they live where I live or further, so they have to take the bus ride home. And if they ain't got no car, [they] can't do a sport or do anything if you can't find someone to pick you up.

Unfortunately, transportation wasn't the only obstacle these teens faced. Violet, for example, also used to be involved in an afterschool program at her public school. She said a change in the art program this year required students to bring their own supplies from home, forcing her to stop attending the program. "I can't get art supplies," she said. "I can't even get a job."

Teens also said their involvements were restricted due to a perceived lack of safety. All of the teens discussed parents whose fears for their safety limited the control they were given over their involvements. For example, Amelia spoke often of her protective father:

> When I show [cattle] over the summer, a bunch of my friends will go out and just, like, drive around or whatever, or just walk around the fair and my dad's like, "No, you can't do that." I was like, "Why?" "Cause you have a show in the morning." "Dad, I'll get up," and he won't let me, which makes me look like I'm really lame. [laugh] 'Cause I have to be like "No my dad says I can't." Or that whole "be home before it's dark" rule or "be home before it's 7:30." Like you can't go out and have fun before 7:30 at night and then come back and just expect me to be all right with it.

Poorer black teens were especially warned and curtailed in their involvements. Amy said her neighborhood is "not real safe," explaining that she had witnessed a gun pulled on a friend in the next neighborhood, and had heard of other violence happening there. "I usually walk over there just to get to the store," she said, "and people be over there fighting, shooting, killing, all kind of stuff, stealing, and I really don't like walking that way." Annie said her parents feared she would "fall in the street" if she walked beyond the neighborhood. LaToya frequently mentioned that her mother did not let her go "outside" because of her concerns for her safety as young female. Such comments highlight factors mediating the opportunities, and, by extension, limiting the control teens have over their offline involvements.

As discussed in previous chapters, as young women, the teens had little control over their lives. The country is imagined as full of space, but, with few options for traversing these spaces, complicated or absent public spaces, and little to do outside, my rural interlocutors commonly reported feeling crowded in their involvements, with a lack of privacy and little to do. Poverty increased this crowdedness, as some teens spent much of their time in small homes shared with many people, some with sibling-watching responsibilities, all with few funds or opportunities for involvement. Living in social media enabled these teens to escape from their everyday crowdedness to feel self-focused, autonomous, independent, and, as such, to feel free and in control.

Involvement with social media enabled them to find ways to gain control. In their media migration, teens found spaces where they were allowed self-focused me-time. They participated in public spaces without needing adult chaperones or permissions and without having to negotiate adult fears. They interacted socially outside of restrictions presented by distances, curfews, expectations, and, often, rules. For example, all but one of the teens who were not allowed to date formed and maintained romantic relationships through social media. Amy, for example, used Facebook to send a message to someone she liked when he was in the hospital. They continued to talk and get closer during his time out of school, and when he was better, they made plans to meet face to face with friends in her neighborhood. Sarah and Amelia grew to appreciate their current boyfriends through tweets. And LaToya accepted a friend request on Facebook from a friend of a friend, which opened up the possibility for flirting. "He started liking my pictures and inboxing me," she said. "And I liked his statuses and he'll post something on my wall like 'You're pretty, I like you,' whatever. And then we started talking, and we were talking for a while, and then we started going out. And then we broke up." All of the other teens in this study had at least one story of flirting in social media—something they all said their parents would not tolerate offline.

Within these environments, media migration proved helpful in making the teens feel more in control of their life by having both things to do in social media and the power to actually do them.

ADOLESCENCE, GIRLHOOD, AND MEDIA MIGRATION INVOLVEMENTS

Social media proved instrumental in the ways these teens navigated, engaged with, and expanded their worlds. As minors and females, these teens reported they have few opportunities for meaningful involvement offline. They longed to participate in things that felt important, that benefited from their involvement, and that provided them important insights. Beyond lacking opportunities, parental fears limited teens' involvements. Parents have reason to fear for their daughters. Parents are responsible for their children's safety and well-being, and they receive many messages throughout the day that validate their sense that their child will not be safe in the world on their own. Many of these messages about youth danger are overblown or even fabricated, but some of them are accurate—teens indeed do have a very hard time surviving on their own in today's society. Parents of females are told their children are even further vulnerable, and some adults struggle to balance daughters' freedom and boundaries within patriarchal power structures that they know harbor misogynistic attitudes, practices, and discourses that even they are not immune to. And parents of non-white youth must fear for their children's lives within the state-sanctioned violent realities of their nation's white supremacy. Parents are charged with protecting their daughters, and they want to do so. But we must understand that the regular policing and normalized material conditions that justify girls' limited offline involvements direct and shape their interests and involvements online.

Crowe and Bradford write that "as material space is increasingly denied to young people (through contemporary discourses of risk, danger and vulnerability) they have found new means and channels within which to express themselves,"[23] and the teens in this study demonstrate as much. They said their involvements in social media helped them feel more informed, esteemed, and in control of their lives. They were delighted by this. However, these teens' descriptions of their highly social and externally concerned and motivated involvements in social media raise concerns, calling into question the extent to which they were, in fact, truly in control and working for the advancement of their own self-focused interests in these spaces.

Social media represents a space that provides teens information, and it also gives them understandings of what information is interesting, valid, and important based upon feedback (or lack thereof) from others on the site. High-quality information that is hard to otherwise find exists within social media. However, information does not have to be of high quality to be present and shared in this space. In *The Daily You*, Joseph Turow writes of how commercial interests within social media devote paid staff to creating advertisements well disguised as interesting "news" and information in their quest of drawing users' eyes and clicks. Indeed, in many ways, social media benefit from the production and dissemination of fabricated, shocking information that gets shared in its forums. And while social media's allowed anonymity can help users seek for information, it can also help source and spread incorrect, misleading, and bad information without recourse, as was observed in this research with Annie and other teens.

Beyond offering content, social media is a space where people learn about the world, about one another, and about how they are expected to behave to be part of society.[24] These teens' social media involvements helped them to meet certain needs for information, relevance, and control they faced as marginalized adolescent-aged rural girls while these involvements cultivated new interests and desires. In Facebook and Twitter, the teens in this study report learning from others, as Cassidy states, "how to be, and how not to be." These issues of socialization and information quality will be taken up in far more detail in a later safety chapter. For now, though, it is important to stress that teens stated their social media involvements were directed by their interests in knowing more about a world they felt largely shut out of, and in finding ways to be meaningfully involved in this world. Media migration provided them with information that made them feel they had understandings of the world they felt they could not otherwise access. It bolstered their sense of purpose, importance, and control. These feelings are not negligible, but it is important to consider how these girls' lack of permissions and opportunities offline fueled their online involvements, and to ask what sort of information and involvements teens are provided *within* these spaces.

The teens in this study, reporting highly limited opportunities for meaningful involvement offline, said that they engaged in social media to be taken seriously, to identify ways to succeed in the world, and to find ways to feel greater control over their lives. Social media was, in brief, a means to mediate partial rights they experienced as rural female adolescents. Media migration opened up opportunities for them, as minors and females, to seek out and acquire useful information, feel socially relevant, exercise control over their involvements, and to gain social permissions they were regularly refused as contained and surveilled rural, female adolescents. It gave them a way to get around and to resist frustrating constraints they experienced offline.

Yet while media migration comforted them and helped them believe they could individually advance by retooling their involvements across new media spaces, the freedoms and control teens felt online did not transform their worlds offline. What media migration did offer was specific ways to engage in the world that involved and entwined them further in peer and social preoccupations while providing an escape valve for their social discontent. As a result, teens' offline opposition to unfair treatment lightened as they turned their attention online, conceding they gain meaningful involvements and fuller rights there. Within marginality, they said this felt like a windfall.

The next chapter will look more closely at social media as it relates to these young people trying to negotiate and provide information about themselves to the world. Specifically, it will look at how and why these teens, through media migration, performed identities in and across social media to advance their interests in being socially known outside of the partial realities they were able to embrace in US adolescence and in girlhood.

NOTES

1. For example, the 1993 Illinois Street Gang Terrorism Omnibus Prevention Act http://www.ilga.gov/legislation/ilcs/ilcs3.asp?ActID=2052&ChapterID=57. While the majority of adolescent gang members are white, Judith Greene and Kevin Pranis of the Justice Policy Institute find a disproportionately high arrest and incarceration rate of youth of color under this type of legislation, http://www.justicestrategies.net/sites/default/files/publications/Gang_Wars_Full_Report_2007.pdf.

2. Eric Caoili, "CityVille has the Largest Facebook Audience Ever," *Gamasutra*, last modified January 31, 2011, https://www.gamasutra.com/view/news/32231/CityVille_Has_Largest_Facebook_Audience_Ever.php.

3. After sending notice to players in early March of 2015, Zynga shut down CityVille the next month in April 2015.

4. See Gaston, 2006; Howe and Strauss, 2003; Long, 2005; McHale, 2005; Oblinger and Oblinger, 2005; Palfrey and Gasser, 2008; Prensky, 2001, 2005, 2006; Skiba, 2003; Tapscott, 1998.

5. "Internet addiction" is a term frequently associated with young social media users. The DSM does not recognize this diagnosis, however, and international studies commonly find comorbidity of depressive symptoms—including anxiety—with concerning Internet involvement (see Ha, Yoo, Cho, Chin, Shin, and Kim, 2006; Kratzer and Hegerl, 2008; Lee, Han, and Yang, 2008), suggesting a short-sightedness and lack of contextual consideration in the use of

this term. A belief in teens' uncontrollable innate peer-orientation has recently begun appearing in parental and mainstream sources to explain teens' avid social media use. For example, picking up on a point made in her influential 2014 book *It's Complicated* ("most teens aren't addicted to social media; if anything, they're addicted to each other"), in a July 11, 2016 article in *The New York Times*, digital media scholar danah boyd wrote: "This is why many of our youth turn to technology. They aren't addicted to the computer; they're addicted to interaction, and being around their friends" (para 10). http://www.nytimes.com/roomfordebate/2015/07/16/is-internet-addiction-a-health-threat-for-teenagers/blame-society-not-the-screen-time.   Age-based grouping is a relatively new invention in the US emerging in tandem with the "discovery" of adolescence, and, to be sure, the importance young people place on peers is high within the limited contexts for social involvement and social importance availed to them. To date, however, social science has yet to show that there are in-born, physiological qualities in youth that set them up for "addiction" to peers in ways that would not also be expected for adults. As another example of this discourse, in an article titled "When Should You Come between a Teenager and Her Phone," the Child Mind Institute cited clinical psychologist Beth Peters, stating: "To adolescents, the social network and contact with friends is the paramount developmental task and focus" (para 9), http://childmind.org/article/when-should-you-come-between-a-teenager-and-her-phone/.

6. See, for instance, Audrey Watters, "Girl Scouts Research Shows How Social Networking Impacts Girls' Self Image," November 5, 2010. Retrieved from http://readwrite.com/2010/11/05/girl_scouts_research_shows_how_social_networking_i/. An April 19, 2013, news report by Fletcher in *The Sacramento Bee* told of two teens arrested after a 15-year-old who had been banned from the Internet later than 10 pm drugged her parents' milkshakes with prescription sleep medicine to get around their monitoring. It quotes a local police spokesperson as explaining the situation akin to tantalizing summaries on the back pages of pulp fiction novels: "The girls wanted to use the Internet, and they'd go to whatever means they had to."

7. For example, in challenging the framing of youth as inherently digitally inclined, researcher Ezsther Hargittai (2010), who has found technological skill to vary widely across individual teenagers, suggests they more accurately be referred to as "digital naïves." As mentioned above, research has not established addiction as a sufficiently causative force to explain Internet use. As we should be asking what causes this addiction, we should also be asking what causes girls to "go wild," or, more, perhaps importantly, what causes us to see girls' actions through these lenses.

8. James Côté and Anton Allaher (1994) write that adolescence is a socially produced and productive holding period in which industrial society deprives youth of economic, political, and civic rights for the sake of exposing them to what they describe as a "long period of indoctrination into acquiescence and acceptance of existing power structures as normal, natural, good, and benign" (26).

9. See Larson (2002), Males (2012), and Mortimer, Vuolo, Staff, Wakefield, and Xie (2008).

10. See, for example, Everett S. Lee, *A Theory of Migration* (Philadelphia: University of Pennsylvania, 1966); Donald S. Massey, Joaquin Arango, Graeme Hugo, Ali Kouaouci, Adela Pellegrino, and J. Edward Taylor, *Worlds in Motion: Understanding International Migration at the End of the Millennium* (Oxford: Clarendon Press, 1998).

11. Esther Dyson, George Gilder, George Keyworth, and Alvin Toffler, "Cyberspace and the American Dream: A Magna Carta for the Knowledge Age," *Release* 1, no. 2 (1994).

12. Michael Hauben, Rhonda Hauben, and Thomas Truscott, *Netizens: On the History and Impact of Usenet and the Internet* (Hoboken: Wiley- IEEE Computer Society Press, 1997).

13. Kathryn Montgomery, Barbara Gottlieb-Robles, and Gary O. Larson, "Youth as E-citizens: Engaging the Digital Generation," *Center for Social Media*, 2004, accessed November 16, 2016, from http://www.centerforsocialmedia.org/ecitizens/youthreport.pdf.

14. Howard Rheingold, *The Virtual Community: Homesteading the Electronic Frontier* (Cambridge: MIT Press, 2000).

15. Ibid.

16. John Perry Barlow, *A Declaration of the Independence of Cyberspace* (Davos: Electronic Frontier Foundation, 1996), accessed October 5, 2016, from https://projects.eff.org/~barlow/Declaration-Final.html.

17. See also Larry Lessig, *Code and Other Laws of Cyberspace* (New York: Basic, 2000).

18. Interestingly, two of the teens said they migrated away from MySpace for similar reasons: MySpace took longer to load onto their computer than Facebook. This was frustrating enough to make them use MySpace less, and feel more willing to leave the efforts they had put in there for a site that was quicker to access.

19. Other teens mentioned the geographies of their social media use shaped by the reach of the Internet. For example, Amelia used her wi-fi–equipped iPod and her laptop, which she bought but shared with her older brother, to access the Internet. While Amelia had Internet access at home, it did not reach her bedroom, so her social media usage was bound to shared, rather than to private, spaces.

20. In March 2013, the Pew Center on Internet & American Life reported "the cell phone has become the primary means by which 25% of those ages 12–17 access the internet. Among teens who are mobile internet users, that number rises to one in three (33%)" (Madden, Lenhart, Duggan, Cortesi, and Gasser, 2013, 7).

21. "91% of teens go online from mobile devices at least occasionally, and 94% of these mobile teens go online daily or more often, compared with 68% of teens who do not use mobile devices to go online" (Lenhart, 2015, 16).

22. For example, in this particular Pew report, rural youth make up only 12% of the 789 teens surveyed in this "nationwide" report. There were 50% fewer rural teens than urban teens in the study, and rural teens represented less than a fourth of the number of suburban teens involved. The Pew's work on youth and Internet is taken quite seriously by those studying teens and Internet involvement, but this study's low representation of rural teens in a "nationwide" sample highlights a common overlooking of the experiences of rural teens in research on "teens" and "youth."

23. Nic Crow and Simon Bradford, "'Hanging out in Runescape'": Identity, Work and Leisure in the Virtual Playground," *Children's Geographies* 4, no. 3 (2006): 343.

24. See Sonia Livingstone, *Children and the Internet* (Cambridge: Polity Press, 2009).

Chapter Four

"I Don't Want Them Knowing My Business. And They Don't Have To"

Negotiating Identities

I am sitting at the corner of a wooden desk facing 17-year-old Noel. It is mid fall, and we are in a janitor's closet in the basement of her high school talking loudly to be heard over the pounding from boys' afterschool basketball practice in the gym above us. I first met Noel two months ago. At that first meeting, Noel came across as serious and reserved. She responded to my questions with short answers made up of carefully chosen words, and she did not offer feedback on areas of her life without being specifically asked. In our more recent meetings, Noel had begun telling me about events from her past week without probing. Today, things are different. Noel is quiet again and her thoughts are guarded. She replies to my questions politely—but briefly—with her eyes fixed on the floor in front of her. Eventually, I let her know that I am sensing a difference in her, and I ask her why. She responds with silence followed by a deep exhale. She then recounts an interaction she had with her father earlier in the week woven through on- and offline spaces.

After dinner a few days ago, Noel tells me that her stepfather insisted that her teenage sister take down a post reading "I love you" that he noticed she had written on her best friends' Facebook page. "He read it," Noel explains, "and said, 'people are going to read it and think you're a lesbian.'" Noel tells me that her sister did not disclose that she has a secret boyfriend to her parents who forbid their daughters from dating, but her sister did tell them that she only likes boys and that her best friend was just a friend. Despite this explanation, her stepfather was not willing to believe her sister even when Noel also tried to tell him that comments like this between close friends were typical in Facebook. "[E]verybody does that," Noel says, exasperated. "Especially if they're best friends. He said 'other people won't know that,' so he made her delete it."

In that fall meeting, Noel told me her stepfather neither understood the subtle nuances of his daughters' social interactions, nor did he try to understand. Interested in protecting his daughters, he drew upon the world that he knew to force interpretations of situations onto parts of their life that had their own meaning, and Noel said he could not be convinced to do otherwise. Explaining or negotiating with him were never options; "It's always the same," she said. "We're just kids."

Noel said that her stepfather's unwillingness to believe her sister's explanations about her social realities and his negative comments about being seen as a lesbian caused her to rethink her own interactions with him. She felt more cautious about what she shared with him since this experience. Honesty felt more risky. Her stepfather's unwillingness to believe his daughters led him, in Noel's words, to "freak out," creating worries where there were none, prompting Noel to stay silent around her parents, and to be more conscientiously strategic in her social media involvements. After this experience, Noel remained active on Twitter, where her parents could not see her expressing herself in ways that felt powerful and valid, but she carefully curated the identities she made visible on Facebook, where her parents could track her activities. "I don't want them knowing my business," she said. "And they don't have to."

Noel and the other teens in this study regularly told me they felt misinterpreted, misrepresented, and, as such, metaphorically mapped by others— even close others—as being different than who they really are. For example, after our second meeting, 15-year-old Violet gave me her address in an unincorporated area of her town, Brown, telling me that people say her house is a little hard to find. "I live in the middle of nowhere," she told me, with an apologetic look. I told her not to worry, that I was happy to come to her house, and that I was sure I would be able to find it. But later, her statement proved prescient; the online mapping programs told me her rural route address did not exist; in fact, even the rural route her house is on could not be found.

MapQuest's erasure of Violet's home and Noel's explanation of her dad exemplify the ways my interlocutors often found themselves drawn by others in ways that disregarded their own realities and self-understandings. Each described such experiences, sprinkling them within their days' recaps and within stories of amusing things that happened after school, of worries over impending exams, of fun weekends, online fights with friends, offline fights with parents, school dances, football games, subtweets, and long bus rides. Whatever the context, the concern expressed for these representational inaccuracies was deep and seismic. Instances were brought up and discussed with passion, sometimes anger, and, typically, with a sense of injustice. The teens felt strongly that this semi-erasure wronged them. It was unfair but, at some point, a turn in tone always occurred reining in these emotions and replacing them with a quiet acceptance. With this, my interlocutors generally concluded: "It's just how it goes." "That's what happens." Parents could not be convinced to change their minds about how to see their daughters. They and other adults would always see them as "just kids." Teens knew others' misrepresentations did not make logical sense, but they also knew they lacked allies in overturning the dominant discourses that discredited them. Without people in their corner, they said their frustration felt pointless. Who were they to think they deserved better?

Most of the time, these young women described their life as pleasant, if a bit dull and confining. Still, they found it unsettling to have others tell them who they are—and who they are not—while also being told some of their own self-framings were not valid. And while sometimes, these representations could be socially countered and rescripted in ways that cast them in a more desirable light, many times, they could not, encouraging these teens to employ tactics off- and online to try to "get around" the undesirable social understandings others held of them, migrating to new spaces where their preferred identities would be more visible and appreciated.

Identity involves both individual representation and social understanding. This chapter examines the ways teens strategically used social media to try to resist marginal identities by moving from spaces that proved hostile to their ability to be visible in desired ways into other realms that promised less constraint, monitoring, resistance, and judgment. However, to understand how teens perform and make visible the identities they value, it is important to note that social media, as infrastructures, demand that users be on show, promoting themselves in very specific ways. Consider, for example, the way Facebook protocols and interfaces define and shape user identity with profiles, news feeds, status updates, likes, photos, comments, and friend counts. Facebook "About" pages offer finite fields, allowing users to represent themselves by specifying work and education history, birthday, relationship status, languages known, home location, religious and political views, movies, music, photos, contact information, family members, and favorite quotations; users cannot, however, add more fields to customize their page in ways that show, for example, their ethnic pride, or their love of polar bears. As such, Facebook puts users and their social interactions on display to be widely seen in ways defined and, in many ways, socially mapped by the platform. Furthermore, while privacy settings can be selected to allow only the user to view information from their page, this is not common. The typical settings release user updates either to all or select "friends," or to the public, reinforcing an expectation of being seen by others. Similarly, tweets can be limited to followers or broadcast to the public, and, in both cases, Twitter promises to disseminate and display user expressions. It was within such parameters that my interlocutors attempted to establish control over identities through media migration.

IDENTITIES

Identities Offline

The teens I met with let me know that they were regularly restrained in owning non-demeaning identities and in claiming certain realities due to factors that ultimately could be categorized in five areas: popularity, white supremacy, sexism, interests in protecting parents, and adolescence. The sections below discuss how the teens encountered and navigated these identities both off- and online.

Popularity

While US culture holds the colloquial idea that young people are "naturally" focused on those their own age over adults, the past 110 years of US adolescence has seen a concerted and effective segregation of youth from adults,[1] leading to a social context for identities to develop with heightened import placed on peers and "teenage" values. In this context, popularity matters, and the teens in my study responded to this reality.

Peer groups were part of my interlocutors' daily lives, and the teens recognized that those in "popular groups" were given preferential treatment not only from peers but also in school, thereby increasing their visibility as important and competent. As Marcin explained:

> Just farmers, cheerleaders, and football players get favored in school. . . . They get special treatment. They can do what they want. And they get more attention in school. Some teachers will tell you to be quiet and not talk, but they sit there and talk the entire hour, and the teacher doesn't even give them a warning or nothing. She acts like she doesn't even hear. Farmers, football players, cheerleaders. And, like if they won a game, they'll talk about them on the announcements. Nobody else gets mentioned on announcements.

Molly, a junior born and raised on a farm, agreed with Marcin's assessment. With a shrug, she told me: "Us in the country group? We kind of get to pretty much do whatever we want at school."

In contrast to those like Molly, students who saw themselves outside of the popular groups believed they had to do more just to be noticed. Marcin, for example, recognized she was different from the farmers, cheerleaders, and football players at her school, but she was less concerned with her social standing than she was displeased about being overlooked, and, by extension, rendered less visible and less important in school. "If you're a farmer, you're automatically cool . . . Sometimes, I guess I wish that I could be treated like the farmers do," Marcin said. "It did happen to me once. . . . They read my name during announcements. Well, they read everyone's name who made honor roll, but I did too, so they read mine. That felt pretty good."

Naomi also struggled to stand out, a problem that was magnified by ongoing budget cuts that forced her school's teachers and other adults in school to take on more—more students in class, more paperwork, more duties—leaving them less time to connect to individual students. Naomi respected her school, and, in general, felt supported in her learning. She also recognized the daily demands teachers faced conflicted with the attention she wanted, and needed:

> Well, if you were a teacher and you like, you have like all those papers to grade, and everything to get situated and stuff. Maybe just somebody just wanted to say something, but maybe you just have to blow it off. Like [pause] like I would understand that sometimes. But sometimes people just want to be listened to.

Naomi could understand that teachers had limited time and attention, but she and other teens were frustrated knowing that certain students, the popular students, were given a spotlight to shine and be noticed in school while the unpopular students lacked the social clout needed to gain valuable attention in this space. Violet, for example, said she regularly felt as if she were being told she was socially subpar to others in her school by the people whose opinions and social assessments mattered. "I am definitely not cool," she said. She explained:

> I don't know how to describe it, but [pause] you know that feeling like when you're in a group of like seven feet tall people and you're like only five feet tall and you feel like the odd one and you're not meant to be there, it's kinda like that, I guess. They make me feel like less than them.

Interestingly enough, while those outside of the popular groups assumed all was great for those inside these groups, students in the so-called popular groups also struggled for positive recognition among their peers. Sarah, a cheerleader and athlete, explained:

> Like with sports, you want people to be like "oh this chick is good. We need to look out for her." Or kind of stand out from everyone so people from other teams know who you are. It's hard to stand out because people are so into bringing other people down.

All of the teens wanted to be recognized as competent and as deserving of individual attention and admiration from time to time, but with peer groups based on parents' occupations and on sporting prowess gained from years of involvement, they knew it was not easy or even possible to just "join" the popular group. And with a well-established social pecking order in schools—some of which assembled the same students for more than a decade—they knew of few ways to otherwise garner the perks of popularity in their daily lives. They longed to access the attention and accolades that they saw other peers regularly receiving. My interlocutors' understanding of how they were viewed by the important audiences in their day-to-day lives informed their social media use.

White Supremacy

The US operates within systems of racial privilege that regularly normalize whiteness and discriminate against people of color.[2] Latina and Black teens in this study recognized white supremacy as limiting and negatively impacting their identity. Violet explained how her father was often treated poorly by others because he was "not white like everybody else"; she too experienced occasional "bad looks" and rejection from students because of her heritage, making her reluctant to talk about her ethnicity. "I'm half Guatemalan, but one time, one of the people who are in the country clique told me to 'go swim back to Mexico,' which was very racist. I'm not even Mexican." Four of Violet's classmates in her entire school identified as Black, and three—including Violet—identified as Hispanic. Violet knew that making this part of her identity visible threatened her ability to be seen as a "welcome," "normal," and "good" person in her school. As such, Violet chose to keep this part of who she was under wraps so it did not add to her being seen in a negative light. "Like, if I met someone new who was white, I would never come out and say I was Guatemalan."

Similarly, following the police killing of a 15-year-old African American boy in a nearby town she used to live in, LaToya discussed social responses to her race, especially when linked to age as a means of diminishing her ability to be visible as credible and "good" in her community:

> I feel like kids are not safe in America. I don't think they are. Especially young Black kids. The police harass you and stop you for no reason at all. But all they look at is what the police report says. They don't see how they harass you.

Teens in this research often reported they were understood in undesirable and inaccurate ways in their school and communities,[3] inspiring their involvement in social media where they felt they could find wider affiliations and escape classmates' and neighbors' demeaning characterizations of them because of their race or ethnicity.

Sexism

The teens reported being left out of activities because they were "a girl." Naomi loved basketball, but she was rarely allowed to join pick-up games on the park court because boys did not want her on their team. Violet's brother had permission to borrow the family car, but she did not. Marcin said the boys' sport teams and farmers received most recognition and power in school. A number of the teens had curfews earlier than their brothers, some of whom were even younger than them. As females, not only was their competence challenged regularly, but their sexuality outside of virginal angel / discredited whore binaries was also denied.[4] The average age a young woman has sex for the first time in the US is 17, and over 30% of ninth graders are sexually active.[5] This creates a dilemma for teens: sexual activity is associated with more adult identities, but female teens are held to a double standard where, unlike their male classmates, they can face very real threats to their social status by being known as sexual.[6] 14 of the 15 interlocutors stated they were or had been in a romantic relationship. Yet while these relationships affected the teens' positive attention, social clout, connection, and affirmation, as females, they also made the teens, as females, subject to dangerous social framings. The teens puzzled over this. Sarah explained:

> 'Cause like for guys, it's like "so and so kissed me" and it gives the girl a bad reputation. But it makes guys be like "oh, he's awesome!" I don't know why that is, because I don't know how one could be like "oh, you're nasty" and the other could be like "oh, you're awesome." Girls get called "nasty" a whole lot more than guys. Guys don't get called that. Girls do a lot.

The teens explained that females could be called names suggesting sexual promiscuity just for kissing, and that the words "whore" and "slut" were often thrown out as harsh yet effective put-downs for a female regardless of her actual carnal involvement. "It's actually a really bad insult, getting called a *whore*," Violet said, but the word was very familiar for these young women, used as a stand in for other insults. Rosie explained: "It means you don't have respect for your body, and showing it off to everyone, you have no morals." Cassidy gave a broader definition: "It means someone doesn't like you."

Like Cassidy, Shelly suggested that being known as a *whore* or *slut* had less to do with internal expression than it did with identity being relational. Those who branded girls with the terms *whore* or *slut* exercised control over girls' identities by associating them with shameful sexuality. In other words, classmates—particularly, but not exclusively, boys—used girls' sexualities to name and shame them, as Shelly indicated when she told me of a classmate who was called a *whore* due to a rumor purporting that she had sex behind the school bleachers:

> I know that's not true. They say it because, first of all, she's a freshman, so people are trying to establish who's who, what clique goes where. And she's dated at least six different guys since school started. And then of course these guys are bad and can't keep their mouths shut and pretty much ruin her reputation. They make things up sometimes, and maybe don't other times. But it doesn't really matter either way.

While all of the teens felt the arbitrariness of these framings were unfair, the actual boundaries between appropriate female sexuality and promiscuity remained very unclear to them, a situation complicated by offline authorities in their lives, namely school and parents. For example, comprehensive sex education programs exist to help young people learn about their anatomy and choices, and to think about rights and relationships related to sexuality. However, the Guttmacher Foundation reports that US teens were far less likely to receive even the most basic sex education in public high school in 2013 than in the past.[7] In fact, most of the teens' high schools taught abstinence.[8] Further troubling matters is that these teens—like most—said they did not talk with their parents or peers to better understand sexual double standards, or to consider the framings and fairness of lines dividing appropriate and inappropriate sexuality.[9] They were left on their own to make sense of their sexuality and of social responses they observed and received. In this absence, most of them indicated that *all* expressions of sexuality from females were potentially inappropriate.

Finding the word "whore" had spreading power and social clout that was difficult to counter, teens might turn to friends for help. Amelia, for example, discussed how a freshman who tried to start a rumor that Amelia was a whore was shut down by her classmates. "I'm basically friends with everyone," she explained, "so nobody believes it. Everyone's like, 'No. That's not how she is.'" Amelia was fortunate that she had people willing to refute the message; unfortunately, the teens told me that once a female was called a whore, others could also unhelpful in undermining her reputation, "especially guys," Marcin said:

> They'll go along with someone calling a girl a whore, especially if it's by another guy. . . . Like, it's cool to call girls sluts, whores. Like, if they break up, "oh, she's a whore. Don't go out with her." They don't need to say it, but they do anyway. I don't know why. Maybe it's just the way guys are. And it makes them get along with other guys.

C. J. Pascoe[10] writes that gender hierarchy in high school operates through males' control of female bodies, and interlocutors saw ready evidence of this in school, where males would regularly damage females' reputations by naming them a whore and, simultaneously, elevate themselves and their respect among their peers.

As much as Marcin and others recognized this double standard, they also noted that many females would laugh and silently condone male classmates demeaning a girl in this way, reinforcing their need to constantly critique and self-regulate their own bodies to avoid trouble rather than rely on guidance or feedback.[11] Going along with name calling, Sarah explained, also moved the potential negative spotlight off them:

> [I]t kind of moves all of the problems that you had, like maybe you just got made fun of for something, and now there's something new to talk about. So you would rather talk about that than people talking about "oh, you said something dumb in Chemistry class."

Sarah had direct experience with this. Three years ago, a boyfriend told intimacies about their relationship that spread around the school and caused her to lose many friends. "We were at such a young age, and my friends are kind of uptight about stuff, they just kind of saw me as dirty for a little bit. So they didn't talk to me for a while." Noting that it took more than a year before her friends returned and apologized, Sarah added that people would still bring up the situation occasionally to try to embarrass her but that, generally, it had faded away because "people were on to the next big drama." Still, this experience caused her to downplay her relationships:

> I just find it easier to date people who are in different schools because he can tell his guy buddies but no one is going to care because it's just some chick from a random town. You have to be careful with how you are in a relationship. That's why, like personally, even sometimes, I will keep things from my best friend. I like to keep to myself now. It's better just to keep things to myself.

Knowing that girls are commonly slandered by males and other females in ways that could be hard to challenge or navigate in offline forums, these teens sought new, safer spaces online.

Interest in Protecting Parents

Like school, home was another location where interlocutors felt that their identities were highly circumscribed, thereby limiting their ability to self-define. As daughters, for example, the teens struggled to balance their need to claim identities with their desire to retain their parents' respect—a task that could be particularly challenging in a culture that did not have high opinion of its youth. As Naomi noted, "I felt guilty whenever I got in trouble for breaking a rule. It's kinda like I let them down." Whereas the teens may have experienced similar feelings at school, in the classroom, they could work to move past stigmas from detentions with good behavior just as they could make up for disappointing academic performances on the next assignment or exam. In contrast, their identities at home were less malleable due to difficulties in regaining parental trust and standing. Home was where they stated they felt the most futility in attempting to negotiate how they were seen and understood, compelling them to render certain parts of themselves invisible. "Sometimes you can't just do stuff in front of your parents," Marcin told me. She continued:

> It makes it easier to just not have them know. You don't have to worry as much. Telling them, you have to worry about the reactions if they don't like it. They'd get mad, and you'd get mad at them. They might ground you, or take away your TV or something. They make it a bigger deal sometimes. Like, these things aren't big deals. They sometimes make it a big deal.

As Marcin suggests, my interlocutors were active in ways that they knew their parents would not like, or approve of, involving themselves in activities they knew ran counter to the ways they were expected to be visible as daughters, and as young women. They went to parties to smoke cigarettes, drink Miller Lite, and say what they wanted to say without censorship. "Parents don't like to think about it," 14-year-old Naomi said, "but I hear kids cuss and say bad things all the time." They wanted to act on their sexuality, but some felt doing so would jeopardize their relationships with their parents; others did anyway. They were interested in meeting new people and in learning about the world. They wanted to be socially involved, to be taken seriously, and to have control over their highly monitored lives. Yet while they let me know that they did all of these things, they worked hard to hide from their parents the fact that they did them.

To continue their social involvements while remaining in their parents' good graces, the teens explained they acted strategically to make visible certain ways of being and hide others while at home. Such performances require certain tactics. "I lie to my mom all the time," Sarah told me from across the table of a local restaurant, looking up from her soda. "And I sneak out a lot." She continued:

> I mean, like right now, I'm not supposed to see my boyfriend, but, tomorrow, I'm going to go after school in my car and drive to his house and see him. I'm just going to say: "Mom, I'm going to my friend Jane's house." It's just, I don't know, it's just the fact that (pause), like, times are changing and adults don't really see it as changing, I guess. Nobody's, like, old fashion or waiting anymore. It's kind of like, this is how things are now.

Like the others, Sarah is socially involved in activities that, as she put it, "people think kids shouldn't do." She sneaks out. She is sexual. She is open to fielding friends' questions on sex, and she believes her mother would not approve of many of the things she does, or allow her to do them if she asked for permission. But with a boyfriend from another school living far away, and a busy after-school schedule, Sarah found her curfew and her mother's directives to not get too serious in stark conflict with her desire to be social and to maintain a relationship with someone she liked.

Sarah clearly valued being able to do what she wanted with her life, but she also discussed not wanting her parents to distrust her or to view her poorly because of these involvements. "It's easier to lie than to tell the truth just because maybe telling the truth can hurt your parents' feelings or make them feel disappointed in you," she explained. Sarah knew her parents would not appreciate the fact that she goes behind their back to pursue a relationship, but she could think of no other way to proceed. "My mom," she said, "she doesn't want me to be in a really, I don't know what you would call it, like in a really important relationship, like a serious relationship. But I'm in one already. She doesn't really understand, and she doesn't want to." Since she did not feel a discussion with her mother would grant her later curfews or more acceptance of her worldly involvements, Sarah explained that sneaking out was needed to claim her unwelcome social and sexual identities. She acknowledged it made her feel more responsible, and more in control of her life.

> Why do I sneak out? You just feel more independent. You feel like you are starting to grow up and be more independent, and your decisions impact how you are . . . [Y]ou know there's consequences, but you kind of already know what the consequences are and you already accept them. Also, I sneak out because if I don't, I can't do things I want to do. My mom's not going to let me, that's for sure. It's just kind of like easier.

When asked about what is made easier, she said she could do what she wanted without her mom making a big deal of it. She was able to act on being social and sexual without risking the loss of her identity as a trustworthy daughter, an identity that she also very much valued.

Marcin expanded on some of Sarah's experiences, noting that the teens in her area were told many things they could not do. "There's so many rules," she explained. "Selling cigarettes to minors, selling alcohol to minors, out too late. There's a lot of rules, but you can go around them as long as you don't get caught." Marcin went on to share that she smoked cigarettes and drank liquor and bought pregnancy tests out of town when she needed them. Amelia also discussed regularly sneaking around her father's rule against taking rides after dark—even to get home from football games and gatherings—from anyone other than an adult. Rides with classmates meant interacting with new people and the possibility of doing fun things that she rarely got to do, like go out to eat. Teens often stayed at events later than their parents, Amelia observed, leaving few people already out of high school to ask for rides. "I always get a ride home from other people, like juniors and seniors," she said. But like many of the other teens, Amelia felt torn between being honest with her parents about the difficulties she faced getting (and wanting) approved rides, and quietly ignoring her fathers' directions to get herself home: "I feel bad for not telling them, but I can't tell [my father], because I knew he'd freak out and then he'd be like, 'well, I can't trust you anymore.'"

As daughters bound to many rules, the teens felt that lying and "going around" rules allowed them to maintain valued relationships with important adults while still being able to act on their interests. These teens knew that their parents worried for them and put rules and limitations around them based on these worries. They knew parents wanted to protect them from harm. But they also believed that behind parental rules was their parents' disbelief that their daughters could negotiate the world without being taken advantage of and, despite their words to the contrary, a distrust in their daughters. Lying and sneaking around were, therefore, tactics the teens used to strategically juggle their identity presentation without upsetting their parents' trust or feelings.

In the process, my interlocutors suggested that they found ways to exercise some much-desired control in negotiating their social visibility by presenting themselves as they wanted to be seen in contexts that mattered to them. Still, these tactics had their limits, increasing the appeal of social media.

Adolescence

Teens also faced serious restrictions upon their identities due to their age. As "Millennials" and non-adult minors, teens are considered unprepared, flighty, primitive, naïve, entitled, and irresponsible, and my interlocutors were ever-conscious of the ways their age diminished both their status and their power, minimizing the control they had in representing and projecting themselves as competent and otherwise worthy of respect.

As female minors, these teens faced strict curfews, assumed asexuality, concerns dismissed as "raging hormones," closely regulated or prohibited dating, medically formalized framings of ineptitude, [12] and both parental and legal limitations on when they needed to have their car home, who they could take a ride from, whether they could buy a tan or rent a car, where they could gain entry to be with other young people, and what they could drink at parties. Amelia, who was almost 16, discussed her driving privileges:

> I wasn't allowed to drive after dark even when I had my permit for about three months. And my dad won't let me turn right on a red yet either. (laughs) I know they just want the best for me and they don't want me to get hurt, but my dad believes that any driver that's 16 or 17, they're not going to be a good

driver. Even if they've had, like, really good training or whatever. But he just doesn't trust it.

When it was not summer, teens were mandated to spend the majority of their days in school and to be under adult supervision at most times when they were not. They struggled to find jobs that would earn them money and interesting activities outside of school that would allow them entry with little money. A number of the teens had parents who had hours cut and jobs lost in the recent recession. One teen's family home was foreclosed upon, forcing them to move. The teens were limited in their ability to take on active roles helping their family within such economic challenge. They reported that job openings were rare, and that adults worked at the Walmart, the nearest fast food restaurants, and many of the other local jobs typically held by teens. Indeed, around the time of this study, the Bureau of Labor Statistics reported that 16–24-year-olds faced the nation's lowest employment rates on record.[13]

Adolescence is recognized as a time of future orientation. All of the teens I met with were interested in their futures, and in taking steps needed to promote their well-being and development. While not all liked school or fared as strongly as others in the classroom, each had ambitions. Each said they hoped to be able to succeed in life, or to "be someone someday," as Violet said. However, they also stated they had limited ability in their day-to-day lives to know about the world they were charged with succeeding in, and few permissions to be involved in this world.

Research finds that young people in the United States experience low levels of guidance and high levels of uncertainty as they plan for occupations and lives which they hope will bring them greater social relevance, control, and rights.[14] In line with this research, many of these teens worried about moving ahead in life, lacking access to family members and school guidance counselors who could help them know how to secure jobs that would allow advancement toward the purpose and financial self-sufficiency central to US framings of adulthood,[15] or how to apply for college. Those who planned to go to college worried about how to tackle the immense expense of even a local school. These worries were warranted, as reduced US government funding, rising tuitions and fees[16] and soaring unsubsidized loans find female college students straddled with historically unprecedented average student debt and student loan delinquency.[17] They are valid concerns as US citizens—particularly those of color—face the highest incarceration rate across the globe;[18] as tough labor and economic conditions since the Great Recession—including falling weekly earnings for young female workers;[19] unemployment rates for 16–24-year-olds more than three times higher than national rates;[20] downward mobility increasing children's likelihood to earn less than their parents;[21] and massive, persistent underemployment for young people with jobs[22] result in more young Americans aged 18 to 34 living in their parents' home now than at any other time throughout the past five generations;[23] and as the country uses its bootstrapping narratives and neo-liberal roots to ignore systemic barriers and to, instead, blame young Americans for their struggles and failings.

The teens I met with were confused about how to be known in the world in ways that would bring them the rights and respect they believed they deserved, and they were quite frustrated in figuring out what to do and how to be to move toward the "futures" they were told they should be spending time and effort planning for. They bemoaned having limited rights to engage, have direction, and be known in desirable ways in the world. They had little trust in their ability to gain more respect on their own, or to negotiate better terms for their life offline with adults—particularly parents—who policed their marginality. Facing routine misinterpretation, devaluing, and refusal of some of their realities, they also said they were frequently not able to trust the way they were socially read. Instead, as young women, the teens reported they were forced to become aware of parts of themselves that were not welcome, believed, or acceptable to certain populations, and they learned to strategically figure out ways to move these expressions underground and into other spaces that offered them less resistance in personally and publicly performing their self-definition to attempt to advance themselves. Teens said they found social media to have more promising life options than what was available to them offline. Social media provided a stage for the teens to assert and manage their appearance in front of different audiences and away from traditional gatekeepers' watch, thereby meeting their interests in having specific identities seen, known, and validated. Given the limitations their age placed on their ability to perform their identities, my interlocutors increasingly turned to social media.

Identities in Media Migration

With little opportunity to rule anything and many limitations, my interlocutors reported taking the Internet up on its well-publicized offers to "rule the air" and "be unlimited" in their lives online. But as was the case offline, the teens were strategic in what Anne Balsamo terms "staging [their] bodies"[24] in desired ways, asserting and advancing their online identities. Teens focused on working to have their "ideal self"[25] *be seen* by others, and they used media migration to perform both visibility and invisibility of identities that would help them maintain important relationships with peers and protective adults while they forged counternarratives to the mismapping they regularly experienced as adolescent girls.

To accomplish this, not only did they work to present themselves in a favorable light online, but knowing that adults monitored them, teens in this study put effort into carefully curating identities in and across social media platforms. Using social media as a stealth tool to choreograph their social presentation, teens created disruptive patterns within and across platforms to distort their identities, obscuring their actual whereabouts while remaining in plain sight much like ocular diffusion camouflage efforts used to protect war ships from enemy submarines in World War I. This specific form of camouflage—termed "Dazzle" camouflage[26]—creates an alternate understanding of an object not by blending it into the background, but by blurring its exact location and definition to keep others from being able to accurately perceive and track it. Knowing they had little ability to be entirely masked or away from their parents' watch without raising concern, these teens used media migration to perform, advance, confuse, and control their identities while simultaneously employing tactics that kept onlookers from noticing that, though they were present, they were often actually elsewhere. The following discussion examines three specific tactics teens used to help in these efforts.

Identity Attenuation

Teens in this study felt powerless to affect others seeing them in specific ways, a situation they found particularly disconcerting because they realized how quickly and widely ideas about them could spread in a small town—from classmates discussing fights to ex-boyfriends who branded them a slut. As Molly explained: "Like if I did something, everybody would find out before I even tell my dad or mom." As such, teens resorted to attenuation in social media to crop, and thus attempt to manage, their online identities, filtering details or leaving things out all together if they thought the information could damage their standing with specific audiences. This tactic was used most frequently on Facebook. For example, knowing her mother monitored her account, Naomi said she thought about her mother and father in the audience whenever she posted Facebook statuses and comments, prompting her to perform identities very carefully on the site. One instance she cites is the type of photos she would post. "[Parents] freak out if you go to the pool and have a picture with your friend with a bikini on," she explained. As a result, she made a point to remove all bikini pictures and other expressions that she knew would trigger parental "freak out" from her profile page, using social media to perform continued invisibility regarding this part of her life. Other teens did the same. Carollynn explained that this shaped how she presented herself on Facebook.

> I know my parents, they get on my laptop sometimes and look at my stuff. I mean, not that I post anything bad anyway, but it's just, I try to keep that in my mind every time I post. I'm like "Ahhh, you better not post this cause my parents might see it and I might get in a lot of trouble."

Violet also made major retractions to her Facebook profile when she realized her mother might be watching her. She explained:

> Well, it sounds bad, but after my mom got a Facebook, I pretty much erased every status I ever made just cause . . . you can't really express emotion in text, so she probably wouldn't understand how I meant things or wouldn't take it the same way that I mean them, so I just didn't wanna risk it.

Meanwhile, Marcin explained how she no longer posts her frustrations with family on Facebook because of this concern:

> If I post some things up there, I know [my mom is] going to make me discuss it. Oh yeah, I know I'm going to have to. So I don't post it. I just feel like she's too overprotective sometimes about that. Like if I said I hated my sister, or I hate this family, it would be a big deal. Or if she thought I was involved in stuff she didn't think I should do. They would say it was starting stuff.

Throughout my time in the field, teens demonstrated they were highly cognizant that adults they knew were watching them through Facebook. While some adults remained quiet, others would give offline feedback on what they observed from teens online, pointing out self-representations they did not like. For example, some parents, worried about the family "looking bad" because of what their daughters put online, told the teens to take down certain posts and to present themselves in certain ways on Facebook to minimize judgment from the parents' family members, work associates, and friends. Violet was instructed to not post song lyrics on Facebook because they reflected badly on her family:

> I had song lyrics on as a status one time and my mom, like from someone else's Facebook, read it and freaked out about it cause apparently it was bad. Like, "your dad's family can see all of this! And we're gonna be looked at as bad people!"

Violet posted the song because she liked it. She didn't particularly affiliate with the lyrics. Still, like Noel's sister, she removed it from her profile.

Marcin also described a friend getting in trouble at home for posting lyrics on Facebook. In response, Marcin chose not to post songs on her Facebook account. And Amelia's insurance salesman father instructed her to watch what she posted because he believed his clients in the community would judge him for what she said. "People seem to be a lot less dramatic on Facebook," she said, "because I think they're friends with, like, their parent's friends, and their uncles and aunts and stuff." With these warnings in mind, teens worked carefully to present themselves well on Facebook, removing controversial presentations to help their family save face and appear in ways they are told represent respectability to others.

Beyond parents, teens censored certain parts of themselves online so as to advance wholesome images toward other adults in their lives, such as teachers. For example, Violet greatly admired a teacher at her school. "I have this friend," she stated. "She's like one of the most inspirational people I've ever met . . . She's never done anything wrong in her life." Violet had recently friended the teacher on Facebook, and she discussed spending a lot of time thinking of the teacher when on Facebook. She explained that having the teacher as a Facebook friend has caused her to want to represent herself differently. "'Cause I look up to her," Violet explained. "I don't want her to think that I'm like not. I don't know. . . . You just don't wanna say something bad." And, with interest in looking good to the teacher, she said she changed the way she made herself visible on Facebook in hopes that the teacher would see her as worthy of her respect and attention:

> I wanna be like her and have little kids looks up to me and think that I'm a great person and wanna be like me so then they'll be good people like, I don't know how to describe that. But I want her to see me like that, like good, like her.

In wanting to impress her teacher, Violet consciously rendered invisible certain identities in her performance of self on Facebook, refusing to post anything that might cause her identity of "goodness" to be less apparent to her teacher.

With awareness of their judgmental adult audience looking on, as well of as their interest in impressing this audience to prove themselves more mature and deserving of responsibilities, my interlocutors reported holding back on "putting it all out there." "People are partially honest on Facebook," said Marcin. "They know teachers and stuff are watching." Recognizing the adult audiences thus promoted the teens to use Facebook less as a diary in which they recorded their private thoughts, crushes, and interests, and more as a résumé to promote their responsibility and trustworthiness.

In addition to self-censoring to enhance the image among adults, teens self-censored in social media to avoid slander. Fights happened regularly on social media, but, outside of those involving their closest friends, most of the teens noted that they abstained from getting involved to avoid ruffling feathers socially. Amelia's comments about a big Facebook fight between friends demonstrated this concern: "I just watched because I did not want to get in the middle of that." Getting involved, she explained, would set her up as a target for insults and negative attention. It would drag her into the fray, and make people have reason to not like her, undermining the work she had done to socially establish herself. Amelia continued:

> You try so hard to fit in with everyone; you don't want to be an outcast. . . . I mean, 'cause in grade school, I wasn't really like, I wasn't really in with everyone. . . . I'm not just gonna, like, throw it all away.

Other teens said that they, too, tried to stay out of friends' online altercations to protect themselves from public ridicule and shaming. Some justified their fears of social reprisal with their experiences online. "I won't start an argument or call someone out on Facebook," Marcin explained. "You get called a whore if you do that." If you try to defend someone on social media, Carollynn noted, "then people will start saying stuff about you too." While she says she loved her friends, Cassidy said concern over strangers turning their animosity her way caused her to stay quiet and look away if one of them was being unfairly treated on Facebook. "We all do it," she said. "It's just not worth it to butt in."

Protecting themselves from others' criticism—adults or their immediate peers—were some of the most common situations in which teens held back information about themselves to better manage and perform their identities, but teens also did so to actively create and shape the ways others saw them. At times it came in the form of omitting details that might inadvertently align them with ideas, values, and even people that might cast them in less favorable ways, as Naomi did with some of her association with the town of Flatville. Flatville was known for its "bad kids" who got in fights and used drugs. Naomi, who lived near Flatville in smaller Brown, made a point to never mention Flatville on Facebook. "I don't want anyone to associate me with them," she said of Flatville teens. Even though Naomi visited Flatville often, by not mentioning the town, she worked to render invisible the connection she had with it and its rowdy teenage residents, projecting herself as a different type of kid who was worthy of respect.

Teens' concerns for their futures likewise informed their decision to attenuate certain behaviors or affiliations online. Often discussing how Facebook use hurt their identities down the line, my interlocutors explained how they worked to present themselves to others. In discussing pictures a friend posted on Facebook that she thought were inappropriate, for instance, LaToya said, "I tell them 'you should take that down. . . . People are going to look at you differently,'" indicating ways they were being—and could be—judged by the images and representations they posted on Facebook. As LaToya explained: "I don't post a lot of pictures that I shouldn't because I don't want people to see me as something I am not." When asked what she did not want to be seen as, LaToya struggled for an answer. "I don't know how to put this. I don't want people to think that I'm a bad influence, or I just don't like people to see me, umm." She paused, looked down, and started laughing. I urged her to continue. She looked to the side and said: "I don't want people to see me as a whore, so I want to have a different look to myself than that."

Not wanting to be seen in certain ways, LaToya and the other teens employed codes and acronyms to perform public invisibility of identities in social media, sending messages parents could neither detect nor decipher—actions social media scholar danah boyd refers to as "social steganography" used to achieve private communications and unobserved performance of taboo identities in highly public forums.[27] For example, rather than post controversial subjects on Facebook, my interlocutors would use hashtags such as "#frustrated" to allude to taboo subjects they were experiencing, but chose not to address fully on the site. They tweaked privacy settings, removed their names from Twitter handles, and created second Facebook accounts they thought their parents could not find to heighten invisibility. LaToya explained: "The ones with their moms [friended], they'll watch what they put on Facebook, or they make another page." And they whispered proclamations in other ways, such as when LaToya posted a stylized picture of herself on Facebook with the letters "FWM" written in bright purple script after a break-up. "It means to Facebook that I'm single but I'm ready to mingle," she said in attempts to politely explain the abbreviation for "fuck with me." LaToya said her mother did not seem to notice these letters, and, even if she did, she believed her mother would not know their intent enough to see them as something to be concerned about.

But codes could not always be used. Recognizing that being slandered was still a danger on Facebook, the teens expressed concerns about appropriate versus inappropriate displays of sexuality and of self in social media. In response to this, they spent a lot of time thinking about the potential implications of their presentation online, and they put effort into not being controversial. Marcin, for example, said she only posted certain types of images of herself to try to decrease the chances that people would call her a whore:

> It would be really easy to just label me a whore if I put up too many pictures on Facebook. Mostly head shots, just head shots are really good. Because it's just your face, it's not really anything else. Cause if it was lower, you could see down their shirt. And people would call you a whore. Someone could comment, "Oh, I can see your bra" or something. People use that word online a lot, whore. That and the "b" word.

Teens were concerned and uncertain of how they would be perceived by others in social media, and, like offline, they knew it was easy for females to be socially shamed online regardless of what they wore or how they acted. When in doubt of what others might approve of, they said they censored themselves more, echoing studies that find female teens to be far more cautious and risk averse in social media than males of their age.[28]

Facebook opens options for users to present different selves and engage in wide identities exploration. Thinking about how others would read their presentation online, teens made themselves less visible in certain areas of social media, cropping themselves out of specific affiliations and interactions to manage their social presentation in these explorations. This helped them to assert desired social understandings while distracting others' attention away from their less desired or more controversial identities.

In looking out for their present and future selves, these teens reported (and showed) that they are often choosing to sit quietly on the side lines by purposefully and actively disassociating themselves in social media rather than to risk unwanted negative attention and trouble. Knowing that adults needed to be protected from some of their realities and that both adults and peers might not back them if they encountered social shaming, they are choosing to silence themselves. This was especially the case concerning conversations they knew many people were watching, and for potentially controversial topics they were unsure of how others might respond to. In social media, teens said widely watched and potentially controversial interactions occurred quite often, especially as they broadened their audiences of friends and followers.

Of course, knowing the potential for isolation and stigma, teens chose not to interject themselves in social interactions that might get messy offline, also. But the widened social potential and social display of social media raised new concerns that stoked girls' self-monitoring and self-censorship. Teens selectively displayed cherished identities online and commonly downplayed those that made them a "minority." For example, fearing racist backlash, Violet never posted pictures of her father on Twitter. Also, it was rare for the teens to tweet or post about their poverty. And while all of the teens said they would "definitely" stand up for a very good friend who was called a whore in an altercation in school, only about half said they would do so in social media where they knew their words would remain long after being expressed for the scrutiny of an anonymous, and sometimes brutally vicious, lurking world.

In some ways, these teens are savvy to try to avoid damaging slander online by steering clear of controversial associations. Online involvement does not free teens of offline prejudices; with normalized stereotyping, doxxing, heteroprejudice, threats, slut-shaming, rape jokes, cloaked white supremacist websites, revenge porn,[29] and few options for recourse,[30] racism, sexism, and other forms of hate abound in social media. Teens' awareness that they are easily discredited and limited in their ability to fight against such injustices is part of what fuels their media migrations. But teens also pay a price for attenuating their presence, even in forums where controversy abounds and where slander is often able to exist with impunity. The widespread use of a site that tolerates and disseminates negative portrayals of females has implications for how teens will come to understand themselves and others, and it also can shape how others will come to understand teens. Specifically, fear of social reprisal online creates a "chilling effect" that finds teens compromising their own values, sense of self, and identities as a silent fee for participation, and that encourages them to disconnect when they would otherwise be affirming important connections.

For example, a teen deciding to not defend a friend while others watch represents a cost to their identity as a loyal friend. Choosing to attenuate rather than to engage in this instance challenges teens' ability to be known and trusted as loyal. Remaining silent does not validate social understandings of them as a friend. Instead, it alters who they can say they are to this friend, and, in this, it redefines who they are as a person. Furthermore, encouragement of such (in)action in social media forges patterns of identity-shaping social norms affirming teens' social disconnection for the sake of survival and advancement as it creates expectations of friends not standing up for friends in social settings, as well as for tolerance of misogyny and sexist speech. There are very real negative repercussions that encourage teens to choose silence on- and offline, and teens' self-censorship in their media migrations impact how others know them, and how they know themselves.

Identity attenuation aided teens in presenting themselves in desired ways to audiences assembled within social media platforms as it freed them of certain social concerns. And while their efforts to crop out parts of their lives on social media provided some social filtering of undesirable affiliations and identities, this was insufficient in asserting some of their more controversial realities, highlighting another tactic the teens used in media migration: augmentation.

Identity Augmentation

Another way teens filtered their identities in concern for receptivity was through augmentation, using social media to highlight and broadcast certain realities about themselves and, in so doing, affirming specific ideas and understandings they wished to have as part of their identity. For example, in an effort to stay in her parents' good graces, Noel made a point on Facebook to only host wholesome posts and pictures herself as a responsible "good girl." Amy, knowing how much her grandmother loved to play online bingo, shared her Facebook password and account with her grandmother. In this, Amy not only helped her grandmother earn more points for her bingo account, but she gained an opportunity to demonstrate her love and generosity toward a cherished adult. Other teens did the same. They used social media to "like" posts and pictures, to retweet, to share pictures showing them with specific people, and to mention others in posts, helping to affirm good relationships with friends and family they value even as they reinforced characteristics they wanted others to attribute to them, such as family-oriented, responsible, smart, popular, interesting, and so on. For example, teens said that expense, time, geographic distances, and a lack of phone numbers commonly prevented them from being able to keep families and friends abreast of their life, so posting pictures on Facebook enabled the teens to share their family-friendly goings-on with local and distant connections and to stay on their radar. As Cassidy explained, seeing family photos on Facebook makes you feel you are "sharing each other's lives." By keeping family members informed of important happenings such as dances, haircuts, birthdays, and holidays, teens used social media to affirm their connections with family members and take part in "kinkeeping,"[31] remaining visible in positive ways despite the distances and infrequent in-person visits that separated them.

Beyond this, teens amplified flattering portrayals of themselves on social media, carefully curating their profiles to reflect the ways they wanted to be seen and socially recognized. Early in our meetings, for example, Carollynn told me she posted actively to Facebook to affirm who she was. "The things I put on Facebook are about me. . . . It's to express myself. That's how I feel. Like, 'this is me.'" Similarly, Annie took time to spell words correctly, and she reviewed her posts and IMs to catch any spelling errors before hitting send, promoting an image of herself as polished and adroit. Annie also told me she never used swear words offline, so she did not use them online in Facebook. "I don't want people to think I'm that type of person," she explained. When probed to expand on this, she replied quickly, "I don't swear. I don't do things like that. People know I get good grades and that I'm nice and friendly. I'm not someone who wants to be known as talking bad." Being seen as "talking bad" was a concern for Annie that she addressed by making conscious efforts to appear "good" in her social media posts. These efforts mattered, she said, because they broadcast the type of person she was.

Teens augmented other types of affiliations in their media migrations. After hearing on Facebook about the shooting of unarmed teenager Trayvon Martin, LaToya and a friend took pictures of one another in black hooded sweatshirts holding a bag of Skittles candy and an Arizona iced tea. They captioned these pictures "I am Trayvon Martin," and posted them to their Facebook pages as a sign of protest. "I put it up because people know what we mean. I feel that justice should be made. I feel it's not fair, his killing," LaToya said. As a female minor in her community, LaToya knew of no way to join the movement objecting to unchecked violence toward Black youth like her. She used her picture to amplify her opinion and affiliation with those calling for justice. Similarly, other teens socially signaled their affiliations with recognized musicians, actors, brands, and activities on social media. For example, Molly posted a picture of herself with a large group of classmates at a restaurant. "We had like seventeen people and it was crazy," she said. "I wanted everybody to be jealous that I was eating at Buffalo Wild Wings."

Teens also used social media to jockey for social standing. "A lot of people want to be popular," Cassidy said. She explained that she and her friends used social media to promote their status by showing others they were valued:

> Like I went and hung out with this person and hung out with this person. And we went and did this. Did you do that? No, you didn't! So I'm cooler than you are because I went and did this stuff.

Appearing cool to classmates was an interest of all of these teens, and this interest became more acute once they started high school, which forced them to leave familiar peer groups and school staff and enter an unfamiliar context where they were less known. "My teachers there all knew me so well," said Naomi of the school where she spent her first eight years. "You could go and talk to them whenever. And now I come here and. . . . I'm just another kid."

For Naomi and others, entering high school called previously set identities into question, and required them to do new work to establish who they are socially. Teens said social media was helpful in allowing them to acceptably broadcast parts of their lives that might impress others and improve their social status. "Because that's just the big thing," Sarah explained, "to get out with all of the cool people, no matter what you say or what you do. And posting it on Twitter or Facebook."

Social standing was also linked to being attractive, for, to these teens, being attractive meant being worthy of others' attention. As a result, LaToya said she only posted pictures on Facebook that presented her as attractive. "I just think that if they saw me as pretty," she said, "they'd be like, 'Oh, well she's pretty,' and then they'll want to talk to me and try to get to know me." And even though LaToya confessed that she wasn't always sure what "attractive" meant, she did recognize that social media played a part in the ways people were depicted and, thus, valued. She explained:

> It's important to look pretty on Facebook because when people see me on Facebook, I want them to say, "oh, you're pretty." Because I don't like people to call me ugly, I mean, I know I'm not ugly, but I don't know. When someone calls you a name, you're like "Oh, really?" This boy called my friend fat yesterday, and she got self-conscious! She started running! And I was like, "you're not fat!" And, yeah. So, people call me fat, and sometimes you think "Am I really fat?" and then you start thinking you're fat and so you just start doing all this extra stuff just to make yourself not [fat].

Lastly, teens used social media to project themselves in ways that gained the attention of peers outside of their usual circles. Most of the teens had fewer than 125 students in their entire high school, and most had been in class with the same 20 classmates throughout their entire life. This led to deeply entrenched and peer-policed identities that welcomed little change; teens said they were quickly called out as "fake" when showing themselves in a new way, and they always knew who would support them and who would ignore them in their daily lives. But social media opened up new options to be recognized. Unlike prior research suggesting that young women are generally not interested using social media to meet strangers,[32] these teens welcomed the chance to expand their social life. One way they did this was by attracting "likes," nice comments, and retweets from the things they posted on social media. Teens explained that having posts and statuses noticed meant that people appreciated your thoughts, and appreciated you. This recognition seemed especially important for these young women who often struggled to find people willing to listen to their ideas, let alone say that they liked them. As such, teens reported that having a stranger notice their ideas was particularly exciting.

To help foster such validation, each of the teens formed new relationships with Facebook "friends of friends." A Facebook status posting opened up the possibility of having one of your friends' friends seeing you as similar or fun; they might even start to talk with you. Facebook provided a forum to be visible to peers in ways found difficult offline due to the presence of cliques, but teens said these conversations could be difficult on Facebook due to the presence of protective and punitive adults. Twitter also created opportunities for new people to notice and unexpectedly respond to a posting, and teens noted that Twitter came with promises of fewer parental eyes watching how they self-defined to others. Like with Facebook, a sharp tweet or good picture could introduce you to new teenagers in the area who could be met up with in person later. This encouraged them to use the interface to host and broadcast their flirting, mingling, and courting. Twitter also passed on celebrities' tweets and micropublication "facts" and aphorisms, providing teens useful social information to share with others at school to better their social standing. And it welcomed teens sharing ideas and acts that were generally considered taboo. Teens said that amplifying these identities often made them appear—and feel—more worldly and in-the-know. Consequently, Twitter was described as having the potential to increase your popularity offline. Sarah explained:

> Saying "oh, I'm with this person" or "I'm with that person." "We're going to this place," "We're driving to the movies." "I'm hanging out and going to a party." Maybe, if you . . . write out there "I'm getting drunk tonight," or "I'm gonna get high tonight," maybe that might make you feel like you're cool, for others to know these things about you.

Teens were eager to be known in positive ways. And expecting judgment, devaluing, and misogyny from people they already knew, they welcomed the opportunity to meet new people who might, instead, see them as they knew themselves, or as they otherwise wished to be seen. Social media provided forums for such work by helping teens socially spotlight parts of themselves they deemed desirable to specific audiences in hopes of making these identities more visible. But as with attenuation, augmentation had its limits. Bricolage helped teens extend, and blur, the possibilities.

Identity Bricolage

Dick Hebdige defines bricolage as the appropriation and performative reassemblage of objects to "erase or subvert their original straight meanings," and teens' use of social media echos this definition by challenging dominant discourses of who they were so as to broaden identities beyond narrow and inaccurate framings they were permitted offline.[33] To do this, they engaged in what Anthony Giddens terms "time-space distancation"[34] to disconnect their identities from both local environments and physical presence, and to divide these deconstructed social expressions to different social media sites. This separation allowed teens to discreetly locate and manipulate parts of their identities on certain social media sites while existing as a re-assembled whole across these platforms. The teens in my study might drive 45 minutes to visit the mall; others might attend away-games, cattle shows, and parties. But as rural youth they had few physical places in their own community where they could be known outside of the ways they were always known: "Bob's youngest," "Terrence's little cousin," the "girl who runs track," "that whore," "one of the Jones girls," or "the kid who lives down by the old post office." In general, social media provided them with new spaces to inhabit and to use as well as to stretch the performance of their identities[35] beyond both offline interpretations and individual social media audiences. But the teens quickly realized that individual media sites had particular advantages—and disadvantages—requiring teens to work across, rather than just within, social media platforms to craft and use a network of social media systems that provided different functionalities. Bricolage made this possible, offering teens different communities outside of their physical environment to receive their realities.

For example, Violet used Facebook to connect to a community that shared her experience of having to deal with racism. She explained:

> It's better to have yourself around people that are like I wouldn't say bad just because they're racists. I guess they're not bad people, but people with a better mindset. . . . I've been to a lot of schools and bigger cities and this is the smallest city I've ever lived in, so I have friends on Facebook from places I used to live and a lot of them are different races and stuff and they're not all just white, country kids from my school who think the same stupid way about me.

Helping her feel more comfortable claiming a part of herself that was regularly devalued offline, Violet's online peer group normalized her experiences and gave her a place to feel more authentic and respected. While it did not give her a structural analysis of race or power, this extended presence allowed her to depersonalize her social exclusion and find strength with others who also struggled in similar ways. Yet because of limitations presented by Facebook, Violet—like other teens—extended her presence *across* social media platforms. Like Facebook, Twitter gave Violet a forum she lacked in her physical space, but this one had the added benefit of being a parent-free space:

> Twitter is like [pause], when your parents leave the house and you can have a party. And you do and say what you want. But Facebook is like when Mom and Dad are home. You have to like, watch yourself. . . . You can say what you want when your parents aren't around. But when they are around you have to watch what you say. And Twitter, since most parents don't have a Twitter account, or they don't monitor their kids' Twitter account and the kids just say whatever.

Outside of Club Penguin, Facebook was the first social media site used by the teens. This was where their friends were and, at one time, this was where they were not under parents' watchful gaze. While their early Facebook days found them posting statuses, liking videos, tagging pictures, and "truth is"-ing solely for peers, they later realized the social landscape had changed: more adults, fewer friends, less controversy to bring up in class the following day. Therefore, while a few of the teens continued spending most of their time on Facebook, many teens relocated to Twitter. "It used to be that you know everything about that person just by going on to their [Facebook] wall," said Sarah. "Now, you know from Twitter." She stated that this made her decide to move away from Facebook.

> On Facebook now, it's just boring. It's just kind of like eighth graders, like lower-grade people on there now, and the adults. And the adults, all they post is pictures of cats and things like that. And so you go through it, and nothing interesting. Nothing that you can say to your friends the next morning and talk about or anything like that. Like a crazy scenario, like so-and-so is pregnant, and stuff like that. And then you talk about that later the next day. Facebook used to help you know about things going on. Twitter does now.

A number of the teens agreed with Sarah's assessments, reporting that Twitter connected them to others who they looked up to and believed welcomed their realities. According to Amelia: "I think it's more so my generation that has Twitter, and celebrities more than adults." But teens also migrated to Twitter for whom they believed were *not* in attendance: their parents. "[W]hen my parents check my computer," Amelia explained, "they don't really care about Twitter 'cause they don't really know what it is." Others agreed.

Rather than supplanting one platform with another, a bricolage of social media helped teens maintain visibility of acceptable identities on Facebook even as they strategically relocated controversial ideas and images to spaces unmonitored by parents, say a second Facebook account or Twitter. Away from parental monitoring in media migration, teens felt less socially constrained and overtly pursued social and romantic relationships, shared sassy pictures, and broadcast tweets and thoughts on "adult" topics. On Twitter, for example, Sarah cursed and discussed sex, drinking, and parties. "I wouldn't use Twitter the same way if my parents were on it," she confessed, explaining these expressions as unacceptable to her parents. But without parents around, Sarah said she spent hours on Twitter because she was "treated like a grown-up" and was "able to make decisions and face the consequences." "On Twitter," she said, "kids can be kids."

Existing outside of adult surveillance, censoring, and other reminders of inferiority, teens said they trusted social media to both accept them and teach them how to gain status and be considered "right" in the world.

Carollynn also censored herself on Facebook, but her imagined Twitter audience made her believe she could safely vent family frustrations there:

> Some of my mom's friends from work that I'm also friends with . . . Like, stuff like, if I'm mad at my parents I can comment, I put it on Twitter not on Facebook so they don't tell my mom or something. Yeah it's different on Twitter.

Others agreed. Noting that she and her classmates heard countless warnings about posting inappropriately on Facebook from adults in formal and informal settings, Cassidy stated that Twitter use came—appealingly—with far fewer warnings. Cassidy explained that she knew Twitter was similar to Facebook in many ways, but she didn't feel as concerned about posting to Twitter. In the absence of parents, the space felt more private than Facebook, and Cassidy said that pictures they posted and saw on Twitter were meant for peers. Ironically, as the next chapter explains, Twitter is, by design, a much more public space than Facebook. Still, teens reported feeling less monitored and less inhibited on Twitter. They reported tweeting frequently on Twitter and performing a different side of their identities there than they were willing to show on Facebook. Molly explained:

> People say really different things on Twitter that they might be afraid to say on Facebook. I see a lot of people cussing on Twitter and I don't see them cuss on Facebook. Cause I know they have Facebook, and that they are afraid to get in trouble or something. They voice their opinion a lot more on Twitter.

Like the other teens, Molly also used Twitter in this way. Some of her tweets—such as "This algebra homework and I just aren't getting along"—contained expressions that also appeared in her Facebook posts, but her swearing, push-back against parental constraints, and racially hostile comments were only found on her Twitter account in tweets stating "Bitch shut the eff up," "There are so many low life kids in our school," "I would be game if my MOTHER WASN'T SUCH A BITCH," "This negro is taking forever at the car wash," and "#ReplaceADisneyMovieWithNigga snow white and the seven niggas."

Viewing Twitter as a space where teens could be visible in more adult, knowledgeable ways, teens also felt much more welcome to claim sexual identities on Twitter. Sarah explained:

> People definitely post different types of pictures on Twitter than they would on Facebook. Like, people with beer bottles in their hands, or maybe little bit like scandalous, like their shirt's up maybe, and, because we're always preached to, like, [sing-songy voice] "On Facebook, don't be taking, like, nudie pictures and putting them online, or anything like that." But nothing, like, nudie is on Twitter, but, like pictures, like more scandalous maybe. Their boobs are hanging out, or something like that, trying to look like they're hot, I guess.

All of the teens on Twitter used it to post pictures of themselves that they knew their parents would not approve. For example, Naomi's Twitter account featured pictures from the pool she was not allowed to share on Facebook along with other selfies that were not posted on her Facebook account. Rosie's Twitter account had pictures of her dressed up and posing at a party she was not supposed to attend. Sarah's included shots of her drinking and kissing her boyfriend. The "wallpaper"—or repeated background image—on one teen's profile showed thumbnails of a photo of her straddling her boyfriend on a bed. Not only did teens feel more comfortable posting more sexually provocative photos on Twitter, but they followed micropublications, or newsfeed accounts with names like "Inspiring Quotes," "Relationships!" and "Teen Facts <3" that tweeted jokes and statements about sex, relationships, and "things people do." Teens considered these accounts an important part of their Twitter involvement. One described them as "things you follow on Twitter to show you know how to use it," and another, as something you do on Twitter "to use it right." Struggling to affiliate with their sexuality offline in positive ways, teens viewed Twitter as a forum that made this possible, and even encouraged. As Sarah explains:

> For some people, they don't talk about sex at all face to face, especially around parents. I feel that this confusion could make them feel more like, like "I don't know as much as everybody else." . . . [E]specially in this time and age, everyone's trying to figure out what sex is, or if they should do it or if they

should wait, or what they want to do with their lives, so I feel Twitter has a big influence on it because it makes it sound like it's good. Sex is kind of shown as this exciting, really interesting thing. So it kind of promotes it. Like this.

Sarah pointed to a tweet on her account from a Twitter account named "Sluttygirl" that read: "All I can think of is penis and vaginas in Instagram." Sarah explained that retweeting micropublication feeds like these helped them "state" and identify with controversial sexuality in a way that felt less risky than offline expressions; the tweets were not their own, and this distance not only protected them from being judged by others by their retweets but it gave them an opportunity to be viewed as worldly, wise, competent, and "in the know" about adult matters. Sarah elaborated:

> I think that's what you are kind of supposed to do on Twitter to look right. Like just to say "Oh, I'm out of it, but I'll pretend I know everything there is to know," maybe just like go on these apps and start retweeting. . . . Nobody wants to be known as clueless.

Indeed, my interlocutors stressed that they did not want to be perceived as "clueless"—especially since, as females and as youth with high levels of protection and confinement and low levels of direction, control, and trust, they regularly felt treated as clueless offline. The bricolaged identities they created and used on social media thus gave them power to perform identities they rendered invisible offline, even as they protected their parents.

The history of teens seeking ways to be seen as grown up can be traced to long before the advent of Twitter. Teens in this study appeared to be continuing this trend. Unhappy with offline understandings and with the idea of having to present one identity to everyone they interacted with in social media, these teens reported that they riled against this technical constraint and crafted new ways to use Facebook and Twitter to construct one large social media stage upon which they performed their identities in ways that were difficult to achieve offline due to rigid cliques, groups, and biases. However, identity continued to be highly relational and social here. Unlike claims of users "forging" and "asserting" their "own" identity online, these teens stated they relied heavily on feedback they received from onlookers in claiming who they were in this space. In other words, similar to offline, the highly social and relational aspect of identity formation continued to exist online, shaping teens' identity presentation. Likes, retweets, and favorites provided teens information about their value, which, in turn, reinforced how teens presented themselves to gain social approval. Sarah explained:

> People comment or like them, especially profile pictures. If you put a cute one on your wall, people will like it and comment on it. It's a good self-esteem

boost too. You can think of it that way. Like, if a lot of people like it, you'd be like "Oh, ok. So this is a good picture."

Teens saw social media as a tool to illustrate the parts of their lives they thought would be valued by audiences they looked to for feedback and, ultimately, for approval. Similarly, they read negative or few comments as a sign of what not to do. Cassidy explained:

Sometimes, people will brag about things they did on Facebook to get attention, because Facebook is a place where you are supposed to get attention. If you don't, like if your posts don't get any "likes" or comments, you kind of look like a loser. You kind of feel like one too sometimes.

In this way, teens learned to prioritize and advance self-representations that others liked to see, and they worked to show these sides of themselves to peers by performing them online. Identity is a social process, and some of the teens realized their efforts online had limits. For example, despite Annie's best efforts at proper spelling and clean language on Facebook, she admitted that she was not entirely in control of how she was perceived. "Sometimes," she said, "it don't matter what you do. People just want to think you're bad." Indeed, identities are social constructs, and many social understandings held about girls are rooted in power hierarchies around gender, race, and age that refute actual evidence. Still, in social media, these interlocutors worked to research and to present themselves in ways that they felt would make them avoid negative comments while being attractive to peers. Sarah observed: "It's just being accepted—that's what people want so much, so you'll change who you are. So on Twitter, like, you want to be accepted so much, so you'll say things that you wouldn't normally say."

While they did have extended hours and spaces in which to show themselves to peers in media migration, social media also brought these teens extended hours and spaces to be informed by peers and others of how to be "right" or "wrong" in the world. In response, they used what they learned to brand and attempt to define themselves through conspicuous consumption[36] in association with flattering people, images, sentiments, and activities, seeking personal advancement within accepted offline constraints.

Still, Facebook and Twitter provided stages on which these teens described performing the visibility and invisibility of identities they found desirable, and difficult to claim or negotiate offline. All of the teens were strategic with the identities they presented in these social media forums, using augmentation, attenuation, and bricolage to respond to their known audiences in different "respectable" ways. All explained using Facebook to show themselves as responsible and deserving of respect and trust. Some also used it to include in their social lives distant communities supportive of identities they held that were not well supported or even accepted in their rural communities. A portion of teens used Twitter as a way to "get around" disapprovals they believed they would encounter in expressing certain identities that ran counter to others' understanding of them as young, innocent, hapless, irresponsible, and needing of protection. These girls appropriated Facebook and Twitter as social tools that they worked together to create one large, networked social media system in which to live. In this system, they met the gendered and age-based presentation and behavioral expectations set on them by adults, and they snuck out from under the parental surveillance presented by Facebook's messily merged audiences to claim Twitter as their space to express denied identities. While performance on Facebook focused mainly on appealing to (and appeasing) adult onlookers, those who migrated to Twitter where they felt they could be, in Naomi's words, "most real," negotiated their identities from, and presented themselves mainly for, peer approval.

It is important to note that, despite these differences, these teens' efforts on both Facebook and Twitter were geared toward improvements in their social condition offline. These findings trouble the well-established notion that on- and offline living are necessarily equally valid and valued for these teens, with both contributing similarly to their overall reality. While virtual engagements were initially trivialized as ancillary and even fraudulent when compared to "real" offline life in early Internet studies, the field now generally dismisses any semblance of this idea as "digital dualism." But the teens in this study recognized a significant difference between the real and the virtual that they felt clearly existed in their lives, and both spaces were not equal in their eyes. Challenging the notion that on- and offline are equally part of "living," they felt a divide between these two spaces. In this divide, they all expressed prioritization of their *offline* encounters, rights, and lives over the permissions they experienced online. My interlocutors reported carefully planning and grooming their personas and retaining hope for their polished Facebook performances paying off in more offline privileges in the near future. They played games and interacted on Facebook to feel power and control they wished to feel offline. They excitedly told of their involvement living in Twitter bettering their social reach and relevance offline. And while they appreciated being able to swear and talk about taboo or personal subjects on Twitter, it was not just having this space in their lives that they most appreciated. Instead, it was the shared experiences and connections with peers they were able to form around this that bled offline. Teens recognized that Twitter allowed for this, and it opened up the possibility for users to recognize more granular commonalities with their everyday peers that might be rendered invisible by strict offline groupings. These experiences could stay on Twitter, but they could also spill offline to positively impact their popularity. And this mattered to teens. Unlike others who might be granted more social privileges and permission, on and offline were *not* equal to these girls. As marginal members of society, teens valued the potential they had online to enjoy themselves, but also to hopefully improve their frustrating offline lives.

While popularity could be troubled by media migration, other social identities that frustrated teens offline were far less malleable. For example, my interlocutors had been grounded and encountered other types of negative repercussions from parents for looking inappropriate, and they placed hope in using social media to show themselves in ways that would grant them greater trust and, eventually, privileges from parents. By performing themselves as "good" and deserving of parental trust on Facebook, they faced less trouble from parents wanting them to explain themselves for a status, picture, or comment but, importantly, they aimed to reap the benefits of having more trust and respect offline. I spent at least six months with each teen. Despite their efforts, not one reported having curfews extended or rules changed by parents impressed by their daughters' presentations online.

Looking well beyond typical risk issues, the next chapter will take up some of the complex issues of safety that are raised by these young women's migrations to and through social media as they attempt to negotiate the pejorative marginalized identities and marginal involvements they expect in their offline lives.

NOTES

1. See Nancy Lesko, *Act Your Age: A Cultural Construction of Adolescence* (New York: Routledge, 2001) and Ray Oldenburg, *The Great Good Place: Cafés, Coffee Shops, Bookstores, Bars, Hair Salons* (New York: Marlowe & Company, 1999).

2. See, for example: Michelle Alexander, *The New Jim Crow: Mass Incarceration in the Age of Colorblindness* (2010); Eduardo Bonilla-Silva, *Racism without Racists: Color-Blind Racism and the Persistence of Racial Inequality in America* (2003); Joe R. Feagin, *Systemic Racism: A Theory of Oppression* (2006); David Theo Goldberg, *Racist Culture: Philosophy and the Politics of Meaning* (1993); George Lipsitz, *The Possessive Investment in Whiteness: How White People Profit from Identity Politics* (1998); David R. Roediger, *Colored White: Transcending the Racial Past* (2002); Shannon Sullivan, *Revealing Whiteness: The Unconscious Habits of Racial Privilege* (2006); Howard Winant, *The World is a Ghetto: Race and Democracy since World War II* (2001).

3. Although race is socially, rather than biologically, determined, its social resonance has been well-documented as not easily changed by counternarratives, logic, or evidence to the contrary (Fouché, 2003; Roediger, 1999).

4. See Janice M. Irving, *Talk about Sex: The Battle over Sex Education in the United States* (Berkeley: University of California Press, 2001); Mary Louise Rasmussen, Eric Rofes, and Susan Talburt, *Youth and Sexualities: Pleasure, Subversion, and Insubordination In and Out of Schools* (New York: Palgrave Macmillan, 2004). These binaries thrive in everyday America, inflecting understandings of females, as a whole. They are normalized in narratives about individual, family, and national virtues, and in political efforts aimed at shaming and regulating female sexuality. For example, the latter framing was visible in Rush Limbaugh's use of his radio show to pronounce Sandra Fluke, a law student and self-professed "American woman who uses contraceptives" who called for insurance coverage of birth control pills a "slut" and a "prostitute." A social understanding exists of female sexuality as always inappropriate, shaping how young women claim, make visible, and perform their realities.

5. "American Teens' Sexual and Reproductive Health," *Guttermacher Institute*, September 2016, https://www.guttmacher.org/fact-sheet/american-teens-sexual-and-reproductive-health#1; Centers for Disease Control, "Youth Risk Behavior Surveillance—United States, 2011, Morbidity and Mortality Weekly Report," 61 (SS-4), (2012).

6. See Mary Crawford and Danielle Popp, "Sexual Double Standards: A Review and Methodological Critique of Two Decades of Research," *Journal of Sex Research*, 40 (2003): 13–26; Derek Kreager, Jeremy Staff, Robin Gauthier, Eva Lefkowitz, and Mark Feinberg, "The Double Standard at Sexual Debut: Gender, Sexual Behavior and Adolescent Peer Acceptance," *Sex Roles* 75, no. 7–8 (2016): 377–392; Michael J. Marks and R. Chris Fraley, "The Sexual Double Standard: Fact or Fiction?" *Sex Roles*, 52 (2005): 175–186; Deborah L. Tolman, *Dilemmas of Desire: Teenage Girls Talk About Sexuality* (Cambridge: Harvard University Press, 2002).

7. Laura Duberstein Lindberg, Isaac Maddow-Zimet, and Heather Boonstra, "Changes in Adolescents' Receipt of Sex Education, 2006–2013," *Journal of Adolescent Health* 58, no. 6 (2016): 621–627.

8. Studies such as Irving (2001) find that abstinence and disease avoidance are dominant messages in young people's sexual education, much of which provides few positive messages about exploration of sexual identity.

9. Although puberty instigates sexual drive and reproductive capacities in youth, adolescents are widely recognized in US culture as devoid of sexuality. Rasmussen, Rofes, and Talburt (2004) state that "[c]ontemporary understandings of youth make it nearly impossible for young people to embrace non-normative identities or to take possession of their bodies and their lives" (3). Girls receive little information about their sexuality in American schools and homes. Additionally, females exist within even stricter expectations of asexuality; their expressions of sexuality are commonly read as deviance within Western society. Rather than encouraging exploration of sexual identity, young women are frequently cast as objects rather than owners of sexuality, as victims-to-be needing protection from their sexuality or, if sexually active, as reckless social problems. As reported by Fine, 1988; Hudson, 1989. See also Gilbert, 2004; Moran, 2000; Santelli, Ott, Lyon, Rogers, Summers, and Schleifer, 2006.

10. C. J. Pascoe, *Dude, You're a Fag: Masculinity and Sexuality in High School* (Berkeley, CA: University of California Press, 2007).

11. This section illustrates Foucault's (1977) "governmentality," or hierarchy maintenance through disciplinary power. Writing that disciplinary power manifests in hyper self-awareness and a "conscious and permanent visibility" that results in bodies exercising regulatory control over their individual conduct in an effort not to be seen and known as deviant, Foucault gives some insights into why young women with interests in holding positive social identities might have a hard time being allies to other females choosing, instead, to side with name-callers.

12. For a thorough review of challenges faced in adolescence, see Lesko, *Act Your Age*, 2001, or James Côté and Anton Allahar, *Generation on Hold: Coming of Age in the Late Twentieth Century* (New York: NYU Press, 1994).

13. US Congress Joint Economic Committee Staff, "Understanding the Economy: Unemployment Among Young Workers," (May, 2010), accessed March 3, 2012, http://www.jec.senate.gov/public/_cache/files/adaef80b-d1f3–479c-97e7–727f4c0d9ce6/understanding-the-economy---unemployment-among-young-workers.pdf. Paul Taylor, Kim Parker, Rakesh Kochhar, Richard Fry, Carey Funk, Eileen Patten, and Seth Motel, "Young, Underemployed, and Optimistic: Coming of Age, Slowly, in a Tough Economy," *Pew Research Center* (February 9 2012), accessed November 11, 2016, http://www.pewsocialtrends.org/files/2012/02/young-underemployed-and-optimistic.pdf.

14. See Larson (2002), Males (2012), and Mortimer, Vuolo, Staff, Wakefield, and Xie (2008)

15. Jeffrey Arnett, "Emerging Adulthood: A Theory of Development From the Late Teens Through the Twenties," *American Psychologist* 55, no. 5 (2000): 469–480.

16. Institute for Educational Sciences: National Center for Education Statistics, "Tuition Costs of Colleges and Universities," *National Center for Education Statistics,* accessed October 31, 2017 https://nces.ed.gov/fastfacts/display.asp?id=76.

17. Student debt averaged $37,172 in 2016. Adjusted for inflation, current student debt rates are higher than ever before in this country's history, and interest rates for student loans are set to rise in summer 2017, deepening debt: https://www.newyorkfed.org/medialibrary/interactives/householdcredit/data/pdf/HHDC_2017Q1.pdf   https://www.washingtonpost.com/news/grade-point/wp/2017/05/11/say-goodbye-to-low-interest-rates-on-federal-student-loans-at-least-for-now/. And a recent AAUW report finds that this falls hardest on women, who hold more than two-thirds of this debt: http://www.aauw.org/files/2017/05/DeeperIn-Debt_ExecutiveSummary-nsa.pdf.

18. Laura Collier, "Incarceration Nation," *American Psychological Association,* accessed October 31, 2017 http://www.apa.org/monitor/2014/10/incarceration.aspx; http://www.apcca.org/uploads/10th_Edition_2013.pdf.

19. An independent review of Bureau of Labor Statistics data finds that 2015 saw employment rates moving back toward the typical employment levels on record prior to 2009 for 16-24-year-old full-time women workers, but it also saw these workers' weekly earnings stagnate between 2009 and 2013, and fall slightly from 2014 to 2015. https://www.bls.gov/cps/cpsaat37.htm; https://www.bls.gov/cps/tables.htm.

20. Bureau of Labor Statistics, *Employment and Unemployment Among Youth Summary,* August 17, 2016. Accessed from https://www.bls.gov/news.release/youth.nr0.htm.

21. Raj Chetty, David Grusky, Maximilian Hell, Nathaniel Hendren, Robert Manduca, and Jimmy Narang, "The Fading American Dream: Trends in Absolute Income Mobility Since 1940," *Science* (April 24, 2017). Accessed from http://science.sciencemag.org/content/early/2017/04/21/science.aal4617.full.

22. Underemployment and unemployment rates for young college graduates was higher in 2016 than at the start of the Great Recession 2007 (12.5 and 5.6% vs 9.6 and 5.5%). The situation was even worse for high school graduates (33.7 and 17.9% vs 26.8 and 15.9%), and, in 2016, 15.5% of high school graduates were "idled," neither in school nor employed compared with 13.7% in 2007. Teresa Kroeger, Tanyell Cooke and Elise Gould, "The Class of 2016: The Labor Market is Still Far from Ideal for Young Graduates," *Economic Policy Institute* (April 21, 2016). Accessed May 5, 2016 from http://www.epi.org/publication/class-of-2016/.

23. Richard Fry, "For the First Time in Modern Era, Living With Parents Edges Out Other Living Arrangements for 18- to 34-Year Olds," *Pew Research Center*, May 24, 2016. Accessed from http://www.pewsocialtrends.org/2016/05/24/for-first-time-in-modern-era-living-with-parents-edges-out-other-living-arrangements-for-18-to-34-year-olds/.

24. Anne Balsamo, *Technologies of the Gendered Body: Reading Cyborg Women* (Durham, NC: Duke University Press, 1996), 131.

25. Hui-Tzu Grace Chou and Nicholas Edge, "They are happier and having better lives than I am": the impact of using Facebook on perceptions of others' lives. *Cyberpsychology, Behavior, and Social Networking* 15, no. 2 (2012): 117–121; Amanda M. Manago, Michael B. Graham, Patricia M. Greenfield, and Goldie Salimkhan, "Self-presentation and gender on MySpace," *Journal of Applied Developmental Psychology* 29, no. 6 (2008): 446–458.

26. Tim Newark, *Camouflage* (London: Thames & Hudson, 2007).

27. danah boyd, "Social Steganography: Learning to Hide in Plain Site," *Zephoria*, April 23, 2010. Accessed January 10, 2017 from http://www.zephoria.org/thoughts/archives/2010/08/23/social-steganography-learning-to-hide-in-plain-sight.html. Ito et al. (2010) and Livingstone (2008) both also write on young people's craftiness in clandestine Internet efforts.

28. See Sarah Pederson, "UK teens' safety awareness online—is it a 'girl thing'?" *Journal of Youth Studies* 16, no. 3 (2013): 404–419 and danah boyd and Eszter Hargittai, "Facebook Privacy Settings: Who Cares?" *First Monday* 15, no. 8 (2010) that find females are targeted for most online privacy warnings and, thus, are more wary than males.

29. See Amanda Hess, "Why Women Aren't Welcome on the Internet," *Pacific Standard* (January 6, 2014), accessed from https://psmag.com/social-justice/women-arent-welcome-internet-72170#.wa0uq14bt; Lisa Nakamura, *Cybertypes: Race, Ethnicity, and Identity on the Internet* (New York: Routledge, 2002); Jessie Daniels, "Cloaked Websites: Propaganda, Cyber-Racism and Epistemology in the Digital Era," *New Media & Society* 11, no 5 (2009): 659–683.

30. For example, the Supreme Court recently set precedent in *Elonis v. United States* in ruling that an estranged husband's violently graphic Facebook posts about killing his wife were not threatening or criminal. Elonis won his case, stating his posts (such as "There's one way to love you but a thousand ways to kill you. I'm not going to rest until your body is a mess, soaked in blood and dying from all the little cuts") were fictitious and therapeutic. See Adam Liptak, "Supreme Court Overturns Conviction in Online Threats Case, Citing Internet," *The New York Times* (June 1, 2015), accessed from https://www.nytimes.com/2015/06/02/us/supreme-court-rules-in-anthony-elonis-online-threats-case.html?_r=1.

31. For a review of kinkeeping, see Carolyn Rosenthal "Kinkeeping in the Familial Division of Labor," *Journal of Marriage and Family* 47, no. 4 (1985): 965–974.

32. See Amanda Lenhart and Mary Madden, "Social Networking Sites and Teens," *Pew Internet & American Life Project* (2007), accessed from: http://www.pewinternet.org/Reports/2007/Social-Networking-Websites-and-Teens.aspx; Sonia Livingstone, "Taking Risky Opportunities in Youthful Content Creation: Teenagers' Use of Social Networking Sites for Intimacy, Privacy and Self–Expression," *New Media & Society* 10, no. 3 (2008): 393–411.

33. Dick Hebdige, *Subculture: The Meaning of Style* (New York: Routledge, 1987), 103. Hebdige wrote about youth bringing new meaning to symbols—metal combs, professional dress, safety pins—in asserting subcultural identities through bricolage. Citing John Clark (1976), he writes "Together, object and meaning constitute a sign, and, within any one culture, such signs are assembled, repeatedly, into characteristic forms of discourse. However, when the bricoleur re-locates the significant object in a different position within that discourse, using the same overall repertoire of signs, or when that object is placed within a different total ensemble, a new discourse is constituted, a different message conveyed" (104).

34. Anthony Giddens, *Modernity and Self-Identity: Self and Society in the Late Modern Age,* (Cambridge: Polity Press, 1991).

35. Hebdige, 1987, refers to this as "magical systems of connection" 103.

36. Thorstein Veblen, *Theory of the Leisure Class: An Economic Study of Institutions,* (Teddington: Echo Library, 1899).

Chapter Five

"I Think It's Pretty Private"

Negotiating Safety, Risk, and Recklessness

I pull my car into the empty gravel lot and park next to a freestanding metal sign with vinyl letters announcing on both sides "Plow's Family Restaurant—Open Tu 6–8, W 5–8, F 6–9." "The Plow," as I am told it is called, occupies an unfussy, white concrete block building on the edge of town. Fields run to the horizons on one side of the restaurant. Flatville covers a half square mile on the other side where the town's sole restaurant joins a post office, a library, a park, and a Casey's General Store along the six blocks of slowed two-lane highway marking downtown. Casey's is a gas station and convenience store chain well known for its pizza and its presence in food deserts throughout the rural US Midwest. Today, like most days, Flatville's Casey's is selling gasoline, candy bars, chips, energy drinks, soda, beer, doughnuts, hot dogs, cigarettes, a small assortment of expensive canned and boxed basic groceries, an even smaller selection of toiletries, and pizza from 6 am to 11 pm seven days a week. Its curb typically hosts a number of young male town folk on warm days, and groups of youth can occasionally be found in the park next to Casey's on summer nights. It is just past 5 pm in early November when I drive into town. The park is empty tonight, and I see only two older males outside of Casey's drinking paper-bagged beverages. They sit far from one another looking out over the street, backs to the gas station and the fields behind it.

Rocks skitter away from my feet as I walk to the door. I push it open and am greeted by a voice: "Sit wherever you'd like, dear." Only one table is taken. I settle into a back booth that, like the other seven booths in the room, rests against a wall of farm-related photographs. My table sits under a faded red Alice Chalmers tractor, posing chesty and proud in a field from the center of the large frame.

Sarah arrives early as I am reviewing my notes. She spots me and comes right over, dropping her bag into the booth as she greets me with a big smile and a shake of the head, issuing a greeting as she plops down across from me: "hel-lo!" Practice was cancelled, she tells me, and Sarah is excited about having an afternoon free. "I have so much to do today," she says after we order French fries and drinks. "Things are super busy." We talk about her plans for the day, about the past week, of who tweeted what, of what went on at and after last week's boys' basketball game against their arch rival. At some point, I ask Sarah what the different is between texting and tweeting. "I mean Twitter's a lot different than texting," she replies, "because, like, everyone can see it." She explains that that is part of why Twitter is exciting to her. "Yeah I've had a couple of celebrities, like, reply to me," she says, referring to some tweets she made about television shows that received unexpected attention. "Have you seen that show *Jungle Gold*? It's, like, on [the] *Discovery* [*Channel*]. It's about these two guys that go to the jungle and look for gold." She laughs then follows up on her comment: "Obviously." I say I haven't heard of the show but say that its name seems fitting. She explains that she likes *Jungle Gold*, and tells me that she sent a tweet to the show's Twitter account after their first episode to say that she was a big fan. She was surprised and flattered to receive a personalized response to her message from both cast members of the show. She explains:

> I, like, tweeted them, and they replied to me, both of them did. I was, like, freaking out. And my mom couldn't figure out why I was so excited. I don't, it's kind of exciting cause they're on TV so they're celebrities, I guess, and out of all the people they chose to reply to, they chose to reply to me so it's like: [shakes clenched fist] "yesssssss!"

Sarah reports that getting tweets from celebrities associates you with someone famous and, thus, helps you stand out. Consequently, receiving these messages from *Jungle Gold* cast members and other famous people on Twitter makes Sarah feel recognized while bringing her admiration from her peers and bolstering her social standing in their eyes. That, she tells me, is a primary reason she appreciates celebrity attention on Twitter, even though she feels she has little control over it:

> I don't know why, but I have a lot of celebrities and really big accounts that follow me so a couple of my friends are always like "How do you always get them to follow you?" But I don't know how they follow me cause I don't even follow them first. [laugh]

In brief, receiving tweets from celebrities like *Jungle Gold* cast members makes Sarah feel special, noticed, and significant. "It's almost kind of in my own way," she states, "that I am kind of a celebrity too."

ONLINE SAFETY AND RISK

Fears for safety that have long accompanied females' involvements in US society persist for young women in social media.[1] Parents, for example, are extremely concerned with teens' online safety, and studies find parents worrying far more about their daughters' victimization online than their sons.[2] The narratives mainstream media offers about female minors—their youth, inexperience, innocence, and recklessness, put them at risk of violence and sexual deviance from middle-age male stalkers waiting to abuse girls in online spaces—merely reinforce concerns about girls' safety in online environments. And the teens in this study were well familiar with such concerns.

Stevie, for instance, told me many stories about female teens being brutalized and killed because of their Facebook involvements. Although she said she did not personally know anyone who had experienced this, Stevie offered cases that came from movies, television shows, and books she told me were "based on a true story," providing her with examples she believed to be accurate and illustrative of risks she and other young women faced online. Carollynn echoed Stevie's concerns, noting that being safe on social media involved "keeping away from creepy people." Yet because of warnings from parents, school, and media, the teens also believed just as strongly that they would receive little sympathy if they made a decision that led to being harmed by ill-intentioned adults waiting to trick and entrap them. Teens considered it their responsibility to be safe in social media. "Yeah, it's maybe kinda risky," LaToya said of her social media use. "You just have to be smart and not let anything stupid happen." Therefore, the teens in this study took conscious steps to try to "be smart" to protect themselves in their media migrations.

For example, highly concerned with privacy and safety online, teens adjusted their Facebook settings so that the information they posted would only go to certain people inside and outside of friend lists to feel less risky in their involvements. Social involvement entails risks, and scholars of youth and media have overwhelmingly found that, rather than leap haphazardly into the fray, teens—especially female teens—spend time weighing risks in their social media involvements and acting in ways they have been led to believe will keep them safe.[3] Teens in this study fell in line with these findings, working strategically to try to be safe in social media. However, despite their actions, their parents and the wider society continue to view adolescents in general, and adolescent females in particular, as unsafe. And while such views may be justified, they're not for the reasons people may think.

Between 2004 and 2007, the popular NBC *Dateline* reality television series "To Catch a Predator" offered the unsubstantiated claim that 50,000 potential predators troll the Internet,[4] shocking parents in living rooms across the country during the show's airing in the early days of Facebook, and setting the stage for the program's twelve highly publicized national broadcasts of men exposed for purportedly being willing to have sex with under-aged, primarily female youth met on the Internet. A few years later, the show's evidence was debunked,[5] but fears of Internet "stranger danger" persist, even though statistics show that, in both online and offline environments, sexual solicitations of teens—including the teens in this study—and sexual abuse far more commonly come from a young person they already know than from an adult stranger.[6] Furthermore, national teen victimization rates have fallen across all indicators over the past two decades, hitting record lows recently in 2014; in fact, girls aged 12–17 are far safer now than they ever were in the 1990s.[7]

To be clear, child predators exist online as they do offline, and any abuse of young women is unacceptable. But females' sexual victimization from strangers is overestimated in both spaces.[8] Despite evidence showing females' risks of online sexual victimization being grossly exaggerated, adults and teens see the Internet as teeming with ill-intended strangers and risk. Yet while parents might advise Internet abstinence, teens worked to negotiate the risks they faced online to gain wider and better opportunities. In doing so, they took additional steps that they thought would ensure their safety in addressing three very real concerns for safety they felt existed online. The following discussion looks at each in greater detail.

Information Control

Social media scholars find that teens typically frame online privacy as controlling information and that, while young people generally take on parents' fear of threats existing in public spaces, they—especially girls—are active in negotiating their involvement in these spaces.[9] The teens in this study echoed this research, and they knew that staying safe meant presenting themselves strategically on social media. As such, all of the teens operationalized safety as being able to limit their exposure to select viewers. Social media was considered extremely risky to them because it had the potential for a loss of valued privacy. I asked Amelia what "privacy" meant to her in social media. "From people," she replied. "Being able to keep stuff from them."

This study found young people to be strategic and proactive in their desire to stay safe in social media by attempting to keep important information private, or to control the transfer of their personal information within the platform. As discussed in the last chapter, using attenuation, augmentation, and bricolage in their media migrations helped teens negotiate their visibility to different audiences gathered in and across platforms, as did using Facebook privacy settings, which all of the teens demonstrated knowledge of and engagement with, especially on computers. This was considered important to stay safe in their online involvements. "I just know it's safe," Amy told me of her Facebook use. "Everything I put on there, only I can see it. Or sometimes my friends can see." Molly explained further:

> I have all different settings 'cause I know how some people, like you go search their name and then they have like, everything on there. Mine, if you just search my name you can't really see anything. Yeah it's important because if you let everybody see what you're doing then [pause] you take a chance at people [pause], weird people out there finding you. [laugh]

These tactics helped teens regulate which information they shared, with whom, and why, building and maintaining relationships as they created the privacy they felt would keep them safer. And consistent with research finding girls to have unusually high trust in their technical competence in Facebook,[10] these teens felt very confident in their abilities to control information while there. Yet for all of their discussions about privacy—especially as a way of establishing and maintaining safety through control—these teens' experiences simultaneously demonstrated how artificial the sense of controlling one's information is on social media. Sometimes problems emerged because the teens did not know how to manage some aspects of the platform. For example, although several of the teens discussed blocking people on Facebook when they were on a computer, doing so was far more challenging on a smartphone. Facebook privacy settings also changed a lot with little fanfare and with new features requiring teens to actively opt out of options to keep data that was previously set to semi-private from being public. Privacy was also harder to maintain on platforms like Twitter that encouraged re-tweeting posts in ways that reached well beyond the intended audiences. But even then, the teens were less familiar with the platform's privacy settings. "On Twitter, I have no idea how to change my privacy settings," Sarah explained. "Do they have them?"

Teens regarded information control as critical to their safety in social media. They took steps to selectively curate their identities and involvements in media migration to broaden their lives, but the effectiveness of these efforts was ultimately limited by their narrow—and in many ways, inaccurate—understanding of information control in social media, as this chapter will later discuss.

Reputation Protection

Most adult warnings about social media are aimed primarily at females.[11] Perhaps not coincidentally, girls have been found to be highly concerned with how they appear in social media.[12] In line with this research, teens in this study were very concerned with staying safe by avoiding social stigma and, as a result, protecting their reputation.

Teens in this study believed their social media use could damage the way others understood them and, by extension, their reputation. My interlocutors told me about school assemblies on social media safety informing participants that social media—especially Facebook—could ruin their futures. Not only did these platforms archive activities that could be used against them both today and in the years ahead, but social media sites often made it difficult for users in general, and girls in particular, to know what presentations of self others would consider inappropriate, thereby affecting their reputation. As Marcin explained, "If you're showing a whole bunch of cleavage, yes. You're scandalous. But if you're showing a little bit, maybe not. It's hard to tell sometimes." She continued:

> Maybe because, well, (pause) if it's nude, everyone will think it's scandalous. If you show a lot of cleavage, you're not fully covered. . . . So that could be scandalous. But I don't know. Like if some of your stuff was showing, or if it's accidental, or if you just can't help it, someone can call you a whore. You can be labeled. Sometimes, it's hard to know sometimes if a picture is going to be ok. Like, if you're wearing a tank top and shorts, you're automatically a whore, or something. A lot of people wear that, I guess. So I don't know. It's kind of confusing. If you have a tank top that you can't help the way it is, then that's, I think that's when it's hard to know. Like, mine usually end right here (indicates neckline), but sometimes, they're right here (points a little lower on neckline), which I can't help.

As Marcin described, it is hard for females in US society to avoid being considered—and being labeled—inappropriate, especially considering that appropriateness in female dress is a highly variable and subjective concept prone to random and seemingly arbitrary regulation by peers as well as adults. Clothing that is marketed to young females as "trendy" or "in," for example, suggest correctness, power, and significance by mirroring what adults and popular celebrities are wearing. Even so, adults in teens' lives may have very different opinions about those same clothing, as evidenced in articles addressing daughters' "trashy" dressing and girls who look "like prostitutes," in proposed state legislation charging female leggings as "indecent" articles of clothing, and in the general blame girls and women commonly receive for allegedly provoking males' abuse simply by the way they dress.[13] Unfortunately, clothing is only one of several forums in which females are scrutinized and, thus, required to monitor their behavior and presentation of self if they are to maintain their reputation. Language, activities, sexuality, and interests were all open to evaluation and criticism in offline worlds, but add the possibility of blasting these depictions to untold audiences online and females believed they would inevitably tarnish their image and stunt their potential.

Making matters worse is that these young women, like most adolescent females, are taught to believe that *they* are culpable for any such damage to their futures, and this message comes in different forums. In addition to a society that regularly judges females, schools emphasize the need for females to retain their reputation. Sarah explained:

> We had this assembly in school last week. It was actually pretty good. She talked about how sex, how girls send pictures of themselves, and that they shouldn't do that. And telling how, like, even if we don't have a picture of your face, we can still find you because there's like this geo-graphic, like, you can find them through coordination, like longitude and latitude, and stuff like that.

Yet while schools used shame and admonitions to teach girls about social media's dark side, school assemblies never chastised—or even addressed— boys who "fraped," "doxxed," or otherwise leaked images of past girlfriends through social media to humiliate, defame, and discredit them. Amy explained: "Naw. They never say nothing about what boys do in those things." Similarly, schools seldom ask teens to reflect on the perks boys get for using social media to abuse girls' trust, or to consider how reputation damage disproportionately—and unfairly—burdens girls. Nor are teens asked to examine the fairness of the social media practices that enabled companies and others to archive that which could be used against users in the future. Sarah continued:

> They were telling us that once you say "I agree," that the company is gonna have all your information whether you delete it or not. So, like, one day, the companies, the social workers who check online to see if there's, like, any child pornography, they're gonna look online and they're gonna see, like, your name, and they're gonna say, "well, she shouldn't be doing this," and then you can get a file about all that stuff, and then colleges won't accept you or you can't get a job.

These things are presented to them as simply non-negotiable parts of life, and as acts of others that girls must think about and take responsibility for to protect themselves.

Parents also reinforced the need girls have to protect their reputation online. Amelia explained that her father warned her about the potential to damage her future through her social media involvements. "My dad warns me about that constantly," Amelia explained. "[He says:] 'Everything you say is permanent.'" Amelia recognized the warning, but, seeing social media as a tool to connect with others, she was also concerned that paying *too* much attention to reputation could compromise her future well-being as it related to her social involvement. "I mean, like, it makes it so much easier to say things like, instead of up front telling someone you like them," Amelia said. "Just, like, typing, it's a lot easier." As a result, she and the other teens were not always clear on what was risky and what was not, leaving them confused about how to be involved in social media and also be safe. Facing this, teens did what they could to curate their social media presence responsibly, but, lacking clear or even consistent guidelines, I found them often bracketing worries about the future to tend to more imminent, well-defined reputation safety concerns they felt they could only advance for themselves by getting around parents.

Parent-Free Involvement

When considering risks to privacy and safety in online engagements, research finds young people in the West far more likely to name people who regularly oversee them as threats than to raise concern over more distal or abstract entities.[14] As the research supports, teens in this study connected online safety with parent-free spaces. Telecommunications have historically provoked adult concerns over keeping girls physically and sexually protected and, thus, contained. Noting that the telephone and the telegraph have both been accompanied by significant social panic regarding girls' safety, Justine Cassell and Meg Cramer write that "themes of parental technical deficiency and ensuing parental loss of control in the face of a daughter's appropriation of the technology for her own ends are common in the literature and publicity surrounding all the communications technologies."[15] By opening access to new social spheres, the Internet similarly poses a challenge to parents as traditional guardians and gatekeepers of young females' involvements. But because privacy from parents was rarely available to teens in private family life or even in public community life where they knew others knew who they were and would tattle on them, the teens turned to online communities where they could participate without fear of parental oversight, disappointment, or punishment. For example, although she never adjusted her privacy settings on Twitter as she had on Facebook, Amelia said she felt more secure on Twitter because her parents were not there:

> I feel safer on Twitter than I do on Facebook. Like, I know my parent's friends can see what I post on Facebook. . . . I know they don't have a Twitter. And it's not like my Twitter name's really obvious—it's not my name it's something totally different. It's a nickname of mine so it's not like they can find me in there.

"Privacy means privacy from parents, yeah," Sarah said. Teens named keeping their social media involvements secure from parents as their top safety concern inspired by offline parental monitoring. They migrated away from Facebook to Twitter due to their belief that Twitter was parent-free and mainly hosting users who would be considered peers, or, as Amelia described: "People my age. And celebrities." While recognizing that the actions they could take within Twitter were limited by technical constraints such as word limits, the teens in this study reported that, in providing a space to act more like they want to act than they could in places watched by parents, social media made them feel less risky in their involvements.

Parents are frequently told that supervision is important to keeping teens safe, but teens often view spaces *without* parental supervision as safe, namely because they feel less conscientious of people monitoring and controlling their behaviors. The teens in this study said their greatest concern in social media safety lie in managing their online interactions in ways that allowed them a parent-free space for at least some of their involvements. In doing so, many simultaneously worked to maintain their relationship with their parents by making invisible behaviors they felt their parents either would not want to see or would not be willing to accept from them. As explained in the previous chapter, while most teens accomplished this by migrating between a Twitter account where they could perform their identities as they liked and a Facebook account where they performed in ways they knew would satisfy their parents, they also negotiated safe, parent-free social media involvements in other ways.

For instance, working outside of Facebook's requirement of real names and limitation to only one personal account, teens set up separate pseudonymous second Facebook accounts to interact with different groups. LaToya explained: "The ones with their moms [friended], they'll watch what they put on Facebook, or they make another page." LaToya, herself, did this. She had two Facebook accounts after starting one to be away from her mother. Demonstrating the difficulty these teens experience separating supportive social worlds, LaToya told me that her mother later became friended on both of her accounts. "I got two pages, but my mom's on both pages now," she explained. "I added her when it was close to my birthday so she could post to my wall [laughing]. . . . I really wanted my mom to say happy birthday on my wall." While LaToya's acts here illustrate well the interests she and the other teens in this study had in remaining close to their parents, she and the others found this closeness difficult to maintain while also feeling safe in their social media involvements. And, in fact, shortly after this discussion, LaToya joined Twitter, and she told me she would never tell her mother about her new account because prior experience taught her that her mother "just won't understand." According to LaToya, sharing this social space with her mother and risking getting her mother to accept the interests that drive her to Twitter "is just not safe."

Parents limited involvements and identities and were, thus, the greatest threat teens identified to their safety online. Teens embarked on media migration to seek and tenuously to claim parent-free spaces for at least some of their involvements as they preserved relationships with adults they needed and, for the most part, greatly valued. In doing so, teens considered the presence of parents in assessing, understanding, and negotiating their risks in social media, and they identified parent-free spaces as most safe.

Throughout this study, I have found myself worried about the safety of my interlocutors because of what they told me about their lives. The teens reported having a lack of information of how to succeed in the world, a lack of guidance, and often poor advice from the few adults in their lives who have time for them. They had limited space for acceptance, involvement, and exploration that led them to feel the need to sneak around in ways that left them unable to live their realities in front of caring adults. All of these things led them to turn to the Internet to seek direction and "ways around" the obstacles the encountered offline. There, they "friended" and "followed" friends, fake and real celebrities, strangers, and corporations, developing trust in commercial spaces. There, they felt free expressing their thoughts, anxieties, loves, and identities with no coaching from adults on how their tweets would be publicly archived or knowledge of the expressions they readily provided being sold and used to direct the information they received. It is in these online contexts—not those conventionally linked to "stranger danger" and "girls gone wild" online—that we find the very real safety threats teenage girls unknowingly face in media migrations, as the next section explains.

RISKS IN SOCIAL MEDIA

More than 90% of US teens use social media every day and, of those, nearly a quarter report being on "almost constantly" with the help of smartphones.[16] Offering both a diversion and outside connections, social media can help teens mitigate emotional and physical isolation. Availing teens to a wealth of ideas, connection, and values, it also assists teens in gaining understandings and feelings of significance, while working around those they feel police their marginality. At the same time, social media spends a lot of time with teens, focusing and directing their attention for better or for worse. "[T]o look is to labor," writes media scholar Jonathan Beller,[17] and, indeed, while media migration proves quite rewarding to teens, it does so by enlisting them as laborers in what he and others term an "attention economy" that encourages them to see, to engage with, and to seek out certain things over others. Considering that media migration has the potential to enter teens into online infrastructures that direct their attention and, thus, shape their understandings of the world and of themselves, youth safety in social media is contingent upon our understanding these attractions and potential take-aways. The sections below examine some of the main areas social media directed these young women's attention, and the overlooked implications they have for their safety online.

Popularity

First, social media encouraged these young women to spend their time thinking about and attending to popularity. Teens—especially girls—are typically considered peer-oriented in US society, but such colloquial perspectives ignore the wider contexts youth find themselves relegated to that present popularity and peer admiration as one of the rare options they have to gain relevance and power.[18] Indeed, as minors with limited control, respect, and rights teens yearned to be valued and to feel meaningful in the world. To varying extents, they wanted to be admired and appreciated by people they knew and by those they encountered. But in this their primary goal was to find ways to move beyond the insignificance and powerlessness they regularly felt in marginality. With few options to be recognized as significant in other ways, and strong—yet parent-challenged—cultural encouragement to socially engage, teens recognized in their daily lives that they could improve their status through popularity and through association with popular things. Social media fed this interest, consistently directing them to think about what others liked and to concern themselves with being among these things. In other words, social media infrastructures actively encouraged teens to pay attention to popularity. In numerous ways, they called upon teens to regard and value items, expressions, people, actions, inactions, and themselves through a lens of popularity.

Display

First, in basing identity in display, social media urged teens to consider potential onlookers' reactions when presenting themselves. Early on, teens in this study were quick to say that their social media use was for them and not for others, but this was, in fact, not backed by their fuller explanations or actions. For instance, in our first meeting while discussing her use of Twitter, Molly said: "I just like to express my feeling. I like to use emojis. . . . I don't really get caught up on what people think." In further probing, however, Molly said she actually spent a lot of time thinking about what others might think of her tweets as Twitter was her main way to connect with friends outside of school.

I noticed my friends and I don't really text much. Like, when we were in grade school, it was a huge thing if you had texting and now everybody, just, I hate texting. All my friends just get on their Twitter. They can see how I'm feeling, and if I post something that they question, they'll text me. Or they just ask me the next day at school.

The teens in this study, like teens throughout time, professed being bored often. But they had numerous options of how to use their out-of-school time. Social media encouraged them to give this and other free time to paying attention to—and considering the responses they might provoke and receive from—peers and other imagined audiences who might be watching them. Amelia explained: "I like knowing what people are doing, I mean, I kind of think that's the point of Facebook is knowing what everyone's doing." Within the infrastructure of social media, teens were given options and norms that directed them to think about others watching them and to seek approval in social display. For example, Shelly explained that, on Facebook, "everybody posts 'truth is' things when they're bored, and then friends and other people like it. Well, it's usually, like, younger kids who post ['truth is']. But when someone you know puts up a picture, you need to like it too. It's just what you do." Teens were encouraged to think about popularity in display by social media platforms that sent them updates of others' thoughts and goings-on in tweets and newsfeeds whether they were physically present or not, that provided buttons and options to embellish identities with actual metrics of popularity, and that provided teens with new social forums to take part in and to reflect upon in scrutinizing the potential implications of their actions.[19] And this focus kept teens logged on and opting to be part of the crowd in their free time. Shelly told me that she is on Twitter "almost always" since most of her friends moved there from Facebook. I asked why, and she replied: "I can see what they're doing and stuff."

A report by the Pew Center on Internet & American Life finds teens shaping their social media pages based on friends' feedback, with actions taken in the hopes of gaining social approval, and posts removed for receiving few overt signs of popularity.[20] The teens in this study aligned with these findings. LaToya discussed what she considered when posting on Facebook:

If you have a boyfriend, you want to impress your boyfriend, you have friends, you want to impress your friends. You have people you don't like, you want to make them jealous of you, like, teenagers, they do it a lot. Like, you try to out-dress somebody.

Teens curated their presentation in social media platforms to optimize their chances for desired responses from the respective recipients of their display. And in turn, social media platforms connected teens' online identities to conspicuous numeric displays of popularity—such as number of friends, likes, followers, and retweets—that teens said opened up opportunities for them to gain even greater popularity. Amelia explained, "I think if you have more followers, then more people will follow you back for some reason cause, I mean, [pause] I don't know why. I just feel like that's what happens."

And teens learned that indicators of popularity in social media came in non-metric forms, as well. In seeking popularity, teens' attention was commonly channeled to material goods and consumerism they believed appealed to others, and teens were encouraged to identify with status-infused symbols in what marketers call "lifestyle branding." For example, Violet followed Doritos, Diet Pepsi, and Christian Dior nail polish on Twitter, and these brands appeared as part of her online identity. Annie worked many weeks to earn enough points to own a McDonalds building in CityVille, the gaming app she accessed through Facebook. "You can tell a lot about a person by what they 'like' on Facebook," Naomi told me. "Like, if they like bad TV shows or rap music, you can know that about them. . . . Or you can 'like' to show people that you like good things." This type of affiliation made teens feel part of a larger community, and they welcomed the chance to gain social connectedness and status by claiming personalities and values flaunted by global goods they knew their peers both recognized and appreciated. "Everyone knows I am all about Flaming Cheetos." "BW3 is, like, our place." "I put their song lyrics on my Facebook page because that's how I am. . . . That's how I feel. Like, 'this is me.'" "H&M is my store." Teens incorporated brands into their public presentation in social media, explaining them as a part of their identity as they attended to popularity through display.

Sharing

Beyond self-presentation in display, in the service of popularity, social media encouraged teens to direct their attention to engaging in a specific type of sociality—exchanging, or "sharing," information—with specific groups of people—mainly peers and those known for fame. And they were encouraged to attend to certain acts in social media because of this. Teens' sharing kept them thinking about what others liked and might like. For example, LaToya, who used a free app to digitally manipulate photographs, posted, or shared, these pictures on Facebook to get them noticed. She explained:

> When you share with people, it makes you feel good, but when you make them and don't share them, it's like "I just made this, and I get no credit for it." That's mainly why I post them, so people can see them. If I just kept them to myself, I'd be like, "well, this is boring."

Notice from others helped teens feel relevant and liked, and teens said this could be achieved by posting and passing on things others knew, liked, and could connect to them around. This worked for LaToya. Asked how people responded to her pictures, she smiled and replied: "I get likes on it, or people IM me and say 'can you make me a picture?'"

Outside of individually crafted offerings, teens said social media gave them abundant assistance in locating shareable content by creating a clear-inghouse of videos, articles, people, ideas, news, and images with indicators of high views, follows, and likes to let them know others considered them "popular," and by allowing them to affiliate with and share this content. On Facebook, the teens talked about following links to funny stories and videos liked and shared by friends, reading memes shared by friends and by busi-nesses their account "liked," checking out pictures on third-party apps like Pinterest and posting them to friends' pages, and listening to YouTube music videos that showed up on their newsfeed. They sometimes also attended to advertisements that referenced their friends' names, suggesting they shared them and gave the content approval. "See this post here?" Annie asked, clicking on a Pepsi advertisement video on the side of her screen showing pop star Nicki Minaj and listing two names as "like"ing it. "My friend said it was good, so I bet it is." On Twitter, they learned about songs, videos, gossip, products, and new Twitter accounts from friends, celebrities, and other accounts they followed, and they shared popular content to both display themselves and to get noticed.

Celebrity

Celebrity was the final way teens worked toward popularity in social media. The teens in this study were uncertain of careers to work toward that might bring them fulfilling lives they hoped to have in their future. Most who knew what they wanted to be were unsure of how to access those careers. Indeed, with soaring college costs, narrowing post-recession markets, parents lacking experience and working multiple jobs, and overburdened school guidance counselors with time only for graduating seniors, adolescent girls may find few options. Most teenage girls, however, recognize fame, celebrity, and their accompanying popularity as success. Accordingly, these teens looked to celebrities and other famous entities for informal—but very real—guidance, and social media provided the forum for getting and sharing that information.

Involvement with celebrities is built into the technical infrastructure of Twitter. In order to set up an account during the time of this study, teens were first required to select at least five "well-known people" to follow from a scrolling list of options under categories starting with "Music," "Sports," and "Entertainment."[21] In addition to "well known people," new users were also required to follow at least five others to set up a Twitter account. One could enter Twitter accounts in a search field here to find friends' accounts, or those that just sound interesting. However, since names are commonly obscured in Twitter handles, this can be a less-than-simple task. Twitter offered a long list of famous people to follow instead to quickly meet this requirement. Perhaps relatedly, the teens with Twitter accounts spoke frequently to me of learning about the relationship status, interests, and recommendations of celebrities that they were excited to share with others in ways they felt made them appear knowledgeable. And teens looked to social media to learn about the lives of celebrities they admired. Violet explained:

> Like Drake and J. Cole? I'm following them on Twitter and they have, like, concert dates and their CDs are coming out and tour dates and stuff. I think it's interesting, like I don't think there's really any other way to know about this. I mean, there's Internet, but that's so much more complicated. . . . And just to talk to celebrities, even though it's probably not a celebrity, it's someone posting about it. A lot of it is helpful information. Like, I've been to two concerts for Drake and one for Drake and J. Cole. [My boyfriend] found out about them on Twitter.

After following a few fake Twitter accounts for J. Cole, Violet said that the actual musician followed her back. "It was like 'J. Cole is following you.' I tweeted at him. I was like 'oh my gosh, you're amazing!'" I asked if she received a reply from the musician after that. "No," she responded. "But it was awesome."

Social media acts that involved celebrities took on heightened importance to teens, attracting their attention and their further online involvement. Naomi joined a community group supporting a local child with terminal cancer after it enlisted celebrities to tweet messages with the group's name. "Like the real celebrities, not the parody accounts," she explained. "They'd tweet group's name and everyone would know about it. It was like a trend for link an hour one day. It was so exciting." Though Naomi did not attend any of the in-person rallies or events hosted for the child by the group, she retweeted these messages and felt part of the group. "I just tweeted 'cause I didn't have a ride. [laugh] And like, of course I said prayers and stuff for him, I mean, I feel like that helped a lot too."

Beyond paying attention to famous celebrities, teens aspired to *be* famous celebrities and, once again, social media provided teens platforms in which to perform and broadcast themselves to audiences they would be otherwise unable to reach and gain admiration from. Interest in popularity motivated teens to put enthusiastic effort both into celebrities and to their own varying levels of "microfame" while on social media. In his book *The Attention Merchants*, Tim Wu[22] writes that social media cultivates an attention economy where individuals—especially those dissatisfied with the status quo—learn that they can gain attention from others. And with its quickly spread tweets and followers, Twitter, Wu argues, avails the best possibilities for working toward that goal by helping users cultivate attention and a sense of influence. The teens in this study would agree. Like Sarah at the start of this chapter, teens' sense of importance was bolstered by notice from those who were considered "big." Amelia spoke with pride of having one of her tweets about disliking early morning winter cattle feeding favorited and forwarded by a multinational feed company she followed. "It kind of made me feel like I was famous," she said with a smile.

Attention given to celebrities benefited teens with interests in popularity as it created new interests that benefited celebrity-hosting commercial outfits and media. Teens followed celebrities' accounts on Twitter, and some micro-pubs also retweeted celebrity tweets. Celebrity accounts posted pictures and messages, in addition to passing on "secrets" for clothes, shoes, soft drinks, makeup, and other products behind their desirability, and thus ideas of how to buy control of your image in the world. For example, a glance at three recent tweets on Naomi's account from Nicole Polizzi, otherwise known as "Snooki" on the popular reality television show *Jersey Shore*, showed one with a link to an Instagram picture of Polizzi's baby and the comment "Happy Thanksgiving! Lorenzo's first!!!!!!" and two tweets with links to an online store selling Snooki-related products. Another that included a link to *Jersey Shore* merchandise read: "#cybermonday is almost here and save money on your @snookislippers. Get Free Shipping on US orders :)."

Celebrity tweets commonly also recommended other accounts to follow to become more popular. Take Sarah's Twitter account, that contained a retweet from pop singer Beyonce Knowles reading: "OMFG ! I just followed @CuteLoveMsgs and gained 1,843+ new followers :o YOU REALLY NEED TO TRY IT NOW !<3." Sarah said she gets frequent tweets with these kind of offers from celebrities. In the past, she followed suggestions like these from *American Idol* and *Idol* alum, country music singer Carrie Underwood, but she does not do so anymore. She explained:

> Twitter will say "follow this person and you'll get 256 new followers!" And I was like "why not?" because at first, I thought it worked, but then I realized, no, you don't ever get followers. No. Actually, no. I've never gotten followers that way.

Still, Sarah admitted she continued to follow the accounts that failed to give her followers because of the cumbersome steps required to unfollow an account on a cell phone.

Social media's focus on popularity brought teens notice, admiration, and social clout that held value and led to very real forms of power within youth culture, and within teens' wider society. Indeed, the same display, sharing, and celebrity stressed online were highly esteemed offline throughout teens' wider culture. However, this focusing of their attention also raises concerns for teens' safety. In social media, teens were regularly encouraged to think about popularity, status, and reputation in their involvements and identities through sites' broadcasted metrics of likes, followers, views, retweets, points, and emojis that displayed positive affirmations in high numbers and in comments expressing social validation. Social media's focus on popularity enmeshes teen users' sense of control and power with a mercurial sense of "never enoughness" and with the successful practice of capitalistic accumulation—a practice that culturally undergirds Western life.[23] And the accumulation of symbols of popularity in social media motivated teens' further involvement with both consumer goods and with social media itself.

Status-gaining interaction with celebrities on Twitter inspired teens' further investment in these celebrities, as well as with their recommendations and with social media platforms that offered interaction opportunities. As mentioned above, these sorts of interactions led teens to seek out celebrity-endorsed products, links, and accounts in social media. Additionally, all of the teens passed on Facebook posts and tweets from celebrities that they felt others would like to know about and appreciate. In this, teens eagerly volunteered themselves to broker, or to pass on and trade, information gleaned from social media about celebrity culture to their peers, donating valuable "word of mouth" marketing labor in exchange for this attention and affiliation. And social media–mediated interactions with a particular celebrity strengthened teens' identification and involvement with this celebrity. Take Sarah. After receiving tweets from the stars of *Jungle Gold,* Sarah explained that she became an even bigger fan than she was before; as a result of receiving the tweets, she decided to follow not just *Jungle Gold*'s Twitter account but also both cast members' accounts. She also gave more attention to the actual show. "Now, I just watch it every week." In a similar vein, Facebook users with more friends have been found visit the site much more frequently than those with few friends, suggesting that the quest for greater symbols of popularity fuels greater social media use,[24] with teens developing dependence on the very mechanisms they turn to in seeking greater independence and power.[25]

Teens' social media lifestyle branding raises other concerns. As we are less likely to question or critique what see as part of ourselves, teens' affiliation with conspicuous corporate goods in social media platforms complicates the identity work they call upon social media to help them with. And teens might have good reason to critique some of these affiliations since consumer entities thrive by manipulating customers' desires to drive their involvements and identities. Indeed, as teens blurred their boundaries in media migration to advance interests in gaining information, feeling relevance, and exerting control over their life, they befriended marketing forces in similar camouflage silently seeking to control them, and to keep them insecure and dissatisfied to best sell them new items and fast fixes. Teens were not aware of this. Furthermore, they did not know that affiliations made with commercial entities on social media opened up possibilities for their personal information to be shared with unintended outside entities, including predatory marketers. For example, after "liking" Burger King on Facebook, Violet noticed a post in her newsfeed that said Burger King was hiring. Though transportation would have been difficult, she clicked the link and filled out the application. Violet said she never received a call back for an interview, but she did begin receiving phone calls. She explained:

> I filled out this, I thought it was like an application, but apparently it was just a survey or something. Some Internet thing. Now once a month I have this place calling me, trying to get me to sign up for something. Yeah, one time I got a call from a place asking me if I would like to further my high school education, like, I'm still in high school. I'm only a junior. I don't really need to further anything right now. I don't remember ever giving them my phone number.

I asked if the form she filled out was on Burger King's site. "I thought it was Burger King's site," she replied. "Maybe it was not the official Burger King site. I don't know." As will be discussed in more detail later, as teens worked to bolster popularity by voluntarily linking their identities to globally recognizable items in social media, multinational marketers also worked hard to brand items to teens to gain their support, and, in many ways, their identities.

Furthermore, social media's influence in directing attention to popularity threatens teens' psychological well-being. As members of societies and cultures, we are all shaped by observation and external feedback, but research notes that too much social comparison can be harmful. For example, studies repeatedly find that females who compare themselves with others on personal appearance report higher rates of body dissatisfaction than those who do not.[26] Such studies raise concerns over the likelihood of girls'—especially less popular girls'[27]—development of body image and mental health problems as they attend to social medias' encouraged social referencing. Social comparison occurs for a number of reasons, but it has been found to increase when one feels on display, as gender scripts ascribe to females in US society, and as was the case for these teens online.[28] Uncertainty and unhappiness also provoke more social comparison,[29] and, as discussed, the girls in this study regularly struggled to gauge appropriate dress, expression of sexuality, and many other areas within their daily lives. And social comparison rises with depression,[30] raising additional red flags for adolescent-aged girls who report more anxiety and depression than either boys or adults with rates rising precipitously over the past decade.[31] Other research suggests that, rather than installing confidence, more frequent social referencing reinforces both conformity and further reliance on social comparison,[32] compounding safety issues presented to teens online, especially in light of research finding that young women's beliefs about their worth fluctuate widely based on feedback they receive on social media.[33]

And as young women are urged by social media to focus on social approval while gaining opportunities for wider involvements and identities online, it is important to note that they remain routine recipients of social oppression and devaluing. For example, a 2014 study by the Pew Research Center found young people aged 18–24 face the most threatening behavior of all age groups online, with young women in this group far more likely to experience severely threatening behavior online than male peers.[34] Misogyny and denigration of females is normalized across social media platforms. Sites devoted to assessing young women's physical appearance through advertisements and actual judging objectify females in social media, and women—and particularly young women—are consistently found more subject to abuse and harassment than males when online.[35] Females have been threatened so much through social media that it has been given a new genre when it happens to writers ("harassment lit"). Online misogyny commonly silences women and causes them even further preoccupation with how others see them.[36] At the same time, young women find themselves increasingly unpopular within traditional misogynist and newer Millennial discourses on- and offline that paint them as entitled, clueless, incompetent, and unworthy of empathy or support. Opposing normalized jokes, stereotypes, threats, and other demeaning rhetoric is necessary in challenging systemic forces underlying racism, sexism, classism, ageism, and homophobia. Resistance often requires non-popularity, at least initially. Fighting injustice involves forming contentious relationships with the status quo that pose a conflict to those urged to be most concerned with gaining social approval and popularity. Not doing so continues to keep these teens marginalized, and, as such, very unsafe.

These teens turned to social media seeking greater direction, control, and significance as they worked to assert desired identities and gain wider involvements. There, they negotiated risks and were continually reminded by social media environments that how others perceived them—something that was always in flux—mattered most. It demanded their focused and constant attention. While teens' encouraged focus upon popularity in social media raises issues of safety, it also ignites and deepens risks teens face in other areas where social media guides their attention.

Narrow Definitions of Privacy

Teens' attention was directed to narrow definitions of privacy in their social media use. Teens generally felt they knew how to control the information they displayed and shared online, and social media guided them to understanding privacy as involving limitations on audience members' ability to see them. This was encouraged through available platforms settings and controls that affirmed their concerns for protection from parents and "creepy" individuals. Teens wanted to know the rules for the social media platforms they engaged in, and they understood that Facebook had privacy controls that could be used to ensure that the information they posted was available only to "friends" rather than to the general public. The presence of these settings caused teens to think that they understood how to control their information in these platforms. In tending to settings and controls, teens felt they were doing what they needed to do to stay safe, and they felt competent in doing so. However, these controls did not give teens reason to think about their involvement in social media being tracked, surveilled, and judged by "creepy" others. Indeed, these settings gave teens a narrowly partial—and, as such an inaccurate—understanding of privacy in their social media sharing and, in doing so, promoted a false sense of power and control to teens that threatened their safety.

Social media encourages an artificial sense of privacy, as the teens in this study reveal. Most of the teens were familiar with the idea that social media platforms stored and sold their actions and interactions. LaToya knew the most. "So many people can access your Facebook, like, companies pay a lot of money just to go and get into your Facebook," she said. But when asked more about it, she and other teens who had ideas about this type of data collection thought it was related to their privacy settings. LaToya believed that closer monitoring of her settings would decrease companies' involvement with her account. The others did also.

Twitter was a different story. None of the teens knew how to adjust privacy settings on Twitter, especially on their phones, and although settings can be changed to make correspondence more private, Twitter is, by default, public, with all tweets ever sent out archived in the Library of Congress,[37] allowing anyone to read anyone else's information on and from Twitter accounts. Such public-ness thus challenges teens' ability to be involved in a space they define as safe. With pseudonymed account handles, Twitter felt safe to teens, but they recognized that a main concern they had for safety— information control—was not as simple as in Facebook.

Teens may have felt they have constructed a well-fortified wall in Twitter to protect themselves in public space, but the walls they constructed are hardly well guarded. Certainly parents might not be able to find their daughters' Twitter accounts directly since they do not use their "real" names, but these accounts can easily be tracked down through association; for example, users often can be found through their association with Twitter friends since many use at least a part of their "real" names on their Twitter accounts to help their friends identify them.[38] Additionally, even with privacy settings set to allow only followers to see tweets, teens discovered that the information they sent easily found its way out of this defined space through followers' retweeting. Similarly, information they chose to not follow often broke through in followers' retweets. One afternoon while observing Sarah using Twitter, she showed me such an instance retweeted to her from a comedy micropub:

> Oh, well then! I didn't know I had this. This is very bad. It says "Slutty." Oh, this was retweeted by one of my—yeah, it says "this girl looks very" um. "This girl look very fuckable." I'm following Comedy Tweets, and then Comedy Tweets retweeted that, so now I can see it.

While each of the teens expressed concern that they knew little about how to adjust or control Twitter privacy settings, their belief in having a "safe" space for involvement outside of their parents' purveyance made this concern quickly dismissible.

But teens' narrow understandings of privacy in their social media use had implications for their well-being and security. In fact, even on Facebook where they felt they were on top of managing their information, it was actually very hard for users to be in control of their information in ways that kept them safe, even within their own definition. "Data mining?" Sarah asked in response to my question asking if she had heard of this term before. "I don't know what that means." She talked through what she thought it meant on Facebook:

> Is that like, keeping things online in case anyone wanted to, like, really look for it, they could see everything you posted online? I know that I change my security to, so only friends or followers can see it, so I think it's pretty private. I've never seen anything called, like, data mining on there when I change things on my security.

Sarah, LaToya, and the others had an idea that Facebook stored their data. However, as Sarah described, since they did not see an option for this in her privacy settings, they thought they were generally safe and protected from anything too concerning. But privacy settings do not influence data collection or sales to outside advertisers.

This is not just a misunderstanding of naïve youth; both privacy settings and policies change frequently on social media platforms, and policies are written in ways that make them very difficult to understand, keeping most users unclear of what they have agreed to. One recent study found social media privacy settings to be highly misunderstood even by adult users who were given time to study privacy policies; another study found Facebook's policy on data use far less understandable than known difficult texts, such as rules for a bank rewards program and government notices, and they were deemed to be entirely incomprehensible by more than half of the adults they studied.[39] Teens knew they could use settings and media migration tactics of attenuation, augmentation, and bricolage to keep information from individual friends and strangers. They did not know that, in using social media, they agreed to allow the details of their social media lives to be given over to industries that thought of them as potential profit before they ever thought of them as private people, let alone as minors.

Facebook's "Privacy basics" link leads to a happy and colorful animation surrounding three sentences starting with: "You have control over who sees what you share on Facebook. That way, you're free to express yourself the way you want," and closing with a section of four links titled "You're in charge." [40] One of the links is "Manage your privacy," which leads to a page with twelve other links under the statement: "Learn how to customize your privacy settings so you can confidently share your moments."[41] Not one of these links mentions that, in the user agreement teens accepted to set up their accounts, they agreed to having their involvements, identities, and images on Facebook tracked, analyzed, sold, and held by unknowns strangers who do not need to disclose their intent through perpetuity and who are also able to tell Facebook what they know about the teens.[42] Nor is there mention of the detail on Facebook's "Data Use" page stating, "If the ownership or control of all or part of our Services or their assets changes, we may transfer your information to the new owner," or of the fact that the 2012 Facebook study that silently enlisted more than a half million unaware users into a psychological experiment manipulating their emotional state for a full week was permissible without teens'—or their guardians'—formal consent under the site's terms of use.[43] Teens did not know their social media involvements and identities were not private, and they were not encouraged to consider the sale of their personal information as relevant to personal privacy. In fact, their attention was directed in ways encouraging them to not consider this.

Privacy settings do not change the type or amount of data collected by site owners. That is, on Facebook, you can change settings to keep others from seeing your posts. However, you cannot change settings to keep Facebook from adding these posts to the profile they (or the advertisers they sell to) are creating on you. Consider that all of the teens reported "liking" posts, comments, and videos on Facebook. "Liking" is an affiliative action that is part of constructing identities on Facebook. My interlocutors told me that "liking" a business showed what type of person you were, and that "liking" someone's post was a way of saying you supported and liked them. Beyond this identities work, "liking" is heavily used in the social analysis of data mining to not only contribute to the profiling and targeted marketing of teen social media users, but to predict their "sensitive personal characteristics" not listed on their profiles, such as sexuality, political stance, drinking habits, and drug use.[44] With an interest in popularity and limited understanding online privacy, teens do identities work for themselves in social media platforms. They also do it for corporations.

Or take, for instance, the ways the platforms themselves mitigate users' privacy. Facebook and Twitter both collect user data to sell to their advertisers and others interested in marketing products to target audiences, and users changing their privacy settings do not make adjustments to these practices. Users cannot control how their information is mined, or how it is shared by the host of her social media involvements. For example, Facebook profits from making apps interoperable, or seamlessly integrated into their platforms.[45] Individual users cannot opt out of this integration. As such, services from apps become more accessible and potentially more referenced and useable, to the delight of marketers. At the same time, teens' personal information also becomes more accessible and usable to these third-party marketers in ways that limits teens' control over their own identities. Despite the immediate conveniences they supply, the interoperable efforts of apps are not always beneficent, intended, or, in the long run, convenient to Facebook users. Identifying this as an issue of connectivity that platforms profit greatly from by encouraging users' attention to focus, instead, upon connectedness with individuals, media scholar José Van Dijck discusses user data mining and sale to third-party apps and others as an essential, but hidden, facet of social media sharing.[46]

Teens were not aware that their privacy settings did not control the sale of their information, and they did not understand the norms or reach of this sharing, which was extensive. In *The Daily You*, Joseph Turow[47] writes that Facebook allows partnering data collectors to choose users by individual characteristics such as age, gender, education, region, and relationship status as they buy special access to users, such as being able to contact them through their accounts to wish them the best on their birthdays.[48] Data-driven viral memes asking teens to post and share lists of first concerts and other nostalgic information added to this list, opening opportunities for teens to connect socially with friends while also encouraging disclosure of valuable deeper personal details to add to sellable data. Teens risk further privacy breaches by playing many fun social games offered by social media platforms. For example, Turow explains that apps and games available through Facebook—including those most popular among young women like viral personality quizzes—are entirely exempt from Facebook's privacy policy as they collect detailed historical, attitudinal, and psychological profiles based on user interests, involvements, and friendship networks, "adding yet another set of data points for trying to identify people's potential and value as customers for particular products."[49] Additionally, many third-party games and apps accessed through Facebook and Twitter are able to pull in further data when accessed by cell phone, including information from teens' phone books. In his book *The Panoptic Sort*, Oscar H. Gandy warned that "advances in digital communication technologies . . . allows market research to apply the sophisticated techniques of social science to the surveillance of consumers in order to predict and control their behavior."[50] In other words, the very tools that suggest information, power, and autonomy to adolescent girls become the same mechanisms that track them, collecting data they use to claim teens' attention and shift their involvements to specific ideas, encouraging their continued containment and lack of control.

Or consider, for example, the role of advertisements. Edward Herman and Noam Chomsky[51] wrote that advertising inflects media with messages that ideologically tie products and involvements to notions of freedom and power, and social media provides a multi-billion dollar platform for this work. The Facebook Reports Fourth Quarter and Full Year 2012 Results financial press release reported an advertising income of $1.33 billion—an amount representing 84% of the company's annual total revenue of $1.585 billion, and 41% more advertising income than was earned in 2011. This same report also quotes CEO Mark Zuckerberg as stating: "We enter 2013 with good momentum and will continue to invest to achieve our mission and become a stronger, more valuable company." And Zuckerberg has come through on his company's promise: Facebook Reports Fourth Quarter and Full Year 2016 Results finds the company with $26.885 billion in advertising revenue, representing a 2556% increase over three years and 97% of its $27.638 billion dollar annual revenue within a business model that José Van Dijck defines as depending on "customers' willingness to contribute data and to allow maximum data mining."[52] In having their attention focused on acquiring and managing individual popularity, young women end up being quite willing customers. Indeed, teens with large numbers of friends on Facebook demonstrate more disclosure of personal information on the site than do those with fewer friends.[53] Given that studies show female teens have significantly more Facebook friends than male teens,[54] this means that individuals who are already marginalized due to their age and gender open themselves to more predatory activities that rely on personal information, such as profiling to target propaganda and commercial pitches, while helping Facebook earn astronomical profits by capitalizing on maintaining their narrow and, ultimately, very poor understanding of online privacy.

Sensationalism

Lastly, emphasizing popularity, social media directed teens' attention to sensationalism. Teens were excited to read and share posts, tweets, stories, news, quizzes, listsicles, and other online content that was outrageous, scandalous, or otherwise striking. This material was often "viral," or highly shared, or it had the potential to be shared by them. Some content was created by—and involved—individuals who teens knew, as was the case with "Cinnamon Challenge" videos, break up news, and fights on Facebook, and in racy Twitter images and subtweets that disparaged people without directly naming them. Amelia said subtweeting led to enthusiastic offline group discussion of classmates:

> I follow these two people who fight a lot on Twitter too. So it's kind of interesting to see, like, how it all unfolds and . . . if they talk about each other, 'cause when you sub-tweet, it's when you tweet but you don't mention the person, you just kind just put it out there and kinda hope that the person knows it's about them.

Sensational content was often shocking or surprising, as was the case with many sub-tweets, along with "real life" stories, controversial videos, and retweeted micropublication quotations. Other times, it attracted attention in appearing informative, entertaining, or fun. A YouTube video titled "Golden Eagle Snatches Kid" that went viral on Facebook included a mixture of both. The clip, which appeared on many of the teens' Facebook newsfeeds, showed an eagle swooping down in a Montreal park to grab a toddler and begin to fly off with the child in its talons before dropping it. The description listed for the video stated that it captured a real event: "A golden eagle tries to snatch a baby in Montreal! What if he got away with it!?" One day after the video debuted, a Montreal arts college announced on their website that the video was fabricated as a final project for one of their 3D Animation and Digital Design courses.[55] By then, the video claimed to have been watched by more than a million viewers. As of February 2017, it racked up over 45 million views. While the Internet lit up with discussion over the technical brilliance of this piece, some voiced concern about its wider social implications. In particular, conservationists warned that this predatory staged performance could paint birds as threats to those who did not see the press release stating the video was a hoax. Indeed, at least two states reported a surge in eagle shootings following the video's airing.[56] The video made an impression on teens. "I was sure it was true," Violet said. "It looked so real. We still talk about it." Such sensationalist content appeared regularly as interesting media clips and stories in teens' newsfeeds and timelines, encouraging them to follow links to the wider Internet. They welcomed this exciting content both as personal entertainment and as social currency they could share online to get attention and to know about to gain entry in on- and offline discussions.[57]

Teen social media users are exposed to a range of provocative ideas passed on and vetted by friends, followers, and advertisers. Some of this content appeared to them to be serious news; some of it did not. Regardless of whether or not it purported to be "news," all of this content has the potential to shape viewers' understandings of the world. This is particularly true for younger users who do not have the skills or experience to properly vet information, especially when assessing information quality and delineating facts from propaganda and advertising is made intentionally difficult as in social media. In fact, a wealth of marketing-driven content and other propaganda spread through social media is finely tuned to appear to viewers not as advertising, but as news or fun banter.[58]

For example, Twitter, and to a lesser extent, Facebook, are known to be sources for gathering breaking local, national, and international stories before they hit the mainstream press. But both are also spaces where witty parodies and satires are widely spread to youth and to adults that informally—but powerfully—shape social understandings of youth and of others.[59] Web sites exist that are devoted exclusively to creating nostalgic, shocking, cheeky, and otherwise entertaining stories, news, and quizzes meant for social media sharing, but marketing scholars point out that these sites exist for much more than fun. Many are indirectly selling teens products and motivating them to pass messages on to friends. Social media sites and their sponsors work to have users spend time engaging with hidden sales pitches. In her book *Black Ops Advertising*, Mara Einstein[60] explains that these pitches abound in social media not just as explicit advertisements that appear in news feeds and along borders of pages but also as sponsor-obscured "native advertisements" and "content marketing" that appear as edgy entertainment and aim to get users to affiliate with them by "liking," "following" or otherwise self-branding, and to also help them with the most influential form of marketing: word-of-mouth sharing. Einstein states that the outlet with the most native advertising is VICE, a favorite of Millennials. And Buzzfeed, the home of viral personality quizzes, engaging banter, and celebrity stories, is so rife with native advertising that Einstein notes they are officially registered not as an Internet publication, but as an advertising agency. Einstein quotes Buzzfeed's vice president in Europe as explaining company goals as tied to users' attention being focused on not just sensationalist online content, but also on this contents' potential relationship to popularity and sharing: "It's not about eyeballs on Buzzfeed.com. It's about creating content for brands and distributing that on Facebook, which has more than one billion users."[61]

Teens were attracted to Buzzfeed and other similar sites by sensationalist content they received and passed on via social media. Each month, at least one teen proudly pointed out a funny article they learned about on their newsfeed documenting a "true story" about an exchange-gone-wrong between people. Young women were commonly the brunt of the joke. Molly showed an article she posted on her Facebook page depicting an instant message conversation between a male and an extraordinarily daft young woman. "It's so funny!" she said. "I could totally see it happening. I love these things." One website that sourced some of these articles documenting young people's—commonly young women's—moronic messages, tweets, and posts drew criticism in paralleling other viral humorous—but fake—articles based on purportedly "real" auto-corrected conversations and instant message exchanges.[62] Doubt was raised about the site's own "real" stories, and light accusations were made against the website for fabricating content to attract viewers. On this, one writer making such a charge mused that "maybe it doesn't matter if they're fake or not, because the essence of the blog gets at a larger truth, one that we're all very much invested in believing: Other people are idiots."[63] But in many ways, it does matter if stories passed through social media are fake or not—especially to youth seeking understandings who have limited opportunities for firsthand knowledge and who are turning to social media seeking information on the world to learn "how to be, and how not to be." And it certainly matters that social media regularly circulates memorable anecdotal evidence that support beliefs in young women's ineptitude.

Social media present attention-grabbing and peer-supported images and ideas that influence teens' beliefs about what is real and good, be they images of brand-name goods, raunchy humor, or excessive alcohol consumption. Yet while normalizing these types of images and actions may be disconcerting, more troubling are those that standardize discriminatory and abusive behaviors, including racist, homophobic, xenophobic, and misogynistic practices. In the case of teenage girls that may live in rural communities, these images and presentations may convey if not promote the objectification, trivialization, commodification, and denigration of females, as well as the idea of violence toward females as normal. Efforts to challenge violence against marginalized communities in social media are active but incremental.[64] Furthermore, while those supportive of misogyny and racism might seek out Internet content on these topics, social media increases the chance that those interested in equality will also catch wind of these types of articles due to their sensationalist viral nature, and that they will click to read them out of outrage. Such clicking adds to the coffers of publications and social media platforms paid to host this content knowing that shock, scandal, and controversy represent major currencies within attention economies that "buy" eyes for advertisers. A system like this should be expected to be more likely to host, rather than hinder, sexism and other oppressive spectacles since it gets attention and, thus, "sells." And teens' understandings of normalcy, rights, and safety should be expected to be shaped by this.

Social media's offering of "news" as information deemed popular within a commercial advertising space should also raise eyebrows for those concerned with adolescents independently seeking direction in social media. While the web hosts many vetted and reputable news sources, re-postings of news stories from entertainment sites such as FOX News–partnered *Radar Online* from America Media—owner of *Star* and *National Enquirer* newspapers—were most prevalent in these teens' social media accounts. Misinformation and disinformation shared in sensationalist content present a threat to youth online safety, especially in a time when, for many, seeing is believing. The teens in this study knew they needed to be critical of information they encountered on the web, but they all were unsure of what proper vetting processes entailed. Visual documentation typically serves as solid evidence to back a claim, but, as Montreal's "Golden Eagle" illustrated, this is not always the case. Teens were also not aware of how what was visible to them in social media was neither always in their control nor everybody's reality, but, instead, shaped by algorithms and programmers subject to familiar offline biases curating what they could see and do in the shared space.[65]

Few sources assist teens in making sense of ideas they receive within this new media context where traditional types of evidence now present many possibilities for misinformation and manipulation. Teens in this study were given little advice on how to determine the credibility or aim of online content, and the guidance two of the teens received from adults gave narrow and often dogmatic statements limited only to finding written sources for academic papers. For example, reflecting upon her English class, Shelly explained: "I don't know. There's some good sites and some that aren't [good]. Like, you're not supposed to use Wikipedia like ever, I guess." And seeking parent-free spaces, teens were not asking for help interpreting what they saw. Considering that few serious sources exist to help teens make sense of the commodified ideas they receive within this new media context, and recognizing that social media remains a largely independent activity for most teens, we must be attentive to increasing risks faced by young women seeking direction online, especially considering that social media have now become young people's primary news source.[66]

Authoritative sources matter to teens that turn to the Internet for credible information and direction to gain greater control over their lives—especially when they have few other options for trustworthy guidance. The Internet opens up possibilities for youth here. Unfortunately, inaccurate information circulating online within sensationalist content is one factor that jeopardizes young people's safety for several reasons. First, it can dissuade them from becoming involved in social issues and movements that can address their marginality and lack of rights. Research finds that only a small amount of doubt can effectively dissuade individuals from voicing their support of a cause. For example, a recent study finds that US readers who are exposed to fabricated news stories in which officials deny or cast doubt upon climate change are less likely to believe in global warming, and, thus, less likely to support climate change intervention than those exposed to a neutral story.[67] If, then, youth are continually exposed to stories that negate experiences, misrepresent situations, or otherwise skew details, they will find it harder to know which problems to address, and how to approach them if they are to advocate for principles, practices, and views that matter to them.

The presence of sensational commercially motivated content presented as "news" and other forms of general information raises other concerns for how the world is being presented to teens seeking information, meaning, and control through social media. For example, as Annie was explaining about her difficulties learning about college admissions and scholarships, she noted an advertisement on the side of her Facebook page she had seen many times before in telling me she knew paying for school wouldn't prove to be a problem for her. The ad featured a photograph of a young black woman with her hand over her mouth looking shocked, and read: "$5500 Grants for Students. People can get $5500 to go back to school in 2013! Click to see if you qualify." Annie explained: "First, I'll get a music scholarship to pay for things." She then pointed to the ad. "Or I can get the money for college lots of other ways if that doesn't work out." In such contexts, teens, like those in this study, can feel in control, giving voice to personally relevant matters on Facebook and Twitter, even as companies market products to them through gaming goals, camouflaged targeted advertisements, girl-maligning propaganda disguised as news stories, and pop stars' tweets about things they say are cool. But these acts of agency are only made possible within a larger, controlled structure of information flow, collection, and use over which teens have little power. Ultimately, then, these teens' involvement and performed identities in social media turn them into objects of marketing who are, themselves, very much for sale. And while such efforts have consequences for teens in general, they can be particularly problematic for adolescent girls in rural environments because they may have few resources to turn to in their immediate environment to challenge, buffer, and help make sense of the sensationalist messages they receive, and often welcome. In this context, Jonathan Swift's words from his 1710 essay "The Art of Political Lying" remain meaningful: "Falsehood flies, and truth comes limping after it, so that when men [*sic*] come to be undeceived, it is too late; the jest is over, and the tale hath had its effect."[68]

The teens I met with liked social media for reasons reflective of their social position. As discussed in previous chapters, they reported that social media gave them regular places to hang out where they are able to feel more powerful, more connected, more appreciated, more listened to, more in control, more entertained, and more admired than anywhere else available and accessible to them offline. They said these social media helped them know things that other people know and appreciate. They made it easier to get to know people, and easier to get around rules that keep them from interacting with the world. These teens said social media lets them be more themselves, and more who they want to imagine themselves as being. Because of this, they liked social media and trusted it, showing their appreciation by giving it their time and attention, filling in fields asking them for information, manipulating privacy settings afforded to them, and following most requirements to "not provide any false personal information"[69] in attempts to be a responsible participant. For the most part, they were very good to social media, and they trusted that social media was being very good to them in return.

In some ways, social media were good to the teens. In addition to hosting communications and interactions that were hard for teens to arrange offline due to distance, cost, age, and time—all of which are relevant in a recession-reeling country of families spread out and moving for work across six time zones—social media gave teens occasional encounters with new perspectives on world events they would not otherwise encounter, and reams of information about their peers and favorite celebrities to barter and use as social currency.

But in other ways, social media were not good and did not deserve the trust teens had given them. Social media encourage teens to give up details about their life, and archive it in ways that can be used and shared with others for years to come. Social media are vague in intentions and acts, giving quick, obtuse explanations of the non-monetary fees collected to allow teens involvement in their communities.[70] Social media do not want to talk about things teens might be interested in, like how their personal information will be used, focusing instead on topics it wants to discuss, like "privacy settings and tools." Social media break their promises about privacy, changing privacy-related agreements without notifying users first and not giving teens realistic options to weigh-in or to know about these changes;[71] when they do, social media require so many clicks and searches to make privacy setting adjustments—especially through mobile phones and tablets—that users like these teens say it's often not worth the effort. Social media do not seek teens' approval when using their photos,[72] when presenting them commercial advertisements as world news stories,[73] or when using their identity to advertise to their networks of friends.[74] Social media use celebrities to engage teens in activities or to purchase products they might not otherwise, they help others lie about their popularity, and they create new social demands that teens increasingly believe they can't live without.[75] In brief, teens continue to give social media their trust, and social media responds by exploiting that trust for their own benefit, raising questions about how we can best protect teenage users even as they profess to feel safer online than offline in both their involvements and in advocating for their identities.

While social media offer teens many benefits, they also enter teens into new types of relationships and risks not covered by school assemblies focused on safety. Trust is important in any healthy relationship, and the teens in this study trusted social media as a friend looking out for their best interests. This trust stemmed from a lack of awareness of who their friend social media really is, as well as from their own desperation as marginalized members of society lacking other options they can trust—or even convince—to help them out in meaningful ways. It also stems from girls being told in many ways both on- and offline that they can and should never trust themselves.

Minors are rarely able to choose the spaces they occupy, let alone ensure they look out for their best interests; this is supposed to be adults' job. While seeking popularity, misunderstanding social media privacy policies, and being drawn to controversial content is not unique to youth, their deep trust of social media is; teens believe that social media is beneficent and looking out for their best interests, and research finds that they believe that the law protects them online more than adults do, and more than it really does. [76] This reflects young people's lack of experience with the legal system, but it also highlights their lack of awareness and understanding of, and indeed teens' lack of attention to, the operations of institutions and societal structures directly related to their safety on- and offline. These are important cultural understandings that girls are not being made aware of offline as they make choices to try to self-advocate, and that they will not learn from social media. Serious considerations of online safety must contemplate how these spaces take advantage of girls' marginality by gaining their trust and directing their attention to their own interconnected profit-oriented interests as teens attempt to negotiate the everyday risks they face while making trade-offs they hope will bring them better terms for their life, and for their safety.

NOTES

1. See American Psychological Association Task Force, 2007; Meenakshi Gigi Durham, *The Lolita Effect: The Media Sexualization of Young Girls and Five Keys to Fixing It* (New York: Overlook TP, 2009); R. Danielle Egan and Gail L. Hawkes, "Producing the Prurient Through the Pedagogy of Purity: Childhood Sexuality and the Social Purity Movement," *Journal of Historical Sociology* 20, no. 4 (2007): 443–461; R. Danielle Egan and Gail L. Hawkes, "Endangered Girls and Incendiary Objects: Unpacking the Discourse on Sexualization," *Sexuality & Culture* 12, no. 4 (2008): 291–311; Joan Gittens, *Poor Relations: The Children of the State of Illinois, 1818–1990* (Urbana, IL: University of Illinois Press, 1994); Anne Meis Knupfer, "The Chicago Detention Home," in *A Noble Social Experiment? The First Hundred Years of the Cook County Juvenile Court, 1899–1999,* edited by Gwen Hoerr McNamee (Chicago, IL: Chicago Bar Association, 1999), 52–53; Judith Levine, *Harmful to Minors: The Perils of Protecting Children from Sex* (Minneapolis, MN: University of Minnesota Press, 2002); Mary E. Odem, *Delinquent Daughters: Protecting and Policing Adolescent Female Sexuality in the United States, 1885–1920* (Chapel Hill, NC: University of North Carolina Press, 1995); Patrice A. Opplinger, *Girls Gone Skank: The Sexualization of Girls in American Culture* (Jefferson, NC: McFarland, 2008).

2. Amanda Lenhart, Lee Rainie, and Oliver Lewis (2001) write that "[p]arents of girls are more concerned than parents of boys that their children will be victimized online" (29).

3. danah boyd and Eszter Hargittai, "Facebook Privacy Settings: Who Cares?" *First Monday* 15, no. 8 (2010), accessed May 2, 2017, http://firstmonday.org/article/view/3086/2589; Mary Madden, "Privacy Management on Social Media Sites," *Pew Research Center* (2012), accessed August 2, 2013, http://www.pewinternet.org/~/media//Files/Reports/2012/PIP_Privacy_management_on_social_media_sites_022412.pdf; Mary Madden, Amanda Lenhart, Sandra Cortesi, Urs Gasser, Maeve Duggan, Aaron Smith, and Meredith Beaton, "Teens, Social Media, and Privacy," *Pew Research Center* (2013), accessed October 2, 2017 from http://www.pewinternet.org/Reports/2013/Teens-Social-Media-And-Privacy.aspx. Girls are found to

be more involved in setting social media privacy settings than boys in a number of studies including Mariea Grubbs Hoy and George Milne, "Gender Differences in Privacy-Related Measures for Young Adult Facebook Users," *Journal of Interactive Advertising* 10, no.2 (2010); Mary Madden and Amanda Smith. "Reputation Management and Social Media," *Pew Research Center* (2010), accessed January 2, 2017, http://pewinternet.org/Reports/2010/Reputation-Management/Part-2/Attitudes-and-Actions.aspx; Justin W. Patchin and Sameer Hinduja, "Cyberbullying and Self-Esteem," *Journal of School and Health* 80, no. 12 (2010); and Seoun-mi Youn and Kimberly Hall, "Gender and Online Privacy Among Teens: Risk Perception, Privacy Concerns, and Protection Behaviors," *CyberPsychology & Behavior,* 11, no. 6 (2008). Also see danah m. boyd and Nicole B. Ellison, "Social Network Sites: Definition, History, and Scholarship," *Journal of Computer-Mediated Communication* 13, no. 1 (2007); Chris Jay Hoofnagle, Jennifer King, Su Li, and Joseph Turow, "How Different are Young Adults From Older Adults When it Comes to Information Privacy Attitudes and Policies?" (2010), accessed September 17, 2017, http://repository.upenn.edu/cgi/viewcontent.cgi?article=1413&context=asc_papers; Sonia Livingstone, "Taking Risky Opportunities in Youthful Content Creation: Teenagers' Use of Social Networking Sites for Intimacy, Privacy and Self–Expression," *New Media & Society* 10, no. 3 (2008): Joseph Turow, *The Aisles Have Eyes*, (New Haven: Yale University Press, 2017).

4. In "To Catch a Predator? The MySpace Moral Panic," *First Monday* 13, no. 6 (2008), Alice Marwick explains that, between 2004 and 2007, *To Catch a Predator* issued twelve highly publicized and watched national broadcasts of men willing to have sex with purportedly under-aged youth (primarily female) who they met over the Internet. While being quite gripping and timely, airing just as Facebook began its boom, this series had numerous well-documented flaws. One was the show's active solicitation of "predators," which was later found in 2011 by Sonoma County courts to be entrapment. The show also based its work on statistics stating that 50,000 potential predators were trolling the Internet, justifying public alarm and calls for swift justice.

5. See Marwick "To Catch." Also, after the program ended, journalists from NPR and other sources probed this statistic in interviews with *Dateline* and found it lacking evidence. In a May 26, 2006 interview with Brooke Gladstone from NPR's *On the Media,* Ken Lanning, the retired FBI agent and consultant to *To Catch a Predator,* admitted he had been the source of the statistic and that the statistic was approximated: in the interview, when asked about the 50,000 online sexual predator statistic, Lanning states "I didn't know where it came from. I couldn't confirm it, but I couldn't refute it either, but I felt it was a fairly reasonable figure. . . . I was somewhat curious about the fact [CHUCKLES] that it was 50,000. That number had popped in the past, because I had been an FBI agent for over 30 years. In the early 1980s, this was the number that was most often used to estimate how many children were kidnapped or abducted by strangers every year. But the research that was done in the early 1990s found that somewhere in the neighborhood of 2 to 300 children every year were abducted in this manner. . . . The other one that I specifically [LAUGHS] remembered kind of came in the late 80s, where there were a lot of people who were talking about satanic cults that were supposedly running around the country engaging in human sacrifices. And when you'd try to say, well, how much of this is going on?—once again, [LAUGHS] the same number popped up—50,000 a year. . . . That's what they were alleging. [LAUGHS] This one here was a little bit more obviously problematic to me, because we do have good data on homicide. And at that time, there was somewhere in the neighborhood of 20 to 23,000 murders every year, so this meant that the Satanists all by themselves were killing twice as many [LAUGHING] people as all the other murderers combined." http://www.wnyc.org/story/128722-prime-number/.

6. Offline, see: Howard N. Snyder, "Sexual Assault of Young Children as Reported to Law Enforcement," Bureau of Justice Statistics, 2000, accessed October 3, 2017, https://www.bjs.gov/content/pub/pdf/saycrle.pdf. Online, see: Justine Cassell and Meg Cramer, "High Tech or High Risk: Moral Panics about Girls Online" in T. McPherson (Ed.), *Digital Youth, Innovation, and the Unexpected* (Cambridge: MIT Press, 2007): 53–76; Kimberly J. Mitchell, Lisa Jones, David Finkelhor, and Janis Wolak, "Trends in unwanted sexual solicitations: Findings from the Youth Internet Safety Studies," Crimes Against Children Research Center, 2014, accessed   from   http://www.unh.edu/ccrc/pdf/

Sexual%20Solicitation%201%20of%204%20YISS%20Bulletins%20Feb%202014.pdf. Marwick (2008) notes that, in 2007, evidence emerged that the reality show had fabricated the online predator statistic, choosing the number 50,000 chosen, in part, for being a familiar, highly-circulated, but false, estimate of child abduction and satanic cult human sacrifice rates in the 1980s and 1990s. After the program ended, journalists from NPR and other sources probed this statistic in interviews with *Dateline* and found it lacking evidence. In a May 26, 2006 interview with Brooke Gladstone from NPR's *On the Media,* Ken Lanning, the retired FBI agent and consultant to *To Catch a Predator,* admitted he had been the source of the statistic and that the statistic was approximated: in the interview, when asked about the 50,000 online sexual predator statistic, Lanning states "I didn't know where it came from. I couldn't confirm it, but I couldn't refute it either, but I felt it was a fairly reasonable figure... I was somewhat curious about the fact [CHUCKLES] that it was 50,000. That number had popped in the past, because I had been an FBI agent for over 30 years. In the early 1980s, this was the number that was most often used to estimate how many children were kidnapped or abducted by strangers every year. But the research that was done in the early 1990s found that somewhere in the neighborhood of 2 to 300 children every year were abducted in this manner... The other one that I specifically [LAUGHS] remembered kind of came in the late '80s, where there were a lot of people who were talking about satanic cults that were supposedly running around the country engaging in human sacrifices. And when you'd try to say, well, how much of this is going on? - once again, [LAUGHS] the same number popped up—50,000 a year.... That's what they were alleging. [LAUGHS] This one here was a little bit more obviously problematic to me, because we do have good data on homicide. And at that time, there was somewhere in the neighborhood of 20 to 23,000 murders every year, so this meant that the Satanists all by themselves were killing twice as many [LAUGHING] people as all the other murderers combined." http://www.wnyc.org/story/128722-prime-number/

7. The Office of Juvenile Justice and Delinquency Prevention reports a drop in the serious violent victimization of 12–17-year-olds between 1994 and 2010, stating "The serious violent victimization rate of youth ages 12–17 is less than one-quarter the rate in 1994" with the data reporting declines in victimization for both boys and girls. Melissa Sickmund and Charles Puzzachera, eds. "Juvenile Offenders and Victims: 2014 National Report," *Office of Juvenile Justice and Prevention Center* (December 2014): 39, accessed October 2, 2017. https://www.ojjdp.gov/ojstatbb/nr2014/downloads/NR2014.pdf. The Bureau of Justice Statistics finds rates of violent and serious violent crime against girls aged 12–17 continuing to drop to "all-time lows" in 2014. https://www.ojjdp.gov/ojstatbb/nr2014/. BJS reports that rates of serious violent crime for females 18–24 are also lower on last report than in 2005 https://www.bjs.gov/content/pub/pdf/cv14.pdf. And Justine Cassell and Meg Cramer examine the curious choice to ignore falling victimization rates of youth in the mid-2000s. Cassell and Cramer, "High Tech or High Risk."

8. Of course, First Wave feminists fought similar myths about offline rapists being primarily strangers. Rose Corrigan writes of this in "Making Meaning of Megan's Law." *Law & Social Inquiry* 31, no. 2 (2006): 267–312. See also Stanley Cohen, *Folk Devils and Moral Panics: The Creation of the Mods and Rockers* (London, UK: MacGibbon and Kee, 1980) and Philip Jenkins, *Moral Panic: Changing Concepts of the Child Molester in Modern America* (New Haven, CT: Yale University Press, 1998).

9. See boyd and Hargittai, "Facebook Privacy Settings"; Jeni Harden, "There's No Place Like Home: The Public/Private Distinction in Children's Theorizing of Risk and Safety," *Childhood* 7, no. 1 (2000): 43–59; Sonia Livingstone, "Taking Risky Opportunities"; Madden et al. "Teens, Social Media"; Patchin and Hinduja, "Trends in."

10. Studies have found that young women, as a group, express much lower confidence in their technical abilities than do young men, even when they have the same ability level, but boyd and Hargittai, "Facebook Privacy," 2010 discovered that this is not the case on Facebook.

11. boyd and Hargittai, "Facebook Privacy," 2010; Sarah Pederson, "UK Teens' Safety Awareness Online—Is It a 'Girl Thing'?" *Journal of Youth Studies* 16, no. 3 (2013).

12. Madden et al. "Teens, Social Media"; Common Sense Media, "Children, Teens, Media, and Body Image," *Common Sense Media*, January 21, 2015, accessed October 2, 2017, https://www.commonsensemedia.org/research/children-teens-media-and-body-image.

13. Take, for example, the *Psychology Today* article on how to best address daughters' "trashy" dressing adjudging silver bracelets as "not too offensive," but still falling into this category of scandalous dress (http://www.psychologytoday.com/blog/parenting-is-contact-sport/201010/dealing-trashy-dressing-daughter), or the more credible *Wall Street Journal* lamenting that "we let" teenaged girls dress "like prostitutes" (ttp://online.wsj.com/article/SB10001424052748703899704576204580623018562.html?mod=googlenews_wsj). Or consider the public schools attended by some of the teens in Brown and others across the nation declaring girls' leggings—a mainstay of the current "athleisure" fashion trend—simply unacceptable. (See: http://www.wfsb.com/story/17200855/meriden-board-of-education-holds-dress-code-debate, http://www.startribune.com/local/west/179141451.html?refer=y , http://www.kgw.com/news/Leggings-banned-at-Forest-Grove-school-114376609.html, http://www.wptz.com/news/vermont-new-york/burlington/Vt-school-bans-leggings/-/8869880/18293912/-/bqi3a/-/index.html). A Petaluma, California junior high school principal explained the ban as necessary "because the boys were getting too distracted." She continued: "The goal is to teach kids to respect themselves and dress appropriately" (http://www.huffingtonpost.com/2013/04/09/leggings-ban-kenilworth-junior-high-california_n_3046043.html). Young women's dress is even the subject of attempted legislation: in 2015, Representative David Moore of Montana put forth a bill legally defining females in leggings as indecent exposure. "Yoga pants should be illegal," Moore stated (http://billingsgazette.com/news/government-and-politics/montana-lawmaker-seeks-to-outlaw-yoga-pants/article_71538ba2-d529-5ec3-a289-108de20e9398.html).

14. See boyd and Hargittai, "Facebook Privacy"; Ito Mizuko, Sonja Baumer, Matteo Bittanti, danah boyd, Rachel Cody, Becky Herr-Stephenson . . . . and Lisa Tripp, eds., *Hanging Out, Messing Around, and Geeking Out: Kids Living and Learning with New Media* (Cambridge, MA: MIT Press, 2010); Livingstone, "Taking Risky"; Kate Raynes-Goldie, "Aliases, Creeping, and Wall Cleaning: Understanding Privacy in the Age of Facebook," *First Monday* 15, no. 1 (January 4, 2010), accessed October 10, 2017 http://firstmonday.org/article/view/2775/2432.

15. Cassell and Cramer, "High Tech," 60.

16. Amanda Lenhart, "Teens, Social Media & Technology Overview 2015," *Pew Research Center*, April 2015, accessed January 3, 2017. http://www.pewinternet.org/files/2015/04/PI_TeensandTech_Update2015_0409151.pdf.

17. Jonathan Beller, *The Cinematic Mode of Production: Attention Economy and the Society of the Spectacle* (Hanover: Dartmouth College Press, 2006).

18. For a fuller discussion on this, see Nancy Lesko, *Act Your Age: A Cultural Construction of Adolescence* (New York: Routledge, 2001).

19. Which, as a result, provides motivation for further sociality and backing to notions of adolescents as obsessively social.

20. Madden et al. "Teens and Technology."

21. The other pages have options from categories ranging from "Fashion" to "NASCAR" to "Government." It has been widely recognized that users face an overwhelming amount of information to choose from in Internet spaces like Twitter. Space matters even in the "immaterial" Internet, and, while "search" is a complex issue, studies have pointed out users' tendency to select from early options presented by browsers and other informational navigation systems and services when searching for information and making selections on the web. Because of this, new Twitter users might be expected to choose their required five "well-known people" from the long first page of options, which sets them up for following celebrities from the music, sports, and general entertainment industries. See, for example, Eszter Hargittai, Lindsay Fullerton, Ericka Menchen-Trevino, and Kristin Yates Thomas, "Trust Online: Young Adults' Evaluation of Web Content," *International Journal of Communication* 4 (2010), accessed May 12, 2017, http://ijoc.org/index.php/ijoc/article/view/636 and Karen Markey, "Twenty-five years of end-user searching part 1: Research findings," *Journal of the American Society for Information Science and Technology* 58, no. 8 (2007).

22. Tim Wu, *The Attention Merchants: The Epic Scramble to Get Inside Our Heads*, (New York: Alfred A. Knopf, 2016).

23. A wonderful discussion of this is found on Ben Grosser's website. Benjamin Grosser, "Facebook Demetricator," accessed October 31, 2017 http://bengrosser.com/projects/facebook-demetricator/.

24. Madden et al., "Teens and Technology."

25. See Sherry Turkle, *Alone Together: Why We Expect More from Technology and Less from Each Other* (New York: Basic, 2011).

26. Taryn A. Myers and Janis H. Crowther, "Social Comparison as a Predictor of Body Dissatisfaction: A Meta-Analytic Review" *Journal of Abnormal Psychology* 118, no. 4 (2009).

27. See Sampasa-Kanyinga Hugues and Lewis F. Rosamund, "Frequent Use of Social Networking Sites is Associated with Poor Psychological Functioning Among Children and Adolescents," *Cyberpsychology, Behavior, and Social Networking* 18, no. 7 (2015): 380–385; Evelyn P. Meier and James Gray, "Facebook Photo Activity Associated with Body Image Disturbance in Adolescent Girls," *Cyberpsychology, Behavior, and Social Networking* 17, no. 4 (2014); Jacqueline Nesi and Mitchell J. Prinstein, "Using Social Media for Social Comparison and Feedback-Seeking: Gender and Popularity Moderate Associations with Depressive Symptoms" *Journal of Abnormal Child Psychology* 43, no. 8 (2015); and Andrew K. Przybylski, Kou Murayama, Cody R. DeHaan, and Valerie Gladwell, "Motivational, Emotional, and Behavioral Correlates of Fear of Missing Out," *Computers in Human Behavior* 29, no. 4 (2013). Also, a 2015 study out of the University of Glasglow by Heather Cleland Woods sponsored by the National Citizens Service found that teens are more likely to go on social media to diffuse anxiety than to talk to adults.

28. Paul J. Silvia and T. Shelley Duval, "Objective Self-Awareness Theory: Recent Progress and Enduring Problems," *Personality and Social Psychology Review* 5 (2001); Diederik A. Stapel and Abraham Tesser, "Self-Activation Increases Social Comparison," *Journal of Personality and Social Psychology* 81 (2001).

29. Leon Festinger, "A Theory of Social Comparison Processes," *Human Relations* 7 (1954); Caterina Giordano, Joanne V. Wood, and John L. Michela, "Depressive Personality Styles, Dysphoria, and Social Comparisons in Everyday Life," *Journal of Personality and Social Psychology* 76 (2000).

30. Stephen R. Swallow and Nicholas A. Kyiper, "Mild Depression and Frequency of Social Comparison Behavior," *Journal of Personality and Social Psychology* 82 (1992).

31. Ramin Mojtabai, Mark Olfson, and Beth Han, "National Trends in the Prevalence and Treatment of Depression in Adolescents and Young Adults," *Pediatrics* (November 2016), accessed May 12, 2017, http://pediatrics.aappublications.org/content/early/2016/11/10/peds.2016-1878.

32. Jennifer Crocker, "The Costs of Seeking Self-Esteem," *Journal of Social Issues* 58 (2002); William O. Bearden and Randall L. Rose, "Attention to Social Comparison Information: An Individual Difference Factor Affecting Consumer Conformity," *Journal of Consumer Research* 16, no. 4 (1990); 461–471.

33. Patti M. Valkenburg, Jochen Peter, and Alexander Peter Schouten, "Friend Networking Sites and their Relationship to Adolescents' Well-Being and Social Self-Esteem," *CyberPsychology & Behavior* 9, no. 5 (2006). Also, teens' acceptance of peer validation in social media leave them more open to being tricked. Scams have been found to be far more efficient when sent through what appeared to be a friend's social media accounts than from one appearing as a stranger, and females have been found particularly susceptible to this type of fraud in being more accepting of information and directives spread to them by trusted networks—See Tom N. Jagatic, Nathanial A. Johnson, Markus Jakobsson, and Filippo Menczer "Social Phishing," *Communications of the ACM* 50, no. 10 (October 2007).

34. Maeve Duncan, "Online Harassment," *Pew Research Center* (October 22, 2014). Accessed March 12, 2015 from http://www.pewinternet.org/2014/10/22/online-harassment/.

35. Deborah Fallows, "How Women and Men Use the Internet," *Pew Research Center* (December 28, 2005). Accessed March 12, 2015 from http://www.pewinternet.org/2005/12/28/how-women-and-men-use-the-internet/2; Robert Meyer and Michael Cukier, "Assessing the Attack Threat due to IRC Channels," in *Proceedings of the International Conference on Dependable Systems and Networks* (2006). Accessed March 12, 2015 from http://www.enre.umd.edu/content/rmeyer-assessing.pdf.

36. Whatever it is called, social media threats have effectively forced females to remove themselves from public involvement to avoid receiving death and rape threats framed as free speech and trivialized by police, to prevent broadcasting of their address and other personal details, and to stop the spreading of lies about them on the Internet that promise to cast doubt upon their character well into the future.

37. http://www.loc.gov/today/pr/2010/10–081.html; http://blogs.loc.gov/loc/2010/04/how-tweet-it-is-library-acquires-entire-twitter-archive.

38. Looking through the list of followers of one of the two interlocutors who told me her Twitter account handle, I very easily identified the accounts of two classmates who were also in this study through friend networks. These teens felt in control of their involvements in what they considered to be a parent-free Twitter. However, locating the teens took minimal time and effort.

39. http://www.pcworld.com/article/255076/fewer_than_half_of_facebook_and_google_users_understood_the_sites_privacy_policies.html; Siegel + Gale (2012).

40. https://www.facebook.com/about/basics.

41. Posts, Profile, Likes & Comments, Tagging, Photos & Videos I'm In, Search, Deleting Posts, Friend List, Comments & Likes by Others, Untagging, Timeline, and News Feed. https://www.facebook.com/about/basics/manage-your-privacy.

42. https://www.facebook.com/about/privacy/. This information is, instead, in a section named "Data Policy." Under "What kinds of information do we collect," in addition to information on other areas, Facebook states: "We collect information when you visit or use third-party websites and apps that use our Services (like when they offer our Like button or Facebook Log In or use our measurement and advertising services). This includes information about the websites and apps you visit, your use of our Services on those websites and apps, as well as information the developer or publisher of the app or website provides to you or us. . . . We receive information about you and your activities on and off Facebook from third-party partners, such as information from a partner when we jointly offer services or from an advertiser about your experiences or interactions with them. . . . We receive information about you from companies that are owned or operated by Facebook, in accordance with their terms and policies."

43. The journal publishing this research writes, "The authors noted in their paper, [The work] was consistent with Facebook's Data Use Policy, to which all users agree prior to creating an account on Facebook, constituting informed consent for this research." http://www.pnas.org/content/111/24/8788.full.pdf.

44. Michael Kosinski, David Stillwell, and Theore Graepel, "Private Traits and Attributes are Predictable from Digital Records of Human Behavior," *Proceedings of the National Academy of Sciences,* 110, no. 15 (2013). Mara Einstein, *Black Ops Advertising* (New York: OR Books, 2016).

45. José Van Dijck, *The Culture of Connectivity: A Critical History of Social Media* (Oxford: Oxford University Press, 2013). See Chapter 3.

46. Van Dijck, *The Culture of Connectivity.*

47. Joseph Turow, *The Daily You* (New Haven: Yale University Press, 2011).

48. Ibid., 145–146.

49. Ibid., 147.

50. Oscar H. Gandy, *The Panoptic Sort* (Oxford: Westview Press, 1989), 67.

51. Edward S. Herman and Noam Chomsky, *Manufacturing Consent: The Political Economy of the Mass Media* (New York: Pantheon, 1988).

52. Van Dijck, *The Culture of Connectivity,* 64

53. Ibid.

54. Beyond this, teens have more friends than adults. Aaron Smith, "6 New Facts About Facebook," *Pew Research Center* (February 3, 2014). Accessed June 16, 2017. http://www.pewresearch.org/fact-tank/2014/02/03/6-new-facts-about-facebook/.

55. Chantal, "Centre NAD reassures Montrealers: No danger of being snatched by a royal eagle" (2012, December 19), accessed December 26, 2012 http://blogue.centrenad.com/2012/12/19/centre-nad-reassures-montrealers-no-danger-of-being-snatched-by-a-royal-eagle/

?lang=en . and reposted http://www.scoop.co.nz/stories/WO1212/S00301/montrealers-reas-sured-no-danger-of-being-snatched-by-eagle.htm.

56. Kathy Hanson, "Eagles Shot in State, Area; Fake Video May Be Cause," *Sawyer County Record* (January 31, 2013), accessed October 20, 2107 http://www.apg-wi.com/saw-yer_county_record/news/eagles-shot-in-state-area-fake-video-may-be-cause/article_6f8a4128-a5d8–5969-abf2–9249c9196362.html. Glen Moberg, "Raptor Expert Says Eagle Shootings Up After Web Video," *Wisconsin Public Radio*, January 23, 2013, accessed June 14, 2017 http://news.wpr.org/post/raptor-expert-says-eagle-shootings-after-web-video.

57. Tim Wu, *The Attention Merchants* (New York: Alfred A. Knopf, 2016).

58. See Einstein, *Black Ops*; Turow, *The Daily You, The Aisles Have Eyes*; Tim Wu, *The Attention Merchants*; Jeff Hammerbacker, an early research scientist at Facebook charged with analyzing users' behavior, explained frustration in his past position with the company to Bloomburg Businessweek: "The best minds of my generation are thinking about how to make people click ads. That sucks." See: Ashley Vance, "This Tech Bubble is Different," *Bloomberg Businessweek*. April 14, 2011: par. 3, accessed September 12, 2017 https://www.bloomberg.com/news/articles/2011–04–14/this-tech-bubble-is-different.

59. See, for example, Steve Bogira, "Parodies Lost: Why Satire Must be Banned from the Internet.," *The Chicago Reader* (December 10, 2012). Accessed September 12, 2017. http://www.chicagoreader.com/Bleader/archives/2012/12/10/parodies-lost-why-satire-must-be-banned-from-the-internet; Kevin Fallon, "Fooled by 'The Onion': 9 Most Embarrassing Fails," *The Daily Beast* (November 27, 2012). Accessed September 12, 2017. http://www.thedailybeast.com/articles/2012/09/29/fooled-by-the-onion-8-most-embarrassing-fails.html; Mackenzie Weinger, "John Fleming links to Onion story on Facebook," *Politico* (February 6, 2012). Accessed September 12, 2017. http://www.politico.com/news/stories/0212/72507.html.

60. Einstein, *Black Ops Advertising*.

61. Ibid., 91.

62. The Tumblr site named "Literally Unbelievable" claimed true stories. For example, fake exchanges: http://www.damnyouautocorrect.com; http://thechive.com/2012/02/23/girl-tattoos-boyfriend-of-1-week-on-her-arm-a-facebook-thread-ensues-12-photos/.

63. Luke O'Neil, "Internet Gullibility Syndrome: Maybe 'Literally Unbelievable' is Unbe-lievable for a Reason," *Street Carnage* (June 13, 2011): para. 7. Accessed September 12, 2017 http://www.streetcarnage.com/blog/internet-gullibility-syndrome-maybe-literally-unbeliev-able-is-unbelievable-for-a-reason/.

64. While both Facebook and Twitter have statements regarding non-tolerance of hate speech, these policies have not been applied to address misogyny or jokes about rape or violence against females—all of which are present in US society, and related to females' subjugation and marginality. For example, Facebook has repeatedly resisted and dismissed as histrionic requests made asking them to address misogynistic and rape-related comedy-oriented accounts' postings as "hate speech." Facebook did eventually cede to public pressure in 2013 calling on it to take a stand against some of the most egregious instances on their site. However, other material remains. Additionally, consider the case of Anthony Douglas Elonis. After his wife left him in 2010, Anthony Douglas Elonis made comments about her on Facebook, including "If I only knew then what I know now, I would have smothered your ass with a pillow, dumped your body in the back seat, dropped you off in Toad Creek, and made it look like a rape and murder." After his estranged wife secured an order of protection as a result of these posts, Elonis posted other comments about her, including that she should fold up the order and "put it in your pocket. Is it thick enough to stop a bullet?" In 2015, the US Supreme Court threw the case out, ruling by a vote of 7–2 that what Elonis wrote did not contain what the law considers actual threats. Similarly, female gamers issued death threats by identified males had their evidence fall on deaf ears when they met with law enforcement. According to the law of the land, a boy telling a girl he knows that he will kill her through social media is not threatening just as the Klu Klux Klan burning a cross on a front lawn is not threatening according to precedent set by *Virgina v. Black*.

65. See, for example, Motahhare Eslami, Aimee Rickman, Kristen Vaccaro, Amirhossein Aleyasen, Andy Vyong, Karrie Karahalios, Kevin Hamilton, and Christian Sandvig, "I Always

Assumed That I Wasn't Really That Close To [Her]: Reasoning About Invisible Algorithms in News Feeds," *Proceedings of the 33rd Annual ACM Conference on Human Factors in Computing Systems* (2015); Frank Pasquale, *The Black Box Society: The Secret Algorithms that Control Money and Information,* (Harvard University Press, 2017); Safiya Noble, *Algorithms of Oppression: How Search Engines Reinforce Racism* (New York: NYU Press, 2018); J. Nathaniel Matias, Aimee Rickman and Megan Steiner, "Who Gets to Use Facebook's Rainbow "Pride" Reaction?" *The Atlantic* (June 26, 2017).

66. Amy Mitchell, Jeffrey Gottfried, Michael Barthel, and Elisa Shearer, "The Modern News Consumer: News Attitudes and Practices in the Digital Era," *Pew Research Center* (July 7, 2016). Accessed May 3, 2017 from http://assets.pewresearch.org/wp-content/uploads/sites/13/2016/07/08140120/PJ_2016.07.07_Modern-News-Consumer_FINAL.pdf.

67. For example, see Aaron M. McCright, Meghan Charters, Katherine Dentzman, and Thomas Dietz, "Examining the Effectiveness of Climate Change Frames in the Face of a Climate Change Denial Counter-Frame," *Future Global Change and Cognition* 8 (2015).

68. Jonathan Swift, "The Art of Political Lying," *The Examiner*, 14 (November 9, 1710), Page 2, Column 1.

69. https://www.facebook.com/legal/terms. Listed as #1 under Registration and Account Security on Facebook's Statements of Rights and Responsibilities: "You will not provide any false personal information on Facebook, or create an account for anyone other than yourself without permission."

70. Somini Sengupta, "Letting Down Our Guard With Web Privacy," *New York Times* (March 30, 2013), accessed June 2, 2017 http://www.nytimes.com/2013/03/31/technology/web-privacy-and-how-consumers-let-down-their-guard.html?pagewanted=all. Also, https://www.facebook.com/full_data_use_policy.

71. Nick Bilton, "Facebook Changes Privacy Settings, Again," *New York Times* (December 12, 2012), accessed September 8, 2017 http://bits.blogs.nytimes.com/2012/12/12/facebook-changes-privacy-settings-again/. Also, Chris Conley, "New Facebook Search Means It's Time to Review Your Privacy Settings (Again)," *ACLU* (January 13, 2013), accessed June 2, 2017 http://www.aclu.org/blog/technology-and-liberty/new-facebook-search-means-its-time-review-your-privacy-settings-again.

72. Sarah Perez, "Facebook Graph Search Didn't Break Your Privacy Settings, It Only Feels Like That," (February 4, 2013), *Tech Crunch*, accessed June 2, 2017 http://techcrunch.com/2013/02/04/facebook-graph-search-didnt-break-your-privacy-settings-it-only-feels-like-that.

73. Alex Weaver, "Coming Soon to Your Facebook Page: Ambiguous Advertising," *Fast Horse* (January 26, 2012), accessed June 2, 2017 from http://fasthorseinc.com/blog/2012/01/26/coming-soon-to-your-facebook-page-ambiguous-advertising.

74. Anthony Wing Kosner, "Facebook is Recycling Your Likes to Promote Stories You've Never Seen To All Your Friends," *Forbes* (January 21, 2013), accessed June 2, 2017 http://www.forbes.com/sites/anthonykosner/2013/01/21/facebook-is-recycling-your-likes-to-promote-stories-youve-never-seen-to-all-your-friends.

75. Kiri Blakeley, "The Justin Bieber Scam," *Forbes* (October 3, 2011), accessed June 2, 2017 http://www.forbes.com/sites/kiriblakeley/2011/10/03/the-justin-bieber-twitter-scam/; Brad Stone and Miguel Helft, "In Developing Countries, Web Grows Without Profit," *New York Times* (April 26, 2009), accessed June 2, 2017 http://www.nytimes.com/2009/04/27/technology/start-ups/27global.html?pagewanted=all&_r=2& Also Austin Considine, "Buying Their Way to Twitter Fame," *New York Times* (August 2, 2012). Accessed June 2, 2017 http://www.nytimes.com/2012/08/23/fashion/twitter-followers-for-sale.html; Lauren Hockenson, "Fake Twitter Followers: An Easy Game, But Not Worth the Risk," *The Next Web* (December 15, 2012), accessed June 2, 2017, http://thenextweb.com/twitter/2012/12/15/fake-followers-an-easy-game-but-not-worth-the-risk/; https://www.facebook.com/facebook?v=info, Facebook's mission is to "make the world more open and connected." See Einstein, *Black Ops Advertising.*

76. Hoofnagle, King, Li and Turow, "How Different are Young."

Chapter Six

Adolescence, Girlhood, and Media Migration

Contrary to notions of teens being at-risk, studies of youth victimization find that teens in the US are safer today than they have been in the past decade. An analysis of data collected by the US Bureau of Justice Statistics concluded that, in 2014, "violent crime victimization among adolescents reached an all-time low, with the rate declining to one-sixth of what it was in the mid 1990s."[1] And challenging the idea that young women are putting themselves in harms' way, the Center for Disease Control's most recent National Youth Risk Behavior Survey reports that, across all indicators related to sexual activity, drunk driving, and use of contraceptives, drugs, cigarettes, alcohol, and seat belts, US high schoolers' riskiness has either stayed consistent or decreased over the past two decades with females less involved in most of these risky involvements than males.[2] Yet despite evidence documenting that the typical dangers facing young people are down, young women in social media are still being defined in a familiar binary fashion: they are either imminently "at-risk" or they are dangerously "reckless." And while the imagery of young women as naïvely out of control is appealing and easy to make sense of, this book suggests this understanding is grossly inaccurate.

In her book *Out in the Country*, Mary L. Gray writes that "youth engage media in far more complicated ways than we assume,"[3] and, indeed, my research demonstrates just how complicated their engagement is. Looking closely at the treatment female youth experience in their day-to-day lives, my work shows how teens travel alone to and through online spaces to set up temporary walls of public privacy that allow them to perform desired identities and involvements away from parents' watchful eyes. In other words, teens intentionally migrate to media not only to escape off-line containment, surveillance, and misinterpretation, but also to strategically attempt to claim social spaces they believe provide opportunities for interacting, performing identities, and crafting counternarratives that can help them mitigate their off-line marginality.

The young women in this study migrated to social media to attempt to negotiate better terms for their life that they were unable to earn, argue for, or otherwise secure offline. In some ways, these teens were pulled to participate in social media. They migrated to social media to access information, social relevance, and control they were regularly denied offline. They migrated to social media to learn about, negotiate, and advance their social understandings and, in doing so, to build their personal standing in forms that brought them rare power through status. They migrated online to capitalize upon social power in ways that might bring them greater permissions and rights offline. But teens' lived realities also pushed them into social media use. They migrated to social media to escape authoritarian conditions they experienced at home and in school (e.g., restrictions regarding acquaintances, curfews). And they migrated to social media to escape shaming, denial of their realities, and the throngs of parents and other observing adults who restricted their ability to act both as they were and as they wished.

This "media migration" gave my interlocutors a rare opportunity to feel connected, meaningful, and actively involved in their lives and futures, providing these adolescent females with a rare form of power allowed to them in US society. But as much as they enjoyed the feelings of connection, control, direction, and purpose that social media promised, the teens most wanted to feel these things in their daily lives, in their face-to-face world. Unfortunately, the fact that these elements are seldom available to them offline makes their accessibility online all that more attractive, and it is in this context that these teens find themselves in perilous positions.

SOCIAL MEDIA, STRUCTURE, AND AGENCY

Promising interactive ways of sharing ideas and information with individuals and groups, social media have changed the ways people connect to and engage with others. Facebook, for example, set out to "give people the power to share and make the world more open and connected," and it has become US teens' main source for news with a mission to "give people the power to build community and bring the world closer together."[4] Twitter aimed to provide a mobile platform for a "real-time information network," and it is now a primary platform these same teens look to for information from both their friends and their nation's leader. Instagram, Pinterest, and Snapchat use images to create customized spaces for expression and social connections that have developed loyal and enthusiastic followings from young people. Users continue to respond to these options, as evident in the growing numbers of people using social media to reconnect with old friends and acquaintances, share their ideas, expand their personal and professional networks, and discover people with like interests around the world. However, as these platforms and their popularity grow, so, too, do the concerns and criticism while teens use social media to try to negotiate the many risks they face in their daily lives.

Early concerns for girls' social media use centered around their vulnerability to individual pedophiles and sexually interested male strangers waiting for them in social life beyond family. These were accompanied by fears about girls' immaturity, frivolous involvements, and potential distractions online. Others have raised critiques of youth productivity online, asking whether teens were spending too much time on social media instead of tending to work they should be doing. Still others have raised concerns about increasing cases of reclusivity as disenfranchised users withdraw further into online forums and messages at the potential expense of real-world interactions, and about the nature of the relationship between this and young women's rising depression rates. Online harassment and concerns for cyberbullying have become more prominent, and people continue to worry about the availability of their personal information that social media makes more readily accessible to would-be criminals. Social media proponents have responded to such concerns by calling for investment in educational technology, more media literacy, and less preoccupation with offline notions of privacy to allow young people better opportunities and wider involvement in the online world. In spite of these efforts, however, there is a little-discussed dark side of social media that needs our attention if we truly aim to protect adolescents. The following discussion highlights some of the problems that make social media a more dangerous environment for teenagers who are desperately seeking ways to "be themselves" and to move toward less marginal identities and involvements.

One problem is that social media is not a neutral environment. Social media technologies are of society—not outside of it. For example, young people's safety in social media is shaped by legislation, and the few gestures made toward protecting US kids from commercial interests on the Internet have been eroded to the point where they are hardly worth mentioning. The Child Online Privacy Protection Act (COPPA) was passed in 1998 to prohibit online advertising to children under 13. In 2012, COPPA was revised to allow both data collection from youth and targeted advertising to them. And the allowance of broad and vague data use policies tied to infrastructures encouraging of greater and greater information sharing enables social media sites such as Facebook and Twitter to collect copious amounts of data on every teen who has an account, to hold this information for years, and to share this however they deem most useful and most profitable.[5] These are human permissions set by people in power that shape the relationships young people are able to have both with technology and within the world. Minors are not able to participate in many parts of society without guardian approval—or at all—due to their age, but their involvements are curtailed, monitored, and sold by profit-oriented companies long before they are even able to vote on such legislation. While we tend to think of media communication technology as a force beyond human bodies and action, what is important here is to remember that "the Internet" is not at all an inaccessible power outside of our selves. Rather, the Internet exists as a result of human-made efforts and decisions. As such, it tends to reflect and reinforce the sexism, racism, classism, ageism, homophobia, and other norms and values evident in the larger society, and it exists to serve certain interests of their owners. It is not neutral.

This is an issue for all in society, especially as they log on believing discourses of incorporeal equality and technological utopianism. However, it presents an even larger problem for young women. Online, my interlocutors "liked" and "friended" and "followed" and "favorited." They posted pictures, stayed aware of ongoing discussions, and performed different identities to different communities. They migrated from site to site to occupy spaces that felt safe to relax and feel respected in. They attempted to better their lives offline through their online actions, and sometimes, they succeeded. These actions had agency, and these teens had power in taking them on. However, the teens' power is limited by the frameworks in which they are working—frameworks that are set up and maintained by others with different or even competing agendas than their participants. And girls' lack of other options made it difficult for them to even want to consider how the Internet might not always be on their side.

Another problem is that social media is set up as an enterprise of capitalism, working with profit in mind. Media scholar Robert McChesney writes that the "elephant in the room" for most research on the Internet is capitalism. Although there have been an immense number of studies on and about the Internet released over the past 30 years, McChesney notes that this research is overwhelmingly devoid of consideration of factors that shape the Internet or involvements within it. Rather, this research "[t]akes the world as it is, accepts it, and assesses it on those terms."[6] McChesney argues that a broader analysis of structures and institutions that have and wield power is required if one hopes to understand through their research the role of the Internet in society, for "[t]he ways capitalism works and does not work determine the role the Internet might play in society."[7]

Social media sites offer users connections, communities, and communication, but their main goal is to make money for their owners, and they do this, in part, by collecting user data, often by any means necessary. This is a problem in general because users must voluntarily donate wide swaths of valuable personal information that will be stored and used to try to manipulate their interests in unknowable ways for years to come as an entry fee to participate in these popular social forums. It is even more of a problem because users are generally unaware they are giving this donation. For instance, the backside of social media's "sharing" ethos involves connectivity with data-interested partners requiring users' consent to pages upon pages of vague terms of service fine-print when they join platforms. But the details of these agreements—and the regular changes made to them—are intentionally downplayed to these users to focus their attention, instead, on potential connections with individuals. For example, after facing outrage for conducting research on nearly 700,000 users without their consent to see if users' emotions could be manipulated with subtle changes to their newsfeeds (spoiler: they could), Facebook quietly added language to their terms of service agreement retroactively giving the company permission to conduct "research."[8]

This is particularly problematic to teenage young women because they migrate to social media seeking opportunities to try to emancipate themselves from regular offline surveillance and inequity that leave them feeling powerless in their daily lives. Once there, they are distracted from the fact that their involvements and identities online are constantly surveilled and monitored—as well as stored, sold, and co-opted—by having their attention focused on quests for popularity, sensationalist content, and privacy from individuals as they unwittingly, but enthusiastically, volunteer their labor in attempts to advance their opportunities. Most social media charge no monetary fee to teens, but they do to commercial entities allowed to secretly lurk in these minors' online social spaces, where they track and attempt to befriend and guide teens' emotions, attention, and involvements to advance their own interests. The boundaries of marginality are socially drawn, and institutions of capitalism have a hand in this effort.

Given that social media will collect data by any means necessary, we need to consider the ways platforms collect this information, especially with regard to teen users. One method social media uses to collect data is by exploiting users' overall trust. Trust in social media is grounded in views of privacy. The more careful a platform appears to be with users' personal data, the more people trust it. But trust becomes slippery when platforms look to surreptitiously collect user information and sell their attention for profit, and this is what these young women face in social media. Trust is no small matter for youth or for social media. Social theorist Anthony Giddens writes:

> [T]rust is directly linked to achieving an early sense of ontological security. Trust established between an infant and its caretakers provides an "inoculation" which screens off potential threats and dangers that even the most mundane of day-to-day-life contain. Trust in this sense is basic to a "protective cocoon" which stands guard over the self in its dealings with everyday reality.

It "brackets out" potential occurrences which, were the individual seriously to
contemplate them, would produce a paralysis of the will, or feelings of engulf-
ment. . . . . Trust here generates that "leap into faith" which practical engagement demands.[9]

Teens in this study chose to engage—and engage loyally—in social media
platforms largely because they trusted these sites and believed that, even with
the risks they took to be there, these sites offered them the best opportunities
they had available. Research finds young and older social media users to
have very similar privacy interests and precautions online, but the young are
distinct in believing they have more protections in the larger world than do
people of their parents' age.[10] Young users feel social media looks out for
their best interests, and that the established law defends their privacy far
more than it really does. In short, the young trust social media more because
they understand both the forces that aim to profit off them and their protections as citizens less.

Social media also collects data by exploiting users' marginality—a trait
that makes teenagers in general, and teenage girls in particular, most susceptible. US society offers a paradoxical and quixotic script for young females to
attempt to perform. They are "our future" yet they need to be controlled.
They are easily taken advantage of but they are also out of control. They are
asexual, but also whores. They are told they are limited only by their efforts,
yet their nation's leader bragged that he and others with fame can do anything they want to their bodies. They are taught they are responsible for both
their own acts and for the violence they have to endure and negotiate from
others. And while they realize this, as marginalized, dependent, and geographically isolated members of a group considered unprepared for full civic
rights and standing, teenage girls have few allies in challenging injustices or
in making sense of their devaluing within dominant national discourses
promising equity for all. With limited opportunities to feel and enact power,
teens are highly susceptible to the lure of social media as they seek greater
social involvement and better opportunities. And these teens enthusiastically
welcomed social media's offers of greater direction, relevance, power, and
control as they tried to negotiate less-marginal identities while tip-toeing
around curfews, reputation damage, and adult fragility. In return, these environments directed and profited from teens' rights-seeking interests, involvements, and identity work.

Victor Turner[11] writes that liminal, in-between spaces represent socio-
cultural moments of powerful potential for personal and social transforma-
tion. In liminality, Turner points out that typical boundings of self in behavior, thought, and understanding are relaxed, enabling new understandings
outside of everyday roles and rituals. In creating a space for existence outside
of the everyday material world, social media have the potential to be very

powerful and socially transformative. Undoubtedly, social media represent new forums in which young women's potential visibility outside of contained and monitored youth- and female-specific spaces challenges social norms built by and maintaining hierarchies of inequity. But in offering standard scripts for performance of—and attention to—identities within plays of commercialism and commodification, this forum primarily presents opportunities for entertainment and leisure that escort these young social media users back into their seats of subjectivity.

Add to this that social media bolsters its data collection capabilities by obscuring privacy settings. Privacy settings change often. So, while the controls may be there, the fact that they aren't easy to find or to navigate makes these settings less effective. Also, privacy settings are superficial on many sites, directing users to consider certain forms of privacy that protect their social standing while actively downplaying attention to other protocols that lessen their ownership and control of their identities. Noting Facebook CEO Mark Zuckerburg's repeated statements that privacy controls are designed to allow users to, in his words, "have more confidence as you share things on Facebook," Laura Brandimarte, Alessandro Acquisti, and George Lowenstein[12] report that high levels of perceived control in social media is tied to users' oversharing of personal information, advancing not only personal expression but also platforms' knowledge and ownership of these expressions. In other words, having a false sense of confidence in one's safety in social media leads to far less safety.

This presents an even larger problem for teens. Using opaque privacy and data use policies and offering controls that increased teens' willingness to share but did little to control their safety, commercial entities entered these young women into relationships with data-interested friends and affiliates that, having collected and retained vast amounts of information on them, then commodify their lives to quietly promote custom-tailored pitches for products, services, values, ideas, and lifestyles to and from them. With permissions deeply embedded in corporate fine print, teens were given few, if any, options for opting out, let alone for understanding what they were entering into. These relationships challenge teens' efforts for respect and visibility in society by giving companies the right to collect, store, and use teens' personal information now and in the future to represent, or map, them as they see fit. It also creates a new container around these adolescents to serve as a release valve for their frustrations while distracting, storing, tracking, and muting their potential negotiation with—and resistance to—larger structures of power within US society.[13] What matters here is commercial spaces' ability to co-opt and profit off of young people's involvements and identities, and, by manipulation of their trust networks, to control their visibility and social power by holding reputation over their head in still-to-be-determined use of their private data disclosed as a result of their desperation to feel both meaningful and non-maligned. At the same time, young women's attentions are directed away from offline conditions that render them marginal as the potential perks of media migration urge them to very literally remove their skins from the game to seek individual advancement. This eases social reproduction of inequities, with teens voluntarily enlisting in surveillance and mismapping while attending to self-regulation within consumptive spectacles of sociality.

Operating within broad, mercurial, and largely inaccessible legal and technical infrastructures of communication and social technologies controlled by many overlapping interests, media scholars note that, in addition to offering space for involvements and sharing, social media increasingly play host to some of the main spaces people rely upon to operate their daily lives.[14] The trust teens placed in social media within this context has serious implications for their well-being. Beyond opening themselves up to false promises,[15] young people's increased trust in and reliance upon social media infrastructure calls into question their ability to use "voice," "visibility," or other acts to effectively negotiate their powerlessness, and ultimately, to have any hope in challenging the marginality they face in adolescence, in girlhood, and in US society.

A Call for Reframing Social Media Risk and Safety

Teens going online today as a way of "getting around" obstacles in their offline lives may, in some of their behaviors, reveal recklessness and riskiness, but to suggest these vulnerabilities are the result of the teens' own personal failings is short-sighted and highly inaccurate. Such analysis also shifts blame away from the people and structures that create and perpetuate genuine dangers for girls both off- *and* online. We need new understandings of girls and young women, and broader, more careful and more critical perspectives on risk. This research thus encourages us to reconsider and reframe the notions of safety and risk as they relate to young women's involvements with social media. In this, it is not enough to say adolescence and girlhood are risky; this is obvious to us (and to them). Similarly, it is not nearly adequate to give social media infrastructures a pass by saying they are here to stay as part of life for these teens. As US females and teens are increasingly monitored, the businesses involved in their lives are bound to fewer controls. This deserves our serious critique. It can and must change. Like young women's social media usage itself, the systems undergirding adolescence, girlhood, and media technologies are, surely, complicated. But they are not at all incomprehensible. And since their related policies and practices are products of people, their basic elements are certainly neither out of our hands nor out of the control of a society that purports to care for its youth. So where do we go from here?

First, we must do a better job in understanding the realities of young women, especially those in rural areas. The current literature on youth and social media focuses heavily on survey-based research considering those in and around cities and universities. The experiences of girls and other minors from rural communities are generally missed in these findings, as are the thoughts they share once they have built more trust than possible in a one-time interaction. Rural girls in the US experience unique geographic conditions that influence their relationships, including those with communication technologies. These perspectives need to be sought out and taken seriously to avoid a continued mismapping of young Americans.

Within this, sharpened attention is direly needed to attend to the sexist, racist, classist, heteronormative, and otherwise marginalizing infrastructures of adolescence and girlhood that motivate young people's identities and involvements in social media and in other realms in the US. Like technologies, adolescence and girlhood are also defined and enforced by people, practices, and processes as part of society and culture. An overlooked story in America is that children have something to do with our future, but they are, more importantly, very real today. The young women in this study were understandably dissatisfied with the ways they are being treated *now*. They disliked the way they are understood in offline life now, and they felt they had no ability to negotiate better respect or options for themselves by voicing their critiques. Because of this, they chose to move to spaces enticing them with promises of more power, greater control, and brighter futures. They knew little about these spaces going in but believed that they must be better than what they had to otherwise endure.

Why should girls have to negotiate so much to just exist in their families, schools, and society? What does it mean for young women to see their best opportunities to be themselves online rather than in their homes and communities? What does it mean for youth to believe they are most able to self-advocate and "hustle" to make something of themselves not in their hometowns, but on social media? What does it say about society that social media use is highest among the very teens most disenfranchised by sexism, racism, and other structural violence? What awaits our country when members of our largest population in upcoming elections turn away from offline spaces to feel meaningful, powerful, and supported? As deliberate efforts continue to successfully erode this country's thin safety net, and as the number of youth—particularly non-white youth—continue to grow, what does it mean that these teens are finding their best life possibilities in media migration?

To understand young women's social media use, it is essential to consider how being a marginal member of society presents it as a good option. With limited opportunities to feel and enact power, the teens in this study turned to social media seeking greater social involvement and better opportunities. There is more than just self-mobilized "choice" going on in any decision teens make to be involved. Economic, social, and political factors shape teens' interests and ability to access the world around them. These influence their choices and their participation, as does the quest to escape powerlessness. Such larger structures of power must be considered and addressed if we hope to better understand and support the actions of young people.

Next, we must ask how social media norms and infrastructures might diffuse young women's frustrations while contributing to their continued marginality. Take, for example, the way youth identities are represented and socialized within social media. In 2016, the US Census reported that young people have been become the US's largest population. Those in the "Millennial" generation born between 1982 and 2000 now outnumber the baby boom.[16] They represent over one-quarter of the population.[17] They are the generation with the largest segment of the US workforce,[18] and, with global forces causing young people to migrate to America in search of greater safety or opportunity, their numbers are growing.[19] The 2016 presidential election year saw almost equal number of Millennials and Baby Boomers in election booths. In 2020, Millennials will be the largest and most influential bloc of voters in the country. As members of such a large group, young people have the potential to harness significant amounts of political power. However, involvement in efforts—be they feminist, anti-racist, reproductive rights, economic, educational, debt-related, age-related, or otherwise—that lead to social movements addressing human rights require more than passive masses. They require individual commitment and willingness to take sometimes-unpopular stances made more difficult by platforms directing teens' attention to popularity and to avoiding association with reputation-damaging controversy. With its dissemination of widely flung ideas through trusted individuals, social media are ideally positioned to cast doubt that could weaken young people's support of movements that could advance their rights. The norms and values set for teens by social media matter due to young people's potential political power, as does the type of information they receive through social media. This is especially true since, for some, what might matter most is discrediting, controlling, and othering young citizens to one another, and priming older voters to see them as symbols of excess or unworthiness to motivate beliefs and votes.

Angela McRobbie and Sarah Thornton remind us that "most political strategies are media strategies. The contest to determine news agendas is the first and last battle of the political campaign."[20] Politicians have used fabricated stories as repeated narratives to craft norms shaping voters' willingness to blame scapegoats with little cultural power, and to direct public anxieties away from more abstract sources of struggle. In this, they have historically called upon media to assist with the social influence needed to advance public opinion, social policy, and even social control. For example, Ronald

Reagan often raised outlandish tales of a Cadillac-driving, steak-dinner-eating, typically non-white, single mother welfare queen in Chicago in his speeches, and these images were intentionally shared to provide fuel backing beliefs in fraud within the public aid system. These narratives influenced voters' call for welfare reform, eventually leading to the dissolution of core threads in the country's already tattered safety net in the Personal Responsibility and Work Act of 1996.[21]

Fabricated projections of soon-to-come crack babies were built upon by the Reagan and, later, the Bush administration who circulated this narrative fable to successfully advance public funding for their "War on Drugs" and to incite social pressure for disproportionately severe and racist penalties for crack cocaine, leading to the prison industrial complex.[22] Narratives on mythical violent black "superpredators" were repeated by the Clinton administration to motivate public support of harsh crime bills and further draconian prison reform. And now we have the well-circulated narrative myth of the Millennial that consistently paints young people—especially young women—as simultaneously arrogant, ignorant, promiscuous, entitled, unprepared, and, at base, undeserving of empathy and support.[23] This narrative is different from its predecessors in taking visual form with images commonly connecting young women to disrespectful self-centeredness through technology, be it by taking selfies at the ballpark or museum, or by being absorbed in social media while in social spaces. However, it is similar in using media to spread emotionally charged false group identities to an anxious and divided populous seeking direction. It is a continuation of a long tradition of media–driven US social propaganda.

The Milliennial narrative circulates on- and offline at a time when young people are experiencing historic labor and educational access difficulties, severe cuts to social services and public funding for their schools, families, and communities, massive debts, and distressing futures. It also comes as this newest generation of youth boasts the most racial diversity in US history, with more than 44% identified as racial or ethnic minorities.[24] By all credible accounts, the floundering US economy is hard on all working Americans, but it is particularly harsh to these young workers—especially to females and to racial and ethnic minorities.[25] Yet there is little outrage as these—like other—realities of females are easily denied, downplayed, and otherwise mismapped within wider national anxieties to blame youth, themselves, for their floundering. And social media play a part in this.

The "entitled Millennial" narrative misrepresents and maligns young people, a marginalized group, to be sure, but a group that has more potential cultural capital than past ideological targets as the children—and, thus the responsibility—of US citizens spanning racial, ethnic, and class lines. This poses problems for this image being spread directly to advance legislative efforts, as previous narratives such as the "welfare queen" have, through politicians whose jobs depend on public opinion. Social media, however, provides an anonymous mouthpiece for circulating this message though shared articles, images, and links that that spread not only ideas but also ideologies. And as this happens, individuals are primed by trusted word-of-mouth information as platforms and their sponsors profit both monetarily and ideologically from social distrust falling upon youth, and from the repeated messages disparaging social safety nets by linking them to youth-coded notions of "entitlement."

As Americans, young women deserve options for education that will not put them in eternal debt, just as previous generations have had. They deserve jobs and healthcare. They deserve to be in control of their own bodies. They deserve to have ways to be meaningfully involved in society. They deserve to be respected for who they are, and to expect to advance in their futures. These are not permissions that go beyond what most Americans expected in previous generations. They deserve to ask for this and more, as citizens, let alone as members of the majority. However, the stories and narratives we hear about youth through media shape beliefs about who is and who is not deserving, and about what (or who) needs fixing to address societal problems.

Speaking to media systems that long pre-dated Facebook and Twitter, the father of modern public relations Edward Bernays stated: "The United States has become a small room in which a single whisper is magnified thousands of times. Knowledge of how to use this enormous amplifying system becomes a matter of primary concern to those who are interested in socially constructive action."[26] As a socializing force, social media have the potential to subtly, but powerfully, influence attitudes, and to impact public policy through public opinion, mobilizing support or stripping already marginal young women of further social care and protections they need. As data- and profit-driven environments, they also have the ability to bypass responsible legal guardians and to track and shape marginal youths' own understandings, interests, involvements, needs, and self-regulation as their identities become owned and performed by others, and their attention is channeled away from larger infrastructures that bound their shared marginality. Media migration provides a new route for girls to be grabbed and used by systems and projects empowered by misogyny, patriarchy, racism, poverty, and other forms of social inequity. This demands our attention.

Next, we must consider the roles parenting and family relationships play in helping daughters participate in a society that often benefits from their invisibility. The US Department of Labor's Fair Labor Standards Act of 1938 defined "oppressive" conditions for children's involvements as compensated work of those under age 16 in any area outside of family agriculture, and that which is "detrimental to [the] health or well-being" of those under age 18.[27]

This act removed many US teens from the world of paid labor and provided a legal foundation to justify the cultural definition of adolescence as separate from adulthood, helping to ensure their seclusion away from central areas of society.[28] Even within such protections, however, young people's frustrations over limited opportunities encourage them into income-generating domains that care little about their health or well-being as youth claim these spaces as their most supportive. This was illustrated by the 2016 Ghost Ship art warehouse fire in Oakland, California, that killed many young inhabitants seeking out spaces for meaningful societal involvement.[29] It is apparent in these teens' media migration, as well. The young women I worked with consistently demonstrated that they are industrious in seeking out new opportunities where a bit of hustle might help them get ahead—especially when faced with demeaning and oppressive options otherwise.

In a culture where being associated with femaleness and femininity is considered an insult and where girls are regularly called "sluts," where young people are being blamed for their country not offering them stable (or any) jobs and for lacking options to gain the air of financial independence viewed as essential to adult identities in the US,[30] where the term "Millennial" has become a dog whistle to Americans conjuring well-primed notions of coddled unpreparedness and greedy narcissism, and where high school graduates face unprecedented levels of debt in seeking to better themselves educationally, girls have a sense that they cannot rely on others to give them respect and power. In homes where teens' displays of "goodness" and responsibility fail to translate into greater trust and social permissions, girls know they can not afford to wait around for others to give them rights. And they are not.

The girls in this study showed that teens are not waiting to be freed of their marginality. Instead, they are doing what they believe they are supposed to do as Americans to succeed: they are putting themselves out in the world in hopes of catching opportunities that will change their luck and avail new and exciting options. They are working hard to contribute in meaningful ways, to earn respect, to be valued, and to have control over their lives. And they are doing it without the help they deserve and the guidance they need from those in power.

The notion that "parents just don't understand" is deeply held in US society. However, daughters have very close relationships with their parents in families across the globe, illustrating that the belief in normal parent-teen discord and disconnect is neither biological nor universal.[31] Girls need their parents. The girls in this study valued their parents. And they would benefit greatly from relationships with adults who they can be honest with and get accurate advice from as they try to make sense of themselves, their wider world, and the options they have for their involvements and identities even as their attentions are continually turned to peers and popularity. But young women struggle to maintain relationships with parents amid dehumanizing fears over their safety and purity. As a result, girls are forced into further isolation as they attempt to independently negotiate and make sense of marginalities that they most clearly see as sourced in the very people who, in fact, care for them most.

This study calls on adults to ask what they can do to allow young women to feel—and, importantly, to be—more valued, honest, trusted, safe, and supported as part of families, schools, communities, and wider society built upon normalized hierarchies of gender, race, and age. At the same time, it asks what is needed to allow parents to deal with their daughters' realities, to be informed of practices and norms emerging in digital spaces, as well as to negotiate the fears that are given to them as protectors of young females framed inaccurately as risky and reckless. The teens in this study expressed deep concern about their futures, and they went to the Internet in part seeking direction they were not given offline. They also told of strong attachment to family, and of disappointment in having to sneak around and to be dishonest to protect parents while self-advocating. Youth fare far better when they have caring and available adults they know they can turn to in their lives, and in their family.[32] This study asks what is needed to help families both advocate for youth in serious ways and support daughters to be able to be themselves offline in ways they now feel is only possible online. Young women need spaces to feel meaningfully engaged. They need adults with time to provide them good advice and feedback. They need places to feel belonging, trust, connection, and honest appreciation. They need to involve and express themselves in ways unconcerned with social comparison, status, and popularity. Psychological theorists stress that everyone needs these things, but they hold particular significance to teens currently subject to the defunding and dismantling of other essential social services and structures of support they and their families need.

Adding to previous examples, as this book was being written, severe state funding cuts led to the closure of the Eagle Bluff youth center where three teens in this study occasionally volunteered to have something to do in their neighborhood, and where their younger siblings and neighbors eagerly took part in homework help and group games after school. Young women are increasingly deprived of options available for—let alone worthy of—their involvement as they are forced to negotiate their identities in a nation headed by leaders who trumpet misogyny, white supremacy, transphobia, and homo-prejudice from national platforms with powerful impunity, and as media sources capitalize upon this type of divisive controversy to gain viewership and earn profits. We must alter material conditions within our society to provide opportunities and respect that young women desperately need but cannot negotiate by themselves to better their lives.

Finally, we must help teens get better information about societal practices that shape Internet protocols so they can better protect themselves. With interests in ensuring their current and future safety, the teens in this study reported putting extensive thought and effort toward trying to "be safe" by protecting themselves in their relationship with social media. However, these teens—like most Americans—are under-informed and misinformed about what safety means in social media. Taking up topics of "stranger danger," sexting, and damaged reputations, adults commonly resorted to generalities and hypotheticals, offering few concrete examples or strategies for how the teens should look out for their best interests online. Further complicating matters was that more pervasive dangers got little if any attention. The teens in this study, for example, seemed unaware of the larger societal institutions that impacted their safety online, let alone how they operated. They were also not conscious of how their involvements and identities were being motivated by their offline frustrations.

These teens' media migrations were borne of economic, political, and social factors that are typically not addressed or even acknowledged in US society. Young people are not taught in school to critically examine media, technology, or the capitalistic forces that fuel parts of our culture we are taught to see as ideal and normal. At the same time, marketers work hard to dissipate any critique by creating associations and affiliations between products and identity—especially youth identity. To be sure, special effort is put into connecting media, technology, and brands with teens in presenting these things as "of" youth. As a result, young people identify personally and emotionally with shows, sites, channels, technologies, and consumer goods, seeing them as things to defend from the devaluing they experience rather than as things they need to question to fully understand. But they do need to question them to really understand them.

Youth have historically done identity work in association with various material goods. This, in itself, is not a problem. But they should be allowed to understand what they are doing. We need to help teens gain critical awareness of the interests in play when they are asked to share and be open in spaces of the Internet, and in their other spaces of involvement as they operate from within power structures that maintain their marginality. As adults, we urgently need this awareness if we want to be able to keep kids safe. And we need to critically evaluate factors behind our tendency to grant trust and generous permissions to entities hosting our children in online spaces we are largely unfamiliar with as we withhold similar rights to girls we raise in offline spaces we are taught to distrust. While social media offers opportunities for counternarratives, we should be asking how our most deeply held social maps of girls are drawn by efforts between media, commercial, and technological infrastructures that benefit from society being distracted from profiteers' increasingly powerful, entitled acts by having public skepticism, concerns, and regulations directed, instead, at young women.

This research raises the issue of education as it relates to young women's safe involvement in the Internet and in society. To be safe, these teens need better information than they are currently getting. They need more help gaining critical awareness of the commercial interests in play when they are asked to share and be open in spaces of the Internet. They need guidance in recognizing and understanding structural forces of capitalism in social media and in larger life that, in Henry Giroux's words, are "designed to influence, shape, and produce future generations of young people who cannot separate their identities, values, and dreams from the world of commerce, brands, and commodities,"[33] and that, through policies and practices, are implicated in many of the struggles they face in marginal adolescence. As a fish, it is hard to see the water you swim in. As a young woman in US society, it is difficult to understand the systems of power that direct your life. Teens require guidance to gain perspective on the world in which they are tasked to be part of and to try to survive and succeed within. And indeed, these young women went online seeking this guidance.

The call for information and media literacy rings out loudly in our schools and communities. This is needed, especially in forms that go beyond vague or dogmatic directives to address the intricacies of authority, power, and accuracy that shape information and media. But teens' social media–mediated lives require so much more than this to allow them to be familiar with the waters that guide them in certain directions through well-established, hegemonic currents. Young people in the US need critical literacy of the capitalism that directs both US society and their own attentions on- and offline. They need literacy of power structures that come from political economy, labor history, sociology, and cultural studies. They need engagement with critical race theory, queer theory, and gender studies to help contextualize the institutional struggles and experiences they are taught to individualize. They need literacy of civics and law. They need media infrastructure literacy to understand how new media exists through policies, networks, systems, algorithms, and profit. These teens' social media use makes clear that these understandings are lacking and sorely needed by them and by those who care about their well-being. Better understandings of these contributors to involvements and identities are essential if we really do want to keep young women safe in US society.

That said, despite the deafening rhetoric, let's be very clear on this: girls are not the problem here. Protection against vulnerabilities youth face in US society and in media migration will not come from their further individual retooling. While girl-blaming and Millennial-bashing provide rare and valuable opportunities for members of an increasingly divided country to ideologically align, these logics are wrong, and they are, ultimately, very harmful. It is not the youth that need to change. In fact, as girl studies scholar Mary Celeste Kearney writes, despite the fact that today's girls are increasingly active and visibly competent in public spaces, "girls cannot on their own make the world a more respectful place for female youth."[34] What will it take for Americans to see girls—black girls, brown girls, white girls, poor girls, rich girls, queer girls, boy-crazy girls, rural girls, city girls, and all girls in between—as whole, and as "us" rather than as "the other"? What will it take for us to move our anxieties off of our girls to, instead, understand "boys will be boys" ideologies and "locker room talk" excuses, white supremacy, neoliberal plutocracy, and austerity-driven corporate deregulation as narcissistic entitlement unworthy of support or empathy in this country? Solutions to the problems that drive young women to media migration—and to the issues raised by media migration, itself—can only come from addressing the everyday systems of inequity that gain power in maintaining girls' marginality. This is what needs to develop. This is what needs to change.

AN ENDING NOTE

Throughout my research, I have been continually struck by the feelings of powerlessness expressed by my interlocutors, and the ways that they discussed their social media involvements in opposition to the disappointing attitudes and opportunities they experienced offline. The story does not have to be this way. Kids do not have to live in social media, traveling through from site to site chased by parents they feel cannot and will not ever understand them. Young women do not need to import their interests, needs, identities, labor, and hopes to online spaces where they feel they might have a greater chance to be respected.

Like many businesses, social media companies like to purport they are just "giving people what they want" in creating the next online social hangout for "creating" and "sharing." But the teens in this study were not hoping for digital spaces that would give them meaningful involvement and the ability to explore, know, and express identities within wider social contexts that respected and valued them. They were hoping for *any accessible, interesting spaces* to accomplish these things. In their absence offline, they said online worked. In some ways, barriers presented to them by rurality cut them off from physical spaces that might otherwise meet these needs. But in many ways, rurality was not the issue. Even if they had a ride and permission, outside of occasional games and parties and random stop-ins to far-away fast food restaurants or malls, there were few places for teens to hang out or to visit repeatedly in their region that made them feel like they belonged, and like they mattered. But they felt like they mattered and belonged in Facebook and in Twitter.

Despite rhetoric stating that "children are our future," this country has made economic, educational, political, and social decisions that makes life hostile and confusing to those we deem young. Defunded public schools leave little teacher time, attention, and tolerance for student support and guidance and fewer accessible options for extracurricular involvement while a curriculum based around high-stakes standardized testing removes critical thought and expression from the classroom. Such economic and educational choices should be understood as making social media's offer of affirming social interactions and of "creative content production" even more appealing to youth.

Political attitudes legislate the narrow and highly limited information those deemed "young" are given access to in and out of school regarding their identities, their sexuality, and the world around them. Such ideologies fuel girls' interest in social media as an information clearinghouse passing on material on topics that they believe they should know about to address their ontological ambiguities, to stay safe, and to gain access into a wider world.

Youth are given highly monitored social spheres for involvement, including parks zoned to render youth deviant. Strategic about their involvement in safe space, this motivates young women's willingness to look outside of their physical area to carve new spaces for less maligning (read: "less risky") involvement on the Internet.

Young women's struggles, competencies, and needs are regularly denied in the US. Advocates propose solutions through greater youth voice and visibility, ignoring that girls' realities are already loudly voiced and highly visible in striking ways, for example, in well-documented and record-breaking youth poverty, homelessness, and un- and underemployment rates; in threats to Title IX and human rights protections; in soaring student debt; in uncontroversial underrepresentation of women, LGBTQ, and non-white elected officials; in overtaxed teachers and underfunded schools; in adults' preference to blame girls for "distracting" males with their clothing and their presence rather than to address misogynistic logics; and in irrefutable scientific evidence justifying the biological necessity of sexual urges for all at puberty.

Nearly one in two children under the age of 17 are now poor or near poor in the US.[35] They, along with older youth and their parents, continue to suffer from a collapsed housing market that lost family savings and homes, expanded poverty, defunded services, and attributed losses to lower-, working-, and middle-class Americans while advancing new frameworks to protect and enrich others. In 2015, the average student graduated from public college with a record $34,000 in debt, representing a 170% increase from ten years ago, and a rate that is expected to continue growing.[36] Public college tuition and fees more than tripled over the past 20 years.[37] This past decade played host to the lowest employment on record for young people between the ages of 16 and 24 since the US government began collecting statistics, the highest rate of young adults aged 25 to 35 living with parents seen in the past century, and a dramatic documented drop in children's ability to earn more than their parents, especially in the Heartland.[38] During this same time, job stability for US workers—and especially for women and minorities—fell.[39] Teachers working to provide youth direction and new immigrants are commonly scapegoated for Americans' lack of jobs as the labor market is automated, deregulated, and downsized to earn greater rewards for the rich. Girls are told not to walk alone. Despite the clear visibility of these problems, it is young people who are considered entitled in this country.

At the same time, young women are called "whores" while being denied rights to their own bodies and ownership of their sexuality as the term "girl" gets hurled as a jokingly cutting insult in spaces ranging from playgrounds to boardrooms by those encouraged to believe females exist for their pleasure. African American youth are suspended, incarcerated, and killed by police at alarming rates, and they are regularly blamed for this violence. Regardless of massive disinformation campaigns, there is ample awareness of everyday hierarchies that continually map girls as lesser in this country, despite their qualities. And just below the hopefulness girls held for proving themselves online lie grim knowledge that there was only so much they could do against these forces. As Annie stated: "Sometimes, it don't matter what you do. People just want to think you're bad." Slanderous misrepresentation—and other hegemonic "fake news"—is old news to marginalized girls.

The girls in this study took on media migration to try to reclaim and rewrite social understandings that devalue them offline, to have ways to meaningfully contribute to the world they are part of, and to find greater justice. However, visibility and voice, alone, will not lessen girls' oppression. Girls' marginalization in US society persists despite individual attempts to game social visibility online, especially when these attempts diffuse shared frustrations and redirect attention and actions to ensure social maintenance. Additionally, considering the plethora of media-circulated images of selfie-taking female Millennials in service of discourses painting them as narcissistically self-absorbed and otherwise unworthy of support, it would not be hard to argue that more visibility is not always more desirable. Marginality also happens regardless of the loudness or clarity of girls' voices. Refuting the belief that girls struggle because they "lose their voice" in adolescence, Dawn Currie, Dierdre Kelly, and Shauna Pomerantz look to wider contexts in arguing that girls, instead, join patriarchal systems that ensure they are not listened to.[40] Without doubt, receiving rights takes far more than being seen or being heard by those in power. It takes addressing systemic variables that deny groups power and that benefit from their subordination, to start. Media migration assists girls in a number of ways, but it certainly does not limit—or even identify—those who profit from their marginality. In fact, as media–migrating girls are urged to concern themselves with social acceptance, sensationalism, and artificial notions of privacy while continuing to see their parents as their main oppressors in life, quite the opposite is true.

Youth media scholar Sonia Livingstone writes that "[s]ocietal decisions downplay children's rights to participate fully in their communities."[41] Indeed, these teens' inability to feel meaningful and relevant served as primary motivation to their media migrations. Absent other options, teens' marginal conditions inspired them into informal economies where they felt more able to negotiate and better their offline situation and standing. As a society, Americans are urged to look away from structural factors to individual analyses that blame girls for their failings and label them out-of-control, reckless, and selfish for wanting rights. This cultural myopia makes girls unsafe both on- and offline. And in locating risk in girls rather than in the wider systems these teens find themselves part of as marginal citizens, it ensures that US girlhood, adolescence, and society will continue to be risky and reckless with its youth, as well.

This research finds that offline conditions created by people, policies, and perceptions[42] directed these young women's involvements and identities to and through media migration. As Jean Baudrillard writes, "We have to describe these things as we see and experience them, never forgetting, in their splendor and profusion, that they are *the product of a human activity* and are dominated not by natural ecological laws, but by the laws of exchange value."[43] The point again here: there are few things "natural" about US adolescence, girlhood, or media migration. And it doesn't have to be like this.

NOTES

1. A 2015 analysis of the US Bureau of Justice Statistics finds that adolescents experienced a record low in violent crime in 2014 with rates of victimization at only one-sixth of the victimization rate in the mid-1990s. "Violent Trends Victimization," *Child Trends* accessed from https://www.childtrends.org/?indicators=violent-crime-victimization.

2. Center for Disease Control and Prevention, "Morbidity and Mortality Weekly Report: Youth Risk Behavior Surveillance—United States, 2016," cdc.gov (June 10, 2016), accessed September 22, 2017 https://www.cdc.gov/healthyyouth/data/yrbs/pdf/2015/ss6506_updated.pdf.

3. Mary L. Gray, *Out in the Country: Youth, Media, and Queer Visibility*, (New York: New York University, 2009) 14.

4. Mark Zuckerberg, "Bringing the World Closer Together," *Facebook* (June 22, 2017), accessed June 27, 2017 https://www.facebook.com/notes/mark-zuckerberg/bringing-the-world-closer-together/10154944663901634/.

5. For example, in 2013, Facebook's Data Use policy stated: "We use the information we receive about you in connection with the services and features we provide to you and other users like your friends, our partners, the advertisers that purchase ads on the site, and the developers that build the games, applications, and websites you use. . . . Granting us this permission not only allows us to provide Facebook as it exists today, but it also allows us to provide you with innovative features and services we *develop in the future* that use the informa-

tion we receive about you in new ways." [emphasis added] There is no mention of future in the March 2017 current Data Use policy. Rather, this section begins with: "We are passionate about creating engaging and customized experiences for people. We use all of the information we have to help us provide and support our Services." https://www.facebook.com/about/priva-cy/your-info.

6. Robert McChesney, *Digital Disconnect: How Capitalism is Turning the Internet Against Democracy* (New York: The New Press, 2013) 4.

7. Ibid., 13

8. Alex Hern, "Facebook T&Cs Introduced 'Research' Policy Months After Emotion Study," *The Guardian* (July 1, 2014), accessed March 10, 2017, https://www.theguardian.com/technology/2014/jul/01/facebook-data-policy-research-emotion-study.

9. Anthony Giddens, *Modernity and Self-Identity: Self and Society in the Late Modern Age* (Cambridge: Polity Press, 1991) 3.

10. Hoofnagle, King, and Turow, "How Different are Young."

11. Victor Turner, *The Ritual Process: Structure and Anti-Structure* (New York: Aldine Transaction, 1969).

12. Laura Brandimarte, Alessandro Acquisti, and George Loewenstein, "Misplaced Confi-dences: Privacy and the Control Paradox" *Social Psychological and Personality Science* 4, no. 3 (January 30, 2015) 346.

13. See Rebecca MacKinnon's *Consent of the Networked: The Worldwide Struggle For Internet Freedom.* New York: Basic Books, 2012.

14. Robert McChesney, *Digital Disconnect*, 11.

15. For example, following in Lisa Nakamura's poignant examination of the false promises of incorporeal equality issued by "Anthem," the first Internet commercial for MCI discussed in her chapter "'Where Do You Want to Go Today?': Cybernetic Tourism, the Internet, and Transnationality," in Beth E. Kolko, Lisa Nakamura, and Gilbert B. Rodman's (Eds.), *Race in Cyberspace* (New York: Routledge, 2000), even the well-circulated offers made more recently by Internet service provider AT&T for users to be "unlimited" online have been found to be untrue, and to be "duping wireless customers." See Wendy Davis "Comcast, Others Side Against AT&T in Throttling Battle," *MediaPost* (June 27, 2017). Accessed July 2, 2017, https://www.mediapost.com/publications/article/303559/comcast-other-broadband-providers-side-against-at.html.

16. "Millennials Overtake Baby Boomers as America's Largest Generation." *Pew Research Center* (April 26, 2016). Accessed September 23, 2017. http://www.pewresearch.org/fact-tank/2016/04/25/millennials-overtake-baby-boomers/.

17. https://www.census.gov/newsroom/press-releases/2015/cb15-113.html.

18. Richard Fry, "For the First Time in Modern Era, Living with Parents Edges Out Other Living Arrangements for 18- to 34-Year Olds," *Pew Research Center* (May 24, 2016), ac-cessed September 27 2017 http://www.pewsocialtrends.org/2016/05/24/for-first-time-in-mod-ern-era-living-with-parents-edges-out-other-living-arrangements-for-18-to-34-year-olds/.

19. Anthony Cilluffo and D'vera Cohn, "10 Demographic Trends Shaping the U.S and the World in 2017," *Pew Research Center* (April 27, 2017), accessed September 2, 2017 http://www.pewresearch.org/fact-tank/2017/04/27/10-demographic-trends-shaping-the-u-s-and-the-world-in-2017/.

20. Angela McRobbie and Sarah Thornton, "Rethinking 'Moral Panic' for Multi-Mediated Social Worlds," *The British Journal of Sociology* 46, no. 4 (1995) 572.

21. See Stanley Cohen, "Folk Devils and moral Panic: The Creation of Mods and Rockers" (New York: Paladin, 1972); Gewndolyn Mink and Rickie Solinger, *Welfare: A Documentary History of U.S. Policy and Politics* (New York: NYU Press, 2003).

22. See Michelle Alexander, *The New Jim Crow: Mass Incarceration in the Age of Color-blindedness* (New York: The New Press, 2014); Dorothy Roberts, *Killing the Black Body* (New York: Vantage Books, 1997).

23. Social media teems with made-up stories masquerading as news articles documenting events such as this story about a Facebook breakup caused by a young women "stupidly" getting a tattoo of a very new boyfriend (http://www.happyplace.com/14442/awful-tattoo-leads-to-amazing-facebook-breakup), condescendingly sexist Twitter micropublications such

as Shit Girls Say (https://twitter.com/shitgirlssay. This Twitter micropublication has also been turned into a book), low-budget, pornography-inspired American Apparel clothing advertisements (http://www.dailymail.co.uk/femail/article-2325474/American-Apparel-branded-sexist-degrading-ads-unisex-shirt-featuring-half-naked-women-g-strings-fully-clothed-men.html) the vacuously attention-seeking "Annoying Facebook Girl" meme (http://memegenerator.net/Annoying-Facebook-Girl), and like-farming, female-on-female shaming postings such as the "Hey Girls, Did You Know" meme and Facebook page.

24. U.S. Census Bureau, "Millennials Outnumber Baby Boomers and Are Far More Diverse, Census Bureau Reports," (June 25, 2015), accessed September 2, 2017 https://www.census.gov/newsroom/press-releases/2015/cb15-113.html.

25. For example, those within the Millennial generation struggle with soaring college costs, exposure to early-interest-accruing unsubsidized school loans, overfilled classrooms, and overworked adults with little time to provide guidance as public school teachers to fight the deprofessionalism and disinvestment in education. At the same time, the job market young workers face continues to be hobbled, offering far fewer stable options than in the past. Specifically, in 2009, young people between the ages of 18 and 24 had the lowest rate of employment on record since the US government began collecting these statistics in 1947. See: Paul Taylor, Kim Parker, Rakesh Kochhar, Richard Fry, Carey Funk, Eileen Patten, and Seth Motel, "Young, Underemployed, and Optimistic: Coming of Age, Slowly, in a Tough Economy," *Pew Research Center* (February 9 2012), accessed November 11, 2016, http://www.pewsocialtrends.org/files/2012/02/young-underemployed-and-optimistic.pdf. It is also occurring at a time when media headlines pass on projections about that could both provoke and distract the much wider economic and geopolitical anxieties that have gripped the country to, instead, scapegoat youth: "Millennials will comprise more than one in three of adult Americans by 2020" writes the Brookings Institute. "Millennials to take over by 2025," reads a *Hartford Business Journal* headline. Another from the *New York Times*: "What happens when Millennials run the workplace?"

26. Edward Bernays, "The Engineering of Consent," *The Annals of the American Academy* 250, no. 1 (March, 1947) 113.

27. US Department of Labor (2011). *The Fair Labor Standards Act Of 1938, As Amended*, (p. 4) https://www.dol.gov/whd/regs/statutes/FairLaborStandAct.pdf. There are interesting variances based on mining and manufacturing, and a long trajectory of attempts before FLSA. For example, according to the Bureau of Labor Statistics, the first child labor law was passed in 1936 in Massachusetts, requiring those under the age of 15 to attend three months of schooling. This effort spread to most other states long before. Also, by 1913, most states outlawed factory workers under the age of 14. https://www.bls.gov/opub/rylf/pdf/chapter2.pdf. Other legislative acts were passed in 1918 and 1922 and overturned as unconstitutional before the FLSA was ratified in 1941.

28. While granting protections to those deemed children, child labor laws also formalized those who were to be considered children by protecting US jobs for certain workers. See research by Gulotta, 1983; Lesko, 2012; Schlegel, 1995.

29. Echoing the 1909 Triangle Shirtwaist tragedy. Also, Bernays, "Engineering of Consent"; Lenhart, "Teens, Social Media."

30. Jeffrey Arnett, "Emerging Adulthood: A Theory of Development from the Late Teens Through the Twenties," *American Psychologist* 55, no. 5 (2000).

31. See, for example, Suman Verma, Deepali Sharma, and Reed Larson, "School Stress in India: Effects on Time and Daily Emotions," *International Journal of Behavioral Development* 26 (2002).

32. Emmy E. Werner and Ruth S. Smith, *Journeys from Childhood to Midlife: Risk, Resilience, and Recovery* (New York, Cornell University Press, 2001); Rutger C. M. Engels, Catrin Finkenauer, Wim H. J. Meeus, and Maja Dekovic, "Parental Attachment and Adolescents' Emotional Adjustment: The Associations with Social Skills and Relational Competence," *Journal of Counseling Psychology* 48, no. 4 (2001); John Borkowsky, Sharon Ramey, and Marie Bristol-Power, eds., *Parenting and the Child's World: Influences on Academic, Intellectual, and Social-Emotional Development* (Mahwah: Erlbaum, 2002).

33. Henry A. Giroux, "Youth in the Empire of Consumption: Beyond the Pedagogy of Commodification," *JAC* 29, no. 4 (2009) 705.

34. Mary Celeste Kearney, "Coalescing: The Development of Girls' Studies." *NWSA Journal* 21, no. 1 (2009): 22.

35. http://www.nccp.org/publications/pub_1170.html.

36. Young immigrants and teachers are blamed for Americans' lack of jobs as the labor market is quietly automated to earn greater profits for the rich.

37. https://trends.collegeboard.org/college-pricing/figures-tables/tuition-fees-room-board-over-time.

38. Paul Taylor, Kim Parker, Rakesh Kochhar, Richard Fry, Carey Funk, Eileen Patten, and Seth Motel, "Young, Underemployed, and Optimistic: Coming of Age, Slowly, in a Tough Economy," *Pew Research Center* (February 9 2012), accessed November 11, 2016 http://www.pewsocialtrends.org/files/2012/02/young-underemployed-and-optimistic.pdf; https://www.bls.gov/opub/ted/2010/ted_20100903.htm; https://www.bls.gov/opub/ted/2011/ted_20110826.htm; Richard Fry, "It's Become More Common for Young Adults to Live at Home—and for Longer Stretches," *Pew Research Center* (May 5, 2017), accessed September 12, 2017 http://www.pewresearch.org/fact-tank/2017/05/05/its-becoming-more-common-for-young-adults-to-live-at-home-and-for-longer-stretches/; "For the First Time in Modern Era, Living with Parents Edges Out Other Living Arrangements for 18- to 34-Year Olds," *Pew Research Center* (May 24, 2016), accessed September 27 2017 http://www.pewsocialtrends.org/2016/05/24/for-first-time-in-modern-era-living-with-parents-edges-out-other-living-arrangements-for-18-to-34-year-olds/; Raj Chetty, David Grusky, Maximilian Hell, Nathaniel Hendren, Robert Manduca, and Jimmy Narang, "The Fading American Dream: Trends in Absolute Income Mobility Since 1940," *Science* (April 24, 2017), accessed April 26, 2017 from http://science.sciencemag.org/content/early/2017/04/21/science.aal4617.full.

39. The Bureau of Labor Statistics no longer tracks contingent labor. However, a non-peer-reviewed study by the National Bureau of Economic Research found the proportion of Americans working temporary or contract jobs jumped from 10.6% in 2005 to 15.8% in 2015, and with women more likely to be doing this work. See Lawrence F. Katz and Alan B. Kreuger, "The Rise and Nature of Alternative Work Arrangements in the United States, 1995–2015," accessed September 2, 2017 http://www.nber.org/papers/w22667.

40. Driscoll, "From Girlhood."

41. Livingstone, *Children and the Internet*: 230.

42. In other words, the important "relations between people." Donald MacKenzie and Judy Wajcman, *The Social Shaping of Technology* (Philadelphia, PA: Open University Press, 2005): xiv.

43. Jean Baudrillard, *The Consumer Society* (Los Angeles: Sage, 1970): 6.

Bibliography

Aapola, Sinikka, Marnina Gonick, and Anita Harris. *Young Femininity: Girlhood, Power and Social Change*. New York: Palgrave Macmillan, 2005.

Alexander, Michelle. *The New Jim Crow: Mass Incarceration in the Age of Colorblindedness*. New York: The New Press, 2014.

American Psychological Association Task Force. "Report of the APA Task Force on the Sexualization of Girls." apa.org. 2007. Retrieved from http://www.apa.org/pi/wpo/sexualization.html.

Arnett, Jeffrey. "Emerging Adulthood: A Theory of Development from the Late Teens Through the Twenties." *American Psychologist* 55, no. 5 (2000): 469–480.

Bailey, D. "Shifting Twitter Demographics: Twitter Less About Teen Drama, More About World Politics," *The Content Standard* (January 14, 2013). Accessed March 23, 2017. https://www.skyword.com/contentstandard/marketing/shifting-twitter-demographics-twitter-less-about-teen-drama-more-about-world-politics/.

Balsamo, Anne. *Technologies of the Gendered Body: Reading Cyborg Women*. Durham, NC: Duke University Press, 1996.

Barlow, John Perry. *A Declaration of the Independence of Cyberspace*. Davos: Electronic Frontier Foundation, 1996. Accessed October 5, 2016. https://projects.eff.org/~barlow/Declaration-Final.html.

Baudrillard, Jean. *The Consumer Society*. Los Angeles: Sage, 1970.

Bearden, William O., and Randall L. Rose, "Attention to Social Comparison Information: An Individual Difference Factor Affecting Consumer Conformity." *Journal of Consumer Research* 16, no. 4 (1990): 461–471.

Beller, Jonathan. *The Cinematic Mode of Production: Attention Economy and the Society of the Spectacle*. Hanover: Dartmouth College Press, 2006.

Bernays, Edward. "The Engineering of Consent." *The Annals of the American Academy* 250, no. 1 (March 1947): 113–120.

Best, Amy L. *Representing Youth: Methodological Issues in Critical Youth Studies*. New York: NYU Press, 2007.

Bilton, Nick. "Facebook Changes Privacy Settings, Again." *New York Times* (December 12, 2012). Accessed September 8, 2017. http://bits.blogs.nytimes.com/2012/12/12/facebook-changes-privacy-settings-again/.

Blakeley, Kiri. "The Justin Bieber Scam." *Forbes* (October 3, 2011). Accessed June 2, 2017 http://www.forbes.com/sites/kiriblakeley/2011/10/03/the-justin-bieber-twitter-scam/.

Bogira, Steve. "Parodies Lost: Why Satire Must be Banned from the Internet." *The Chicago Reader* (December 10, 2012). Accessed September 12, 2017. http://www.chicagoreader.

com/Bleader/archives/2012/12/10/parodies-lost-why-satire-must-be-banned-from-the-internet.

Borkowsky, John, Sharon Ramey, and Marie Bristol-Power, eds. *Parenting and the Child's World: Influences on Academic, Intellectual, and Social-Emotional Development*, Mahwah: Erlbaum, 2002.

boyd, danah. "Why Youth (Heart) Social Network Sites: The Role of Networked Publics in Teenage Social Life" In D. Buckingham (Ed.), *MacArthur Foundation Series on Digital Learning—Youth, Identity, and Digital Media*. Cambridge: MIT Press, 2007. 119–142.

———. "Social Steganography: Learning to Hide in Plain Site," *Zephoria*, April 23, 2010. Accessed January 10, 2017 from http://www.zephoria.org/thoughts/archives/2010/08/23/social-steganography-learning-to-hide-in-plain-sight.html.

———. *It's Complicated: The Social Lives of Networked Teens*. New Haven: Yale, 2014.

boyd, danah and Eszter Hargittai. "Facebook Privacy Settings: Who Cares?" *First Monday* 15, no. 8 (2010). Accessed May 2, 2017. http://firstmonday.org/article/view/3086/2589.

boyd, danah m., and Nicole B. Ellison. "Social Network Sites: Definition, History, and Scholarship." *Journal of Computer-Mediated Communication* 13, no. 1 (2007): 210–30.

Bradford, Clare, and Mavis Reimer, eds. *Girls, Texts, Cultures*. Waterloo, Ontario, Canada: WLU Press, 2015.

Bradford, Clare, and Mavis Reimer. "Girls, Texts, Cultures: Cross-Disciplinary Dialogues." In Clare Bradford and Mavis Reimer, eds., *Girls, Texts, Cultures*. Waterloo, Ontario, Canada: WLU Press, 2015: 1–13.

Brandimarte, Laura, Alessandro Acquisti, and George Loewenstein. "Misplaced Confidences: Privacy and the Control Paradox." *Social Psychological and Personality Science* 4, no. 3 (January 30, 2015): 340–347.

Bureau of Labor Statistics, *Employment and Unemployment Among Youth Summary*, August 17, 2016. Accessed September 22, 2016 from https://www.bls.gov/news.release/youth.nr0.htm.

Caoili, Eric. "CityVille has the Largest Facebook Audience Ever." *Gamasutra*. Last modified January 31, 2011. https://www.gamasutra.com/view/news/32231/City-Ville_Has_Largest_Facebook_Audience_Ever.php.

Cassell, Justine and Meg Cramer. "High Tech or High Risk: Moral Panics about Girls Online." In T. McPherson (Ed.), *Digital Youth, Innovation, and the Unexpected*. Cambridge: MIT Press, 2007: 53–76.

Center for Disease Control and Prevention. "Morbidity and Mortality Weekly Report: Youth Risk Behavior Surveillance—United States, 2016." cdc.gov (June 10, 2016). Accessed September 22, 2017. https://www.cdc.gov/healthyyouth/data/yrbs/pdf/2015/ss6506_updated.pdf.

Chetty, Raj, David Grusky, Maximilian Hell, Nathaniel Hendren, Robert Manduca, and Jimmy Narang, "The Fading American Dream: Trends in Absolute Income Mobility Since 1940," *Science* (April 24, 2017). Accessed April 26, 2017 from http://science.sciencemag.org/content/early/2017/04/21/science.aal4617.full.

Chou, Hui-Tzu Grace and Nicholas Edge. "They are happier and having better lives than I am": the impact of using Facebook on perceptions of others' lives. *Cyberpsychology, Behavior, and Social Networking* 15 no 2 (2012): 117–121.

Cilluffo, Anthony and D'vera Cohn. "10 Demographic Trends Shaping the U.S and the World in 2017." *Pew Research Center* (April 27, 2017). Accessed September 2, 2017 http://www.pewresearch.org/fact-tank/2017/04/27/10-demographic-trends-shaping-the-u-s-and-the-world-in-2017.

Clarke, John, Stuart Hall, Tony Jefferson, and Brian Roberts, "Subcultures, Cultures and Class," In Stuart Hall and Tony Jefferson (Eds.), *Resistance Through Rituals: Youth Subculture in Post-War Britain*. New York: Routledge, 1975. 9–74.

Cohen, Phil. *Rethinking the Youth Question*. London: Macmillan, 1997.

Cohen, Stanley. *Folk Devils and Moral Panics: The Creation of the Mods and Rockers*. New York: Paladin, 1972.

Collier, Laura. "Incarceration Nation." *American Psychological Association.* Accessed October 31, 2017. http://www.apa.org/monitor/2014/10/incarceration.aspx; http://www.apcca.org/uploads/10th_Edition_2013.pdf.

Common Sense Media. "Children, Teens, Media, and Body Image." *Common Sense Media,* January 21, 2015. Accessed October 2, 2017. https://www.commonsensemedia.org/research/children-teens-media-and-body-image.

Conley, Chris. "New Facebook Search Means It's Time to Review Your Privacy Settings (Again)." *ACLU* (January 13, 2013). Accessed June 2, 2017 http://www.aclu.org/blog/technology-and-liberty/new-facebook-search-means-its-time-review-your-privacy-settings-again.

Considine, Austin. "Buying Their Way to Twitter Fame." *The New York Times* (August 2, 2012). Accessed June 2, 2017. http://www.nytimes.com/2012/08/23/fashion/twitter-followers-for-sale.html.

Corrigan, Rose. "Making Meaning of Megan's Law." *Law & Social Inquiry* 31, no. 2 (2006): 267–312.

Côté, James and Anton Allahar. *Generation on Hold: Coming of Age in the Late Twentieth Century.* New York: NYU Press, 1994.

Crawford, Mary and Danielle Popp. "Sexual Double Standards: A Review and Methodological Critique of Two Decades of Research," *Journal of Sex Research,* 40 (2003): 13–26.

Crenshaw, Kimberle. "Mapping the Margins: Intersectionality, Identity Politics, and Violence Against Women of Color." *Stanford Law Review* 43, no. 6 (July, 1991): 1241–1299.

Crocker, Jennifer. "The Costs of Seeking Self-Esteem." *Journal of Social Issues* 58 (2002): 597–615.

Crow, Nic and Simon Bradford. "Hanging out in Runescape: Identity, Work and Leisure in the Virtual Playground," *Children's Geographies* 4, no. 3 (2006): 331–346.

Curry, Dawn H. "From Girlhood, Girls, to Girl Studies." In Clare Bradford and Mavis Reimer, eds., *Girls, Texts, Cultures.* Waterloo, Ontario, Canada: WLU Press, 2015: 17–35.

Daniels, Jessie. "Cloaked Websites: Propaganda, Cyber-Racism and Epistemology in the Digital Era," *New Media & Society* 11, no 5 (2009): 659–683.

Davis, Wendy. "Comcast, Others Side Against AT&T in Throttling Battle." *MediaPost* (June 27, 2017). Accessed July 2, 2017. https://www.mediapost.com/publications/article/303559/comcast-other-broadband-providers-side-against-at.html.

Delgado, Richard, and Jean Stefancic. *Critical Race Theory: An Introduction.* New York: NYU Press.

Duncan, Maeve. "Online Harassment." *Pew Research Center* (October 22, 2014). Accessed March 12, 2015 from http://www.pewinternet.org/2014/10/22/online-harassment/.

Durham, Meenakshi Gigi. *The Lolita Effect: The Media Sexualization of Young Girls and Five Keys to Fixing it.* New York: Overlook TP, 2009.

Dyson, Esther, George Gilder, George Keyworth, and Alvin Toffler. "Cyberspace and the American Dream: A Magna Carta for the Knowledge Age." *Release,* 1, no. 2 (1994).

Egan, R. Danielle, and Gail L. Hawkes. "Producing the Prurient Through the Pedagogy of Purity: Childhood Sexuality and the Social Purity Movement." *Journal of Historical Sociology,* 20 no 4 (2007): 443–461.

———. "Endangered Girls and Incendiary Objects: Unpacking the Discourse on Sexualization." *Sexuality & Culture* 12, no. 4 (2008): 291–311.

Einstein, Mara. *Black Ops Advertising.* New York: OR Books, 2016.

Engels, Rutger C. M., Catrin Finkenauer, Wim H. J, Meeus, and Maja Dekovic. "Parental Attachment and Adolescents' Emotional Adjustment: The Associations with social Skills and Relational Competence." *Journal of Counseling Psychology* 48, no. 4 (2001): 428–439.

Erikson, Erik. H. *Identity: Youth and Crisis.* New York: W. W. Norton and Co., 1968.

Eslami, Motahhare, Aimee Rickman, Kristen Vaccaro, Amirhossein Aleyasen, Andy Vyong, Karrie Karahalios, Kevin Hamilton, and Christian Sandvig. "I Always Assumed That I Wasn't Really That Close To [Her]: Reasoning About Invisible Algorithms in News Feeds." *Proceedings of the 33rd Annual ACM Conference on Human Factors in Computing Systems* (2015): 153–162.

Facebook. "Our Mission." Accessed October 31, 2017. https://newsroom.fb.com/company-info

Facebook, "Statements of Rights and Responsibilities," Accessed October 31, 2017 https://www.facebook.com/legal/terms.

Facebook. "Stats." Accessed October 31, 2017. https://newsroom.fb.com/company-info.

Fallon, Kevin. "Fooled by 'The Onion': 9 Most Embarrassing Fails." *The Daily Beast* (November 27, 2012). Accessed September 12, 2017. http://www.thedailybeast.com/articles/2012/09/29/fooled-by-the-onion-8-most-embarrassing-fails.html.

Fallows, Deborah. "How Women and Men Use the Internet." *Pew Research Center* (December 28, 2005). Accessed March 12, 2015 from http://www.pewinternet.org/2005/12/28/how-women-and-men-use-the-internet/2.

Festinger, Leon. "A Theory of Social Comparison Processes." *Human Relations* 7 (1954): 117–140.

Fleetwood, Nicole. "Busing it in the City: Black Youth, Performance, and Public Transit," *TDR: The Drama Review* 48, no 2 (2004): 33–48.

Fry, Richard, "It's Become More Common for Young Adults to Live at Home—and for Longer Stretches," *Pew Research Center* (May 5, 2017), accessed September 12, http://www.pewresearch.org/fact-tank/2017/05/05/its-becoming-more-common-for-young-adults-to-live-at-home-and-for-longer-stretches/.

———. "Millennials surpass Gen Xers as the Largest Generation in the U.S. Labor Force." *Pew Research Center* (May 11, 2015). Accessed September 23, 2017. http://www.pewresearch.org/fact-tank/2015/05/11/millennials-surpass-gen-xers-as-the-largest-generation-in-u-s-labor-force.

———. "Millennials Overtake Baby Boomers as America's Largest Generation." *Pew Research Center* (April 26, 2016). Accessed September 23, 2017. http://www.pewresearch.org/fact-tank/2016/04/25/millennials-overtake-baby-boomers/.

———. "For the First Time in Modern Era, Living with Parents Edges Out Other Living Arrangements for 18- to 34-Year Olds." *Pew Research Center* (May 24, 2016). Accessed September 27, 2017. http://www.pewsocialtrends.org/2016/05/24/for-first-time-in-modern-era-living-with-parents-edges-out-other-living-arrangements-for-18-to-34-year-olds/.

Gandy, Oscar H. *The Panoptic Sort.* Oxford: Westview Press, 1989.

Geertz, Clifford. *The Interpretation of Cultures.* New York: Basic, 1973.

Giddens, Anthony. *The Constitution of Society: Outline of the Theory of Structuration.* Berkeley: University of California Press, 1984.

———. *Modernity and Self-Identity: Self and Society in the Late Modern Age.* Cambridge: Polity Press, 1991.

Gil, Paul. "What Exactly is 'Twitter'? What is 'Tweeting'?" (2012) Accessed from http://netforbeginners.about.com/od/internet101/f/What-Exactly-Is-Twitter.htm.

Giordano, Caterina, Joanne V. Wood and John L. Michela. "Depressive Personality Styles, Dysphoria, and Social Comparisons in Everyday Life." *Journal of Personality and Social Psychology* 76 (2000): 438–451.

Giroux, Henry A. "Youth in the Empire of Consumption: Beyond the Pedagogy of Commodification," *JAC* 29, no. 4 (2009): 691–756.

Gittens, Joan. *Poor Relations: The Children of the State of Illinois, 1818–1990.* Urbana, IL: University of Illinois Press, 1994.

Gray, Mary L. *Out in the Country: Youth, Media, and Queer Visibility.* New York: New York University, 2009.

Grosser, Benjamin. "Facebook Demetricator." Accessed October 31, 2017. http://bengrosser.com/projects/facebook-demetricator/.

Hanson, Kathy. "Eagles Shot in State, Area; Fake Video May Be Cause." *Sawyer County Record* (January 31, 2013). Accessed October 20, 2107. http://www.apg-wi.com/sawyer_county_record/news/eagles-shot-in-state-area-fake-video-may-be-cause/article_6f8a4128-a5d8-5969-abf2-9249c9196362.html.

Harden, Jeni. "There's No Place Like Home: The Public/Private Distinction in Children's Theorizing of Risk and Safety." *Childhood* 7, no. 1 (2000): 43–59.

Hargittai, Eszter. "Digital Na(t)ives? Variation in Internet Skills and Uses Among Members of the 'Net Generation.'" *Sociological Inquiry* 80, no. 1 (2010): 92–113.

Hargittai, Eszter, Lindsay Fullerton, Ericka Menchen-Trevino, and Kristin Yates Thomas. "Trust Online: Young Adults' Evaluation of Web Content." *International Journal of Communication* 4 (2010). Accessed May 12, 2017. http://ijoc.org/index.php/ijoc/article/view/636.

Hauben, Michael, Rhonda Hauben, and Thomas Truscott. *Netizens: On the History and Impact of Usenet and the Internet.* Hoboken: Wiley-IEEE Computer Society Press, 1997.

Hebdige, Dick. *Subculture: The Meaning of Style.* New York: Routledge, 1987.

Herman, Edward S., and Noam Chomsky. *Manufacturing Consent: The Political Economy of the Mass Media.* New York: Pantheon, 1988.

Hern, Alex. "Facebook T&Cs Introduced 'Research' Policy Months After Emotion Study." *The Guardian* (July 1, 2014). Accessed March 10, 2017. https://www.theguardian.com/technology/2014/jul/01/facebook-data-policy-research-emotion-study.

Hess, Amanda. "Why Women Aren't Welcome on the Internet." *Pacific Standard* (January 6, 2014). Accessed March 12, 2016 from https://psmag.com/social-justice/women-arent-welcome-internet-72170#.wa0uq14bt.

Hirschman, A. O. *Exit, Voice, and Loyalty: Responses to Decline in Firms, Organizations, and States.* Cambridge: Harvard University Press, 1970.

Hockenson, Lauren. "Fake Twitter Followers: An Easy Game, But Not Worth the Risk." *The Next Web* (December 15, 2012). Accessed June 2, 2017. http://thenextweb.com/twitter/2012/12/15/fake-followers-an-easy-game-but-not-worth-the-risk/.

Hoofnagle, Chris Jay, Jennifer King, Su Li, and Joseph Turow. "How Different are Young Adults From Older Adults When it Comes to Information Privacy Attitudes and Policies?" (2010). Accessed September 17, 2017. http://repository.upenn.edu/cgi/viewcontent.cgi?article=1413&context=asc_papers.

hooks, bell. *Black Looks: Race and Representation.* New York: Random House, 1981.

Hoy, Mariea Grubbs, and George Milne. "Gender Differences in Privacy-Related Measures for Young Adult Facebook Users." *Journal of Interactive Advertising* 10, no. 2 (2010):28–45.

Hugues, Sampasa-Kanyinga and Lewis F Rosamund. "Frequent Use of Social Networking Sites is Associated with Poor Psychological Functioning Among Children and Adolescents." *Cyberpsychology, Behavior, and Social Networking* 18, no. 7 (2015): 380–385.

Institute for Educational Sciences: National Center for Education Statistics. "Tuition Costs of Colleges and Universities." *National Center for Education Statistics.* Accessed October 31, 2017. https://nces.ed.gov/fastfacts/display.asp?id=76.

Irving, Janice M. *Talk about Sex: The Battle Over Sex Education in the United States.* Berkeley: University of California Press, 2001.

Ito, Mizuko, Baumer, Sonja, Bittanti, Matteo, boyd, danah, Cody, Rachel, Herr-Stephenson, Becky. . . . and Tripp, Lisa, eds. *Hanging Out, Messing Around, and Geeking Out: Kids Living and Learning with New Media.* Cambridge, MA: MIT Press, 2010.

Jagatic, Tom N., Johnson, Nathaniel A., Jakobsson, Markus, and Menczer, Filippo. "Social Phishing." *Communications of the ACM* 50, no. 10 (October 2007): 94–100.

Jenkins, Philip. *Moral Panic: Changing Concepts of the Child Molester in Modern America.* New Haven, CT: Yale University Press, 1998.

Jiang, Yang, Maribel R. Granja, and Heather Koball, "Basic Facts about Low-Income Children." National Center for Children in Poverty (January 2017), accessed March 10, 2017 from http://www.nccp.org/publications/pub_1170.html.

Katz, Lawrence F. and Alan B. Kreuger. "The Rise and Nature of Alternative Work Arrangements in the United States, 1995–2015." Accessed September 2, 2017. http://www.nber.org/papers/w22667.

Kearney, Mary Celeste. "Coalescing: The Development of Girls' Studies." *NWSA Journal* 21, no. 1 (2009): 1–28.

Kirkpatrick, David. *The Facebook Effect: The Story of the Company that is Connecting the World.* New York: Simon and Schuster, 2010. 199.

Knupfer, Anne Meis. "The Chicago Detention Home." In *A Noble Social Experiment? The First Hundred Years of the Cook County Juvenile Court, 1899–1999.* Edited by Gwen Hoerr McNamee, 52–53. Chicago, IL: Chicago Bar Association, 1999.

Kolko, Beth E., Lisa Nakamura, and Gilbert B. Rodman, eds. *Race in Cyberspace*. New York: Routledge, 2000.

Kosinski, Michael, David Stillwell, and Theore Graepel. "Private Traits and Attributes are Predictable from Digital Records of Human Behavior." *Proceedings of the National Academy of Sciences* 110, no. 15 (2013): 5802–5805.

Kosner, Anthony Wing. "Facebook is Recycling Your Likes to Promote Stories You've Never Seen To All Your Friends," *Forbes* (January 21, 2013). Accessed June 2, 2017. http://www.forbes.com/sites/anthonykosner/2013/01/21/facebook-is-recycling-your-likes-to-promote-stories-youve-never-seen-to-all-your-friends.

Kreager, Derek, Jeremy Staff, Robin Gauthier, Eva Lefkowitz, and Mark Feinberg. "The Double Standard at Sexual Debut: Gender, Sexual Behavior and Adolescent Peer Acceptance." *Sex Roles* 75, no. 7–8 (2016): 377–392.

Larson, Reed. "The Future of Adolescence: Lengthening Ladders to Adulthood." *The Futurist* (2002, November/December): 16–20.

Larson, Reed, Suzanne Wilson, and Aimee Rickman. "Adolescence Across Place and Time: Globalization and the Changing Pathways to Adulthood." In *Handbook of Adolescent Psychology* (2nd Ed.), edited by Richard Lerner and Laurence Steinberg, 297–330. New York: Wiley, 2009.

Lee, Everett S. *A Theory of Migration*. Philadelphia, University of Pennsylvania, 1966.

Lenhart, Amanda. "Teens, Social Media & Technology Overview 2015." *Pew Research Center*, April 2015. Accessed January 3, 2017. http://www.pewinternet.org/files/2015/04/PI_TeensandTech_Update2015_0409151.pdf.

Lenhart, Amanda and Mary Madden, "Social Networking Sites and Teens." *Pew Research Center*, 2007. Accessed January 3, 2017 from: http://www.pewinternet.org/Reports/2007/Social-Networking-Websites-and-Teens.aspx.

Lenhart, Amanda, Lee Rainie, and Oliver Lewis, "Teenage Life Online: The Rise of the Instant-Message Generation and the Internet's Impact on Friendships and Family Relationships." *Pew Research Center*, 2001 Accessed from http://www.pewinternet.org/~/media//Files/Reports/2001/PIP_Teens_Report.pdf.pdf.

Lesko, Nancy. *Act Your Age: A Cultural Construction of Adolescence*. 2nd ed. New York: Routledge, 2012.

Lessig, Larry. *Code and Other Laws of Cyberspace*. New York: Basic, 2000.

Levine, Judith. *Harmful to Minors: The Perils of Protecting Children from Sex*. Minneapolis, MN: University of Minnesota Press, 2002.

Lindberg, Laura Duberstein, Maddow-Zimet, Isaac, and Boonstra, Heather. "Changes in Adolescents' Receipt of Sex Education, 2006–2013." *Journal of Adolescent Health* 58, no. 6 (2016): 621–627.

Liptak, Adam, "Supreme Court Overturns Conviction in Online Threats Case, Citing Internet." *The New York Times* (June 1, 2015). Accessed January 2, 2017. https://www.nytimes.com/2015/06/02/us/supreme-court-rules-in-anthony-elonis-online-threats-case.html?_r=1.

Livingstone, Sonia. "Taking Risky Opportunities in Youthful Content Creation: Teenagers' Use of Social Networking Sites for Intimacy, Privacy and Self–Expression." *New Media & Society* 10, no. 3 (2008): 393–411.

———. *Children and the Internet*. Cambridge: Polity Press, 2009.

MacKenzie, Donald and Judy Wajcman. *The Social Shaping of Technology*. Philadelphia, PA: Open University Press, 2005.

MacKinnon, Rebecca. *Consent of the Networked: The Worldwide Struggle For Internet Freedom*. New York, NY: Basic Books, 2012.

Madden, Mary. "Privacy Management on Social Media Sites." *Pew Research Center* (2012). Accessed August 2, 2013. http://www.pewinternet.org/~/media//Files/Reports/2012/PIP_Privacy_management_on_social_media_sites_022412.pdf.

Madden, Mary, Amanda Lenhart, Sandra Cortesi, Urs Gasser, Maeve Duggan, Aaron Smith, and Meredith Beaton "Teens, Social Media, and Privacy." *Pew Research Center* (2013). Accessed October 2, 2017 from http://www.pewinternet.org/Reports/2013/Teens-Social-Media-And-Privacy.aspx.

Madden, Mary, Amanda Lenhart, Maeve Duggan, Sandra Cortesi and Urs Gasser. "Teens and Technology 2013." *Pew Research Center* (2013). Accessed January 2, 2017. http://www. pewinternet.org/~/media//Files/Reports/2013/PIP_TeensandTechnology2013.pdf.

Madden, Mary, and Amanda Smith. "Reputation Management and Social Media." *Pew Research Center* (2010). Accessed January 2, 2017. http://pewinternet.org/Reports/2010/Reputation-Management/Part-2/Attitudes-and-Actions.aspx.

Maira, Sunaina and Elizabeth Soep. *Youthscapes*. Philadelphia: University of Pennsylvania Press, 2005.

Manago, Amanda M., Michael B. Graham, Patricia M. Greenfield and Goldie Salimkhan, Presentation and gender on MySpace. *Journal of Applied Developmental Psychology* 29, no. 6 (2008): 446–458.

Markey, Karen. "Twenty-five years of end-user searching part 1: Research findings." *Journal of the American Society for Information Science and Technology* 58, no. 8 (2007): 1071–1081.

Marks, Michael J. and R. Chris Fraley, "The Sexual Double Standard: Fact or Fiction?" *Sex Roles* 52 (2005): 175–186.

Marwick, Alice. "To Catch a Predator? The MySpace Moral Panic." *First Monday* 13, no 6 (2008). Accessed February 2, 2017. http://www.firstmonday.dk/ojs/index.php/fm/article/view/2152/1966.

Massey, Donald S., Joaquin Arango, Graeme Hugo, Ali Kouaouci, Adela Pellegrino, and J. Edward Taylor. *Worlds in Motion. Understanding International Migration at the End of the Millennium*. Oxford: Clarendon Press, 1998.

Matias, J. Nathaniel, Aimee Rickman, and Megan Steiner. "Who Gets to Use Facebook's Rainbow 'Pride' Reaction?" *The Atlantic* (June 26, 2017).

Mazzarella, Sharon R. "Reflecting on Girls' Studies and the Media. Current Trends and Future Directions." *Journal of Children and Media* 2, no. 1 (2008): 75–87.

McChesney, Robert. *Digital Disconnect: How Capitalism is Turning the Internet Against Democracy*. New York: The New Press, 2013.

McCright, Aaron M., Meghan Charters, Katherine Dentzman, and Thomas Dietz, "Examining the Effectiveness of Climate Change Frames in the Face of a Climate Change Denial Counter-Frame," in *Future Global Change and Cognition*, 8 (2015): 76-97.

McRobbie, Angela. *Feminism and Youth Culture: From Jackie to Just Seventeen*. London: Macmillan, 1991.

McRobbie, Angela and Jenny Garber. "Girls and Subcultures." In *Resistance through Rituals: Youth Subcultures in Post-War Britain*, eds. Stuart Hall and Tony Jefferson, 209–222. London: Harper Collins Academic, 1976.

McRobbie, Angela and Sarah Thornton. "Rethinking 'Moral Panic' for Multi-Mediated Social Worlds." *The British Journal of Sociology* 46, no. 4 (1995): 559–574.

Meier, Evelyn P. and James Gray. "Facebook Photo Activity Associated with Body Image Disturbance in Adolescent Girls." *Cyberpsychology, Behavior, and Social Networking* 17, no. 4 (2014): 199–206.

Meyer, Robert and Michael Cukier, "Assessing the Attack Threat due to IRC Channels," in *Proceedings of the International Conference on Dependable Systems and Networks* (2006). Accessed March 12, 2015 from http://www.enre.umd.edu/content/rmeyer-assessing.pdf.

Mink, Gewndolyn and Rickie Solinger. *Welfare: A Documentary History of U.S. Policy and Politics*. New York, NY: NYU Press, 2003.

Mitchell, Amy, Jeffrey Gottfried, Michael Barthel, and Elisa Shearer. "The Modern News Consumer: News Attitudes and Practices in the Digital Era." *Pew Research Center* (July 7, 2016). Accessed May 3, 2017. http://assets.pewresearch.org/wp-content/uploads/sites/13/2016/07/08140120/PJ_2016.07.07_Modern-News-Consumer_FINAL.pdf.

Mitchell, Claudia and Jacqueline Reid-Walsh. "How to Study Girl Culture." *Girl Culture: An Encyclopedia*. Vol. 1. Ed. Claudia Mitchell and Jacqueline Reid-Walsh. Westport, CT: Greenwood, 2008: 17–24.

Mitchell, Claudia, Jacqueline Reid-Walsh, and Jackie Kirk. "Editorial." *Girlhood Studies* 1, no. 1 (Summer 2008), v-xiii.

Mitchell, Kimberly J., Lisa Jones, David Finkelhor, and Janis Wolak. "Trends in unwanted sexual solicitations: Findings from the Youth Internet Safety Studies." *Crimes Against Children Research Center* (2014). Accessed May 3, 2017. http://www.unh.edu/ccrc/pdf/Sexual%20Solicitation%201%20of%204%20YISS%20Bulletins%20Feb%202014.pdf.

Moberg, Glen. "Raptor Expert Says Eagle Shootings Up After Web Video." *Wisconsin Public Radio*, January 23, 2013. Accessed June 14, 2017. http://news.wpr.org/post/raptor-expert-says-eagle-shootings-after-web-video.

Mojtabai, Ramin, Mark Olfson, and Beth Han. "National Trends in the Prevalence and Treatment of Depression in Adolescents and Young Adults." *Pediatrics* (November 2016). Accessed May 14, 2017. http://pediatrics.aappublications.org/content/pediatrics/early/2016/11/10/peds.2016-1878.full.pdf.

Montgomery, Kathryn, Barbara Gottlieb-Robles, and Gary O. Larson. "Youth as e-citizens: Engaging the Digital Generation." *Center for Social Media*, 2004. Accessed November 16, 2016. http://www.centerforsocialmedia.org/ecitizens/youthreport.pdf.

Mortimer, Jeylan T., Mike Vuolo, Jeremy Staff, Sara Wakefield, and Wanling Xie. "Tracing the Timing of 'Career' Acquisition in a Contemporary Youth Cohort." *Work and Occupations* 35, no. 1 (2008): 44–84.

Myers, Taryn A. and Janis H. Crowther, "Social Comparison as a Predictor of Body Dissatisfaction: A Meta-Analytic Review" *Journal of Abnormal Psychology* 118, no. 4 (2009): 683–698.

Nakamura, Lisa. *Cybertypes: Race, Ethnicity, and Identity on the Internet*. New York: Routledge, 2002.

———. *Digitizing Race: Visual Cultures of the Internet*. Minneapolis, MN: University of Minnesota Press, 2008.

Nesi, Jacqueline, and Mitchell J. Prinstein. "Using Social Media for Social Comparison and Feedback-Seeking: Gender and Popularity Moderate Associations with Depressive Symptoms." *Journal of Abnormal Child Psychology* 43, no. 8 (2015): 1427–38.

Newark, Tim. *Camouflage*. London: Thames & Hudson, 2007.

Noble, Safiya. *Algorithms of Oppression: How Search Engines Reinforce Racism*. New York: NYU Press, 2018.

Odem, Mary E. *Delinquent Daughters: Protecting and Policing Adolescent Female Sexuality in the United States, 1885–1920*. Chapel Hill, NC: University of North Carolina Press, 1995.

Oldenburg, Ray. *The Great Good Place: Cafés, Coffee Shops, Bookstores, Bars, Hair Salons*. New York: Marlowe & Company, 1999.

O'Neil, Luke. "Internet Gullibility Syndrome: Maybe 'Literally Unbelievable' is Unbelievable for a Reason." *Street Carnage* (June 13, 2011): para. 7. Accessed September 12, 2017 http://www.streetcarnage.com/blog/internet-gullibility-syndrome-maybe-literally-unbelievable-is-unbelievable-for-a-reason/.

Opplinger, Patrice A. *Girls Gone Skank: The Sexualization of Girls in American Culture*. Jefferson, NC: McFarland, 2008.

Pascoe, C. J. *Dude, You're a Fag: Masculinity and Sexuality in High School*. Berkeley, CA: University of California Press, 2007.

Patchin, Justin W., and Sameer Hinduja. "Cyberbullying and Self-Esteem." *Journal of School and Health* 80, no. 12 (2010): 614–21.

Pederson, Sarah. "UK teens' safety awareness online—is it a 'girl thing'?" *Journal of Youth Studies* 16, no. 3 (2013): 404–19.

Perez, Sarah. "Facebook Graph Search Didn't Break Your Privacy Settings, It Only Feels Like That." *Tech Crunch* (February 4, 2013). Accessed June 2, 2017 from http://techcrunch.com/2013/02/04/facebook-graph-search-didnt-break-your-privacy-settings-it-only-feels-like-that.

Proefrock, David W. "Adolescence: Social Fact and Psychological Concept," *Adolescence* 26 (1981): 851–858.

Przybylski, Andrew K., Kou Murayama, Cody R. DeHaan, and Valerie Gladwell. "Motivational, Emotional, and Behavioral Correlates of Fear of Missing Out." *Computers in Human Behavior* 29, no. 4 (2013): 1841–1848.

Qvortrup, Jens. *Childhood Matters: Social Theory, Practice, and Politics.* Aldershot, UK: Avebury, 1994.

Rasmussen, Mary Louise, Eric Rofes, and Susan Talburt. *Youth and Sexualities: Pleasure, Subversion, and Insubordination in and Out of Schools.* New York: Palgrave Macmillan, 2004.

Raynes-Goldie, Kate. "Aliases, Creeping, and Wall Cleaning: Understanding Privacy in the Age of Facebook." *First Monday* 15, no. 1 (January 4, 2010). Accessed October 10, 2017 http://firstmonday.org/article/view/2775/2432.

Reagan, Gillian. "The Evolution of Facebook's Mission Statement." *The Observer*, July 13, 2009. Accessed October 31, 2017. http://observer.com/2009/07/the-evolution-of-facebooks-mission-statement.

Rheingold, Howard. *The Virtual Community: Homesteading the Electronic Frontier.* Cambridge: MIT Press, 2000.

Roberts, Dorothy. *Killing the Black Body.* New York: Vantage Books, 1997.

Rosenthal, Carolyn. "Kinkeeping in the Familial Division of Labor," *Journal of Marriage and Family* 47, no. 4 (1985): 965–974.

Sengupta, Somini. "Letting Down Our Guard With Web Privacy." *New York Times.* (March 30, 2013). Accessed June 2, 2017 http://www.nytimes.com/2013/03/31/technology/web-privacy-and-how-consumers-let-down-their-guard.html?pagewanted=all.

Sickmund, Melissa and Charles Puzzachera, eds. "Juvenile Offenders and Victims: 2014 National Report." *Office of Juvenile Justice and Prevention Center*, December 2014: 0–231. Accessed October 2, 2017. https://www.ojjdp.gov/ojstatbb/nr2014/downloads/NR2014.pdf.

Silvia, Paul J. and T. Shelley Duval. "Objective Self-Awareness Theory: Recent Progress and Enduring Problems." *Personality and Social Psychology Review* 5 (2001).

Sheridan-Rabideau, Mary. *Girls, Feminism, and Grassroots Literacies.* New York, NY: NYU Press, 2008.

Smith, Aaron. "6 New Facts About Facebook." *Pew Research Center* (February 3, 2014). Accessed June 16, 2017. http://www.pewresearch.org/fact-tank/2014/02/03/6-new-facts-about-facebook/.

Snyder, Howard N. "Sexual Assault of Young Children as Reported to Law Enforcement." Bureau of Justice Statistics, 2000. Accessed October 3, 2017. https://www.bjs.gov/content/pub/pdf/saycrle.pdf.

Stake, Robert E. *The Art of Case Study Research.* Thousand Oaks, CA: Sage, 1995.

Stapel, Diederik A. and Abraham Tesser. "Self-Activation Increases Social Comparison." *Journal of Personality and Social Psychology* 81 (2001): 742–750.

Steinberg, Laurence. *Adolescence.* Chicago: McGraw Hill, 1993.

Sternberg, Jason. "Young, Dumb, and Full of Lies: The News Media's Construction of Youth Culture," *Screen Education* 37 (2004): 34–39.

Stockton, Katherine Bond. *The Queer Child, or Growing Sideways in the Twentieth Century.* Durham: Duke University Press, 2009.

Stone, Brad and Miguel Helft. "In Developing Countries, Web Grows Without Profit." *New York Times* (April 26, 2009). Accessed June 2, 2017. http://www.nytimes.com/2009/04/27/technology/start-ups/27global.html?pagewanted=all&_r=2&.

Swallow, Stephen R., and Nicholas A. Kyiper. "Mild Depression and Frequency of Social Comparison Behavior." *Journal of Personality and Social Psychology* 82 (1992): 252–261.

Swift, Jonathan. "The Art of Political Lying." *The Examiner*, 14 (November 9, 1710).

Taylor, Paul, Kim Parker, Rakesh Kochhar, Richard Fry, Carey Funk, Eileen Patten, Seth Motel. "Young, Underemployed, and Optimistic: Coming of Age, Slowly, in a Tough Economy." *Pew Research Center* (February 9 2012). Accessed November 11, 2016. http://www.pewsocialtrends.org/files/2012/02/young-underemployed-and-optimistic.pdf.

Tolman, Deborah L. *Dilemmas of Desire: Teenage Girls Talk About Sexuality.* Cambridge: Harvard University Press, 2002.

Turkle, Sherry. *Alone Together: Why We Expect More from Technology and Less from Each Other.* New York: Basic, 2011.

Turner, Victor. *The Ritual Process: Structure and Anti-Structure.* New York: Aldine Transaction, 1969.

Turow, Joseph. *The Daily You.* New Haven: Yale University Press, 2011.
———. *The Aisles Have Eyes.* New Haven: Yale University Press, 2017.
Twitter. "Mission." Accessed October 31, 2017. https://twitter.com/about.
Twitter. "Our Company." Accessed October 31, 2017. https://twitter.com/about.
US Census Bureau. "Millennials Outnumber Baby Boomers and Are Far More Diverse, Census Bureau Reports." (June 25, 2015). Accessed September 2, 2017. https://www.census.gov/newsroom/press-releases/2015/cb15-113.html.
US Congress Joint Economic Committee Staff, "Understanding the Economy: Unemployment Among Young Workers." (May, 2010). Accessed March 3, 2012. https://www.jec.senate.gov/public/_cache/files/adaef80b-d1f3-479c-97e7-727f4c0d9ce6/understanding-the-economy---unemployment-among-young-workers.pdf.
Valkenburg, Patty M. Jochen Peter, and Alexander Peter Schouten. "Friend Networking Sites and their Relationship to Adolescents' Well-Being and Social Self-Esteem." *CyberPsychology & Behavior* 9, no. 5 (2006): 584–590.
Van Dijck, José. *The Culture of Connectivity: A Critical History of Social Media.* Oxford: Oxford University Press, 2013.
Vance, Ashley. "This Tech Bubble is Different." *Bloomberg Businessweek.* April 14, 2011: par. 3. Accessed September 12, 2017. https://www.bloomberg.com/news/articles/2011-04-14/this-tech-bubble-is-different.
Veblen, Thorstein. *Theory of the Leisure Class: An Economic Study of Institutions.* Teddington: Echo Library, 1899.
Verma, Suman, Deepali Sharma and Reed Larson. "School Stress in India: Effects on Time and Daily Emotions," *International Journal of Behavioral Development* 26 (2002): 500–508.
Weaver, Alex. "Coming Soon to Your Facebook Page: Ambiguous Advertising," *Fast Horse* (January 26, 2012). Accessed June 2, 2017 from http://fasthorseinc.com/blog/2012/01/26/coming-soon-to-your-facebook-page-ambiguous-advertising.
Weinger, Mackenzie. "John Fleming links to Onion story on Facebook." *Politico* (February 6, 2012). Accessed September 12, 2017. http://www.politico.com/news/stories/0212/72507.html.
Werner, Emmy E. and Ruth S. Smith. *Journeys from Childhood to Midlife: Risk, Resilience, and Recovery.* New York: Cornell University Press, 2001.
Wu, Tim. *The Attention Merchants: The Epic Scramble to Get Inside Our Heads.* New York: Alfred A. Knopf, 2016.
Wyn, Johanna and Rob White. *Rethinking Youth.* London: Sage, 1997.
Youn, Seounmi. and Kimberly Hall. "Gender and Online Privacy Among Teens: Risk Perception, Privacy Concerns, and Protection Behaviors." *CyberPsychology & Behavior,* 11, no. 6 (2008): 763–65.
Yousefian, Anush, Erika Ziller, Jon Swartz and David Hartley. "Active Living for Rural Youth: Addressing Physical Inactivity in Rural Communities." *Journal of Public Health Management and Practice* 15, no. 3 (2009): 223–231.
Zuckerberg, Mark. "Bringing the World Closer Together." *Facebook* (June 22, 2017). Last modified June 27, 2017. https://www.facebook.com/notes/mark-zuckerberg/bringing-the-world-closer-together/10154944663901634/.

Index

About the Author

Aimee Rickman is assistant professor of child and family sciences at California State University, Fresno, where she heads the Youth and Social Media Lab. She is an ethnographer and critical researcher of adolescence, girlhood, technology, and culture.

www.ingramcontent.com/pod-product-compliance
Lightning Source LLC
Chambersburg PA
CBHW021818270326
41932CB00007B/237